Living Justice

Love, Freedom, and the Making of *The Exonerated*

Jessica Blank and
Erik Jensen

ATRIA BOOKS
New York London Toronto Sydney

For our families

1230 Avenue of the Americas
New York, NY 10020

For information address Atria Books, 1230 Avenue of the Americas, New York, NY 10020

ISBN-13: 978-0-7434-8345-2
ISBN-10: 0-7434-8345-6
ISBN-13: 978-0-7434-8346-9 (Pbk)
ISBN-10: 0-7434-8346-4 (Pbk)

First Atria Books trade paperback edition September 2006

10 9 8 7 6 5 4 3 2 1

Manufactured in the United States of America

For information regarding special discounts for bulk purchases, please contact Simon & Schuster Special Sales at 1-800-456-6798 or business@simonandschuster.com

Acknowledgments

The Exonerated—and this book—would not have been created without the generous and selfless support of countless people. First and foremost, we would like to thank the exonerated individuals who told us their stories—each and every one of them. Their courage is a gift to all of us.

We would also like to thank Greer Hendricks at Atria Books for searching us out and encouraging us to tell our own story—for believing that this crazy journey could become a book, and for helping us to shape it.

We are also grateful to the Actors' Gang, Chris Ajemian, Shawn Armbrust, the Artists Network, Kara Baker, Bob Balaban, Eve

Battaglia, Jane Bergere, Jordan Berlant, Patrick Blake, the Blank family, the Boehm Foundation, Carolyn Bowles and Craig Roth, Larry Breakstone and Karen Levy, Julie Brimberg, Richmond and Sandy Browne, Allan Buchman, John Buzzetti, Gabriel Byrne, the Center on Wrongful Convictions, Bonnie Cottle, Court TV, the Culture Project, Glenn Daniels, Micki Dickoff, Mindy Duitz and the George Soros Foundation, Wendy Eaton, Robert Edgar, Ginny and Terry Eicher, David Elliott, Curtis Ellis, Cyrena Esposito, Mike Farrell, Barbara and Richard Feldman, the Fortune Society, the Funding Exchange, Leslie Garis, Thom Gates, the Gersh Agency, Lynne Godwin, Nancy and Lou Goodman, Andrew and Jane Gordon, Alan Grabelsky, Colin Greer, Olivia Greer and the New World Foundation, Samuel Gross, Nick Hallett, Carolyn Halliday and CR Schult, Enid Harlow, Dede Harris, Gail Hartman, Jason Helm, Ruth Hendel, Ginny Hepler, Barbara Heyer, Neal and Clara Hulkower, the Innocence Project, Richard Jaffe, the Jensen family, Anna Johnson-Chase, Michael Johnson-Chase, Connie Julian, the Justice Project, Casey Kait, Cathy Kanner and Kanner Entertainment, Jessica Kaplan and Steve Symonds, Moisés Kaufman, Jen Knestrick, Nancy and Jerry Kobrin, Arthur Kopit, the Ethel and Abe Lapides Foundation, Darrell Larson, Gerald Lefcourt, Diana Levy and Bruce Fabens, Arthur Lewis, Roz Lichter, Joe Mantello, Maria Markosov, Larry Marshall, the Mattis family, Jim McCloskey and Centurion Ministries, Marghe Mills-Thysen, Kim Moarefi, Peter Neufeld, the New York State Council for the Arts, Paul Nugent, Nellie Nugiel, Suzanne O'Neill, Jason Pendergraft, Arlene Popkin, Nina Pratt, Sister Helen Prejean, Andrew Price, Greg Reiner, Speedy Rice, Riptide Communications, David Robbins, Tim Robbins, Mordechai Rochlin, Steve Rothstein, Allan Rowand, Joshua Rubenstein, Diann Rust-Tierney, Susan Sarandon, Barry Scheck, Kate Schumaecker, Elizabeth Semel, Olivia Mellon Shapiro, Robert and Elizabeth Sheehan, Alison Shigo, Anne

Smith, Kent Spriggs, Edward Steele, Denny Swanson, Mort Swinsky, Ronald Tabak, Zoe Tanenbaum, Kim Waltman, Robert Warden, Joyce Warner, Helen Whitney, Cheryl Wiesenfeld, Sarah Whitson and Josh Zinner, the crews of the Los Angeles, New York, and national touring productions, and all the extraordinary actors who have workshopped or appeared in *The Exonerated*.

It would not have been possible without you.

Foreword

The desire for revenge is powerful. The biblical imperative of an eye for an eye has been the pillar for many systems of justice throughout the world. Our current president is a proponent of the death penalty, yet he professes to believe in the sacredness of human life—which seems to me a moral contradiction. There is still enormous support for the death penalty in this country. A poll taken by Gallup in 2003 found that 74 percent of Americans support capital punishment, while over 50 percent of the countries in the world have abolished it. It is only through awareness and education that the ugly reality of this institution, which has become a fundamental component of our national fabric, can be exposed and unraveled.

One of the most rewarding things I've done to help tell the truth about this barbarism was join the cast of *The Exonerated*. Last year I played the role of Kerry Max Cook, a man freed after spending twenty years on death row, punished for a crime he did not commit. His words, and those of four other men and one woman whose sentences were overturned, were so skillfully dramatized by Jessica Blank and Erik Jensen that they had the power to reach out and change the opinions of many audience members who were trenchantly supportive of the death penalty. Every person who was moved, even slightly, represents one of the most exhilarating results of the theatrical process—the merging of art and politics in a way that can inspire as well as entertain.

Living Justice is not merely a behind-the-scenes look at the creation of a play, but also a fascinating chronicle of a developing political consciousness. Before they set out on their journey, Jessica and Erik were no more qualified than anyone else to advocate the anti–death penalty cause. They of course had their opinions on the subject—they both felt that it was wrong to kill people, period—but they had no idea about the excessive failures of our justice system that made the already brutal act of execution even more unethical than they had imagined. As Jessica and Erik uncovered layer upon layer of evidence of blatant injustices and inequities, they were arming themselves with the facts, the skeleton structure they would need in order to form their argument. They knew what they needed to do next. In order to drive their point home, to make their audience connect with their message, they had to move beyond statistics, laws, and legal jargon. They had to put a human face on the issue, so that everyone would know what was at stake.

And so they came to travel the country, reaching out to those who had suffered the unthinkable. In *Living Justice* they document their trepidation as they set out to interview these men and women who were robbed of the American promise of freedom simply because they lacked the money, connections, or the right skin color to prove their innocence. Welcomed into the homes and the haunted memories of these exonerated people, the couple forgot their insecurities and became even more dedicated to making their stories known. The result was their highly acclaimed play, *The Exonerated*, in which they let their audience hear what they heard—the words of these folks who had lost so much.

As a reader, I found it so easy to relate to Jessica and Erik, who aren't lawyers or journalists, but rather two people who were simply called to action. There was always the risk of failure for the two of them, a risk that they were well aware of, but they plowed forward nonetheless, driven by their determination to make a difference. I am happy to know that they did not fail—quite the opposite. Theirs is a classic American story we can all be proud of.

Read *Living Justice* to learn about the death penalty, one of the greatest shames of the American conscience. Read it to find out just what goes into getting a play up and running in Manhattan. Read it to see how one couple's still-new relationship survived a road trip replete with bad directions, small hotel rooms, and a rambunctious canine. Or read it to learn how you don't have to sit idle and complain about injustice, how you can translate your talents and passion into something meaningful. Whatever you take away from *Living Justice*, I promise you this: you will be inspired. Now what are you going to do about it?

—Gabriel Byrne, November 2004

February 19, 2000. An anonymous lecture hall at Columbia University. It's a Sunday; class is not in session. There are students here, but not the kind you'd expect: a variously dressed group of lawyers, activists, and college kids spill over into the aisles. Thirtysomething attorneys in suits and ties bump up against graybeards sporting button-covered backpacks; sixtyish New Yorkers and tattoo-covered teenagers pass sheets of paper back and forth to one another. The hard, green plastic seats are filled with the civic-minded, the morbidly curious, even a priest or two. At the front of the room is a lectern with microphone, precariously wired to a cell phone. The nervous young woman leading the workshop apologizes for the technical difficulties as she fiddles with the phone: It's hard, she says, to get phone calls from prison. The inmate has to call his lawyer, the lawyer has to call us, and then on top of it there are these speakers to deal with, the feedback whine, the shaky connection. The dial tone crackles, quivers, and drops out. The phone rings and stops ringing several times before a connection is made; finally the call goes through, it's patched in to us, and a man begins speaking:

My name is Leonard Kidd. I'm on death row for something I didn't do. I want to go home.

Chapter One

The two of us had been dating just over a month. Erik had lived in New York City for almost a decade, making a steady living as an actor in independent films and TV. Jessica'd just shown up in the city nine months earlier, after graduating from college in Minnesota. She was training at an acting studio, making the rounds, spending her days doing political organizing and her evenings doing spoken-word poetry. Both of us had your typical broke bohemian artsy New York lifestyle.

When we'd first met, Erik was deep in the throes of self-imposed bachelorhood. He'd bribed someone to obtain the lease on his East Village apartment, then turned his little rent-stabilized hardwood hovel into a fortress, usually spending his evenings in front of one of Manhattan's few working fireplaces accompanied by a stack of comic books, a script, and his Brittany spaniel Zooey. Erik had a steady, skinny little New York life complete with hundreds of paperbacks, acting work that he got paid for but would happily have done for free, and a dog that didn't smell too bad. He could smoke a pack and a half of cigarettes a day, eat as many Sno Balls as Hostess could ship into Manhattan, and throw laundry on his fire escape without having to answer to anyone (except when the super complained about the tube socks hanging off the downstairs neighbor's window garden).

Jessica, on the other hand, was caught up in a whirlwind of just-moved-to-New-York. She had her starter New York City apartment—which, like many starter New York apartments, was in New Jersey—which she used exclusively to crash out at 4 a.m. after running around the city all day and night. Every day was totally different; not yet jaded, she made new friends every five minutes and was dating, um, a bunch of different people. She knew what she loved (politics, acting, writing) but was still stumbling around trying to figure out how on earth to do all three things and make a living. Happy to be finished with college, not entirely sure what to do next, she let the city lead the way and wound up organizing politically minded artists, studying acting, making the audition rounds, and hanging out at poetry slams.

We'd met through the tangled and tiny social web of young New York actors when Erik crashed his friend Kelly's date with Jessica. Erik had just started a run of a new play, and it had been a tough audience that night. Erik stopped off at Kelly's East Village restaurant on his way home, hoping for some company and consolation. And a free beer.

Kelly was indeed there, sitting with Jessica at a table in the back. Erik said hi to Kelly, spilled a beer on himself, and introduced himself to Jessica. Then he sat down and started describing that night's performance. Kelly knew the drill: When in doubt, blame it on the audience. Then the weather. Then the stage manager.

It wasn't till Jessica got up to go to the bathroom that Kelly had a chance to lean over to Erik and tell him to quit talking about himself so much. "I'm trying to spend some time with this girl, man. You need to step off." From the subtle pressure Kelly was applying to Erik's knuckles, Erik knew he meant it.

When Jessica returned from the bathroom, she found Erik strangely silent. Soon after that, Erik went home to walk the dog, but he managed to slip Jessica his phone number first, ostensibly so he could get her free tickets to his play.

Time passed; Jessica and Kelly didn't work out; she called Erik to take him up on the free-tickets offer. Unbeknownst to her, Erik had used up all his comps by then, but he told her it was no problem to set up free tickets; she should come down to the theater that Friday, maybe they could go have a drink with the playwright after. Then Erik went out and hawked some used books to pay for it. So much for self-imposed bachelorhood.

Jessica showed up as promised, picked up her $65 "free" ticket, watched the play, and went out after with Erik, the playwright Arthur Kopit, and his wife, writer Leslie Garis. We got drunk, ate pie, and talked about theater and writing. Going from one café to another, we lingered behind Arthur and Leslie, talking to each other a mile a minute, overlapping, interrupting each other a lot.

Leslie told us later she'd eavesdropped on us as she and Arthur walked ahead, and that she went home that night so struck by the conversation that she wrote it down. We're still trying to get our hands on that transcript—we have a feeling it might be embarrassing.

We spent the next month and a half or so starting to really like each other, being afraid of starting to really like each other, cataloging each other's strengths and weaknesses, trying to figure out how compatible we were, boring our friends.

One of the areas in which we were still feeling each other out was politics. We were both decidedly left of center—and maybe that was enough common ground—but we came from very different political backgrounds, and our approaches were, well, different. Erik had grown up in rural and suburban Minnesota, the grandson of a highway patrolman, the great-grandson of a judge. Minnesota is a progressive state with a strong populist streak, infused with the belief that if we elect honest, hardworking, good-hearted leaders, and work hard ourselves, things will turn out pretty much okay. Despite having run off to an East Coast acting school and the proverbial "big city" (his father actually used that phrase once) after graduation, when it came to politics, Erik was a child of Minnesota, a registered Democrat who balanced his populist bent with a lot of faith in the system.

Jessica, on the other hand, was the daughter of sixties lefties. Her parents had been early protesters of the Vietnam War, attended MLK's March on Washington, and helped found Vietnam Veterans Against the War. Jessica's mom is a movement educator with a background in modern dance and a devotion to progressive schooling; her dad is a jazz-piano-playing psychoanalyst. They moved to Washington, D.C., in the early eighties so Jessica's mom could expand her practice, and so Jessica's dad could put their family's ideals to work at the Veterans Administration, fighting to preserve benefits for Vietnam vets who'd more or less been discarded by their government, educating the public about the traumas caused by war. Jessica grew up amidst noisy political dinner-table conversation and was an obnoxiously outspoken vegetarian and feminist by seventh grade.

By the time she got to New York ten years later, she was helping organize politically minded artists, getting involved with prison-reform issues and participating in New York's famously lefty slam-poetry scene. She was still a vegetarian and a feminist, too, although hopefully less obnoxiously so than she had been in junior high. Erik, on the other hand, liked Slim Jims, teriyaki beef jerky, salami, and sardines.

Jessica's dragging Erik to an anti-death-penalty conference that February afternoon may have been some sort of subconscious test to see how he'd do around her radical friends—or maybe she just wanted the company. Either way, he showed up, curious and open-minded (and did just fine with her radical friends, thank you very much). The conference took place in the ornately carved chapel at the Cathedral of St. John the Divine and the beige, nondescript lecture halls of Columbia Law School. We shuffled between different workshops all day, discussing the case history of imprisoned writer Mumia Abu-Jamal, the role of artists in creating social change, the new report on the death penalty just released by Columbia University. Finally, we wound up at a workshop that, on the surface, looked similar to the others.

Freshly drawn permanent-marker arrows pointed us into yet another gray-and-tan lecture hall at Columbia Law; we sat down to learn about a group of Illinois men who had been dubbed the Death Row Ten, one of whom was a man named Leonard Kidd. We watched a news segment on the cases and heard a lecture that explained how Kidd's confession—along with those of the other members of the Death Row Ten—had allegedly been tortured out of him by a police commander named Jon Burge. This wasn't just rumor or bad propaganda; it had been proven through an internal investigation by the Chicago PD, and an external investigation by Chicago newspapers. Burge, who had learned his "techniques" in Vietnam, had been fired (with pension), but Kidd—with little other evidence against him besides his "confession"—still languished on death row, unable to get a new trial. Needless to say, we were disturbed by this information; but it seemed no different from more bad news in the paper, or an upsetting report on *20/20*.

But then the call came through. The workshop organizers had arranged for Leonard Kidd to call their cell phone collect from the prison; the phone was hooked up to a speaker so Leonard could speak directly to the audience. His words hollowed out the room. He tried to control the quavering in his voice. He tried to reach out to us; you could hear it over the bad connection. You could hear his will. And his fear. Within moments, tears were streaming down our faces: here was this young man, trapped in an unbelievably tragic and terrifying situation. Not much older than us, likely innocent, caught in a system he and half a dozen lawyers couldn't find a way out of, waiting to be put to death for something he didn't do. Something happened, hearing his voice, right there, in the room, that took our experience out of the realm of newspaper-story, "isn't-that-terrible" abstraction, and into the realm of human empathy—where it belonged.

Soon, prison authorities got wise to the jerry-rigged phone call, and the line went dead. In the quiet afterward, Erik looked around the room. His distance from the activist "scene" gave him enough perspective to notice that everyone in the room was already an organizer or a defense attorney. They all *knew* these stories. They were the proverbial choir, being preached to. Moving as it was to hear Leonard speak, they were not the ones who really needed to have this experience. Annoyed and frustrated by this, Erik started writing notes to Jessica about it on her laptop. Soon we were writing back and forth to each other, brainstorming about how to get around the problem.

At first our brainstorms consisted mainly of complaining that people who didn't already sympathize would never put themselves in a situation where they'd have this kind of experience. Why should they think about it? It's too depressing. But then we started writing back and forth about what exactly "this kind of experience" was. Were we really only talking about getting people in a room where they would literally hear the voices of the wrongly convicted? Or were there other ways to create the same kind of emotional immediacy with the same kinds of stories? Then the conversation really opened up.

We knew something about how good theater could, if done right, allow an audience member to empathize with someone from completely different circumstances, family background, class, race. And we both were interested in documentary theater, a relatively new form being utilized most notably by Anna Deavere Smith, Moisés Kaufman, Emily Mann, and Eve Ensler. Ideas, words, started to flash back and forth between us. Ensemble piece, monologues, not didactic. Real people's words. Somehow at the same time, we both arrived at the same idea: What if we found people who had been on death row who were innocent and made a play from their words?

It seemed a perfect way around, no . . . *through* all the problems we'd been discussing. A well-constructed play could attract audiences who had no political predisposition to the subject matter. If we did it right, we could bring in audiences with diverse points of view—some people who agreed with us coming in the door, sure, but also people who didn't, and people who hadn't previously considered the issue. If we limited our subjects to those who had been on death row—the most extreme, literally life-and-death stories—audiences might attend the play for the dramatic value of the stories alone. And if we kept our focus on cases where people had been declared *innocent* by the system, then we could sidestep much of the polarized ethical debate that so often bogs down conversations about the death penalty and get right to the human issues involved.

We left the conference energized and set to work doing research. We knew from that first conversation that we wanted to create a documentary play, using the subjects' real words. We knew we wanted to limit our subject matter to people who had been on death row and who had been found innocent and released by the court system. But beyond that, we were starting from scratch.

Chapter Two

We spent about two months immersed in reading on capital punishment, wrongful conviction, and the legal system in general—which mostly served to show us how little we knew. We'd both gone off to college and studied theater, so the furthest either of us had gotten in any formal study of the court system was our high school government classes.

Erik remembered his government class well: One day in that class, sometime back in the eighties, Erik had participated in a debate about the death penalty. There were about thirty students in the class, and when the teacher asked, "Okay, who here is against the death penalty?" one lone, skinny arm shot up—Erik's. Then she asked who was in favor of it, and the other twenty-nine arms waved in the air. Erik was, of course, assigned the anti-death-penalty position in the debate, and with the few facts he had at his disposal, he performed valiantly. At the end, the teacher polled the class again. Now, two people were against the death penalty. Erik had reached one person. He tried hard to hold on to the comfort this offered as a couple kids whose minds he *hadn't* changed decided it would be fun to engage in a little after-class debate of their own by slamming Erik's books onto the floor and dumping his backpack in a wastebasket. Jessica had similar experiences as an alienated lefty in high school—she'd paid attention to any political facts she could absorb in class, if only to use them as ammo in heated arguments with the jocks, and her memories of government class were just as vivid.

So from those high school classes—and from reading newspapers in the ensuing years—we thought we understood the American judicial system, at least a little. But our research began to show us that in the real world, things rarely work the way they're laid out on paper. We both had a lot to learn.

We started way back at the beginning. The death penalty as a legal institution dates back to Hammurabi's Code, we read; it also shows up in ancient Rome and Athens. The American death penalty's roots, unsurprisingly, are mostly in British law. The death penalty was implemented fairly rarely in early Britain—until the reign of Henry the Eighth, under whose rule, according to the Death Penalty Information Center, "as many as seventy-two thousand people are estimated to have been executed." The death penalty remained in heavy use in Britain until around 1873, when it declined in popularity and significant reforms began.

In the meantime, though, British settlers brought the death penalty to America; the earliest recorded execution in the colonies was in 1608. In 1612, according to the Death Penalty Information

Center, the governor of Virginia instituted the death penalty for an enormous number of offenses, "such as stealing grapes, killing chickens, and trading with Indians." Beginning in the late 1700s, American opposition to the death penalty grew in strength and volume; early American advocates of death penalty reform or abolition included Thomas Jefferson and Benjamin Franklin. The abolitionist movement gained momentum over the next fifty years: in 1834, Pennsylvania became the first state to ban public executions and began conducting them in correctional facilities (a big move at the time). Over the ensuing two decades, a few states abolished the death penalty for all crimes except treason; around the world, several other countries did the same. At the same time, however, some states increased the use of the death penalty, especially for crimes (sometimes quite minor ones) committed by slaves.

The Progressive Movement brought the first major wave of twentieth-century death penalty reform. Between 1907 and 1917, six additional states abolished the death penalty, and three more strictly limited its application. But then, in the wake of the Russian Revolution, and in light of the serious political challenges being posed by American working classes and socialism, the ruling classes in America started to panic about the possibility of a domestic revolution; a law-and-order mentality prevailed, and the death penalty was reinstated in five of the six abolitionist states. The death penalty remained in heavy use from the 1920s through the 1940s; in the 1930s—during Prohibition and the Depression—there were more executions than in any other decade in American history.

After World War Two, American public support for the death penalty declined again, reaching an all-time low of 42 percent in 1966. At the same time, more countries around the world began to ban the use of the death penalty; in the wake of the Holocaust, international human rights treaties were drafted that declared life to be a basic human right, and over the following three decades, executions all but ceased in the vast majority of the industrialized world. The Supreme Court, citing an "evolving standard of decency," began to reflect this decline in support for the death penalty, beginning in the late sixties. In 1972, the Court ruled in the landmark *Furman v. Georgia* decision that the Georgia capital punishment statute (which was similar in kind to most states' death penalty laws) was "cruel and unusual" and thus violated the Eighth Amendment. This ruling effectively commuted the sentences of 629 death row inmates across the country and suspended the death penalty.

In ruling that the specific death penalty statutes were unconstitutional—rather than the death penalty as a whole—the Court left an opening for states to rewrite their statutes to do away with the problems cited in *Furman*, and to reinstate the death penalty. The first to do so was Florida; thirty-four other states followed, providing sentencing guidelines that allowed for the introduction of aggravating and mitigating factors. Lawmakers who introduced these guidelines argued that this would prevent arbitrary application of the death penalty. Arbitrary application of the death penalty was one of the main reasons the Supreme Court gave for judging the Georgia death penalty statute unconstitutional, and in 1976, the Court ruled in three separate death penalty cases, collectively referred to as the *Gregg* decision, that these new sentencing guidelines were constitutional, effectively reinstating the death penalty in Florida, Georgia, and Texas. Other states followed suit. The first person executed after the reinstatement of the death penalty was Gary Gilmore; he was killed by firing squad in January of 1977, thus ending the de facto national moratorium. Today, capital punishment is on the books in thirty-eight states, with Texas's, Florida's, and California's death row populations the largest, and Texas, Virginia, and Oklahoma leading the nation in the number of executions actually carried out. More than one hundred countries (including all in the European Union) have abolished the death penalty in law or practice, while over thirty-three hundred people are on death row in America, the highest known death row population on earth.

Once we got the history under our belts, we started to study the specificities of contemporary death penalty law, as well as the complex realities of the ways in which that law is applied. Unfortunately, we learned, the arbitrariness the Supreme Court deemed unconstitutional in *Furman v. Georgia* is still very much at work today. To cite just one example, according to Amnesty International, black people and white people are the victims of murder in almost equal numbers—but "82 percent of prisoners executed since 1977 were convicted of the murder of a white person. In Kentucky, for example, every death sentence [from 1977] up to March 1996 was for the murder of a white victim, despite over one thousand homicide victims in the state being black." In many places, the race of the defendant makes a difference, too. The same report points out that "a recent study, made public in June 1998, found that in Philadelphia the likelihood of receiving a death sentence is nearly four times higher if the defendant is black, after taking into account aggravating factors. . . . Blacks make up just 12 percent of the country's population, but 42 percent of the nation's condemned prisoners. In early 1998, of the twenty-six people under federal sentence of death (military and civilian), only five prisoners were white."

And the issue of innocence has become of increasingly urgent concern in recent years: when we started in on our research, eighty-nine people had been freed from death row, and questions about the guilt of many other death row inmates were building in intensity and volume. A few months later, when we got on the road, we would begin to understand the very real, very human meaning of all these statistics.

During our two months of initial research, Jessica started spending more and more time at Erik's fifth-floor walk-up in the East Village. She still had her supercheap starter apartment—but it only took a couple bleary-eyed PATH train rides back to Jersey City after seven hours of death penalty research for Jessica to decide it was a lot easier just to crash out on the piles of newspaper clippings on Erik's couch. More and more often, Erik's roommate, Jan, would come home to find us sprawled out on the living room floor, surrounded by piles of books, website addresses, and newsprint. More and more often, when Jan would start friendly roommate-ish conversations about how her internship was going or her day in class, she would find us unable to talk about anything besides the death penalty, prisons, and wrongful conviction. "Did you know that on average it takes seven to eight years for an innocent person to be freed from death row—and that in Texas, death row inmates, on average, are executed after only three years?" "Did you know that in the last twenty-five years, twelve people have been executed in Illinois, and thirteen have been exonerated?" Jan would smile and nod and act surprised every time. She seemed very tolerant of the four-hundred-square-foot apartment, our endless "Did you know?"'s, and Zooey, the insanely hyper dog who incessantly shredded blankets, humped pillows, and scrambled around the living room, strewing papers everywhere.

There's nothing like death penalty research to get your roommate to move out of your New York apartment. In April, Jan officially left, and Jessica officially moved in. While Jessica worked her bartending job, Erik would traipse to Jersey City and bring boxes of Jessica's stuff back to the East Village, hauling them up the five flights to the apartment. She'd wake up the next day, unpack, and redecorate. At first Jessica was subtle, hinting that the green-painted stainless-steel desk and the black-painted stainless-steel file cabinet were maybe not quite exactly her style. But as the unpacking continued, she grew bolder, and soon Erik's thrift-store bachelor furniture was gone, replaced by much cooler thrift-store nonbachelor furniture—and a lot more space in which to spread out all our research. (Zooey continued to shred things, but due to Jessica's influence, her shredding became much more refined.)

Throughout the researching-and-moving-in-together period, Connie, one of the more senior and accomplished of Jessica's organizer friends, was prodding us along into the next stage of making *The Exonerated.* If it weren't for Connie's incessant supportive pestering, we would probably never really have gotten started. Connie is the unofficial leader of an association called the Artists' Network—a woman who has made it her life's work to organize artists, a daunting task if ever there was one. From what we've seen Connie do over the last four years, it seems as if her self-assigned mission is to identify artists in all media who are making nondogmatic, nondidactic work that nonetheless aims to change political consciousness, encourage those artists, and bring them together. In other words, for people like us, she's an angel.

When we were researching, Connie called us almost every day to ask when we'd have a proposal she could look at. Eventually we just got too embarrassed to tell Connie "not yet," for the twenty-seventh time, so we yanked our noses out of the newspaper clippings and started writing.

* * *

By May 2000, the national debate around innocence and the death penalty was growing more heated. Governor George Ryan of Illinois had declared a moratorium on the death penalty in his state, and another George was running for president—with more executions carried out under his watch in Texas than under any other governor, in any other state, since the reinstatement of the death penalty in 1976. An execution date was set for Gary Graham, a Texas death row inmate whose guilt was in serious doubt, drawing national media attention. And Columbia University released the results of a long-term study that showed a high risk of convicting the innocent in capital cases. America was definitely paying attention.

After two months in "death penalty boot camp" and innumerable urgings by Connie, we finally had a proposal. Only problem was, we didn't know what to do with it.

One night, during one of Jessica's poetry slams, we spotted a sort of Buddha-ish figure hanging off to the side surveying the talent. His name was Allan Buchman; Jessica knew him from around the poetry scene, and Erik knew him from several years back when he'd had a theater company that used Allan's rehearsal space. An enigmatic sixtysomething presence with an always-flickering twinkle in his eye and an affinity for Tibetan silk shirts, Allan is the Joe Papp of the twenty-first century with a yogi twist. A former antique-piano expert with a countercultural background, Allan changed his life entirely in the early nineties, opening a theater and starting a second career as a producer. Allan has both a great willingness to seek out new artists and new work and a great talent for nurturing them, as evidenced by the fact that he was spending a Monday night—the only night theater people ever have off—at a poetry slam, listening for promising young writers.

Jessica had just finished one of her poems when Allan sidled up to Erik and asked him what he was up to these days. Erik mooned around a little about his newfound love, then mentioned that we had this project we'd been working on, and we weren't sure where to take it next. Allan had just opened a new theater space downtown called the 45 Bleecker Theater, a three-hundred-seat former lumberyard. He loosely mentioned that we should "drop something off sometime," so a couple days later, we did. The next day, Allan called us up and asked us out to lunch to talk about the proposal.

When we sat down at a little NoHo café with Allan, our faith in our abilities was lacking; his faith in us was loud and immediate. We started spouting off about our ideas for the play, trying to explain ourselves; about five minutes in, he interrupted us and said, "Great; can you have something up before the elections?"

We said, "Sure." Having absolutely no idea what we were getting ourselves into, we went home from that lunch and promptly started calling every single person we'd ever known. If Connie's prodding had kicked us out of the idea stage into the proposal stage, Allan's deadline catapulted us out of the proposal stage into the "Uh-oh-now-we-have-to-really-do-something" stage. Thanks to that deadline's proximity, there was no time to really think about the "uh-oh" part. We had just enough time to realize that to actually do this thing required skills and resources far beyond what either of us possessed—but not enough time to worry about that fact. If we'd had even a minute to sit down and think about it, we probably would've been paralyzed.

We knew that if we were going to have something ready to go before audiences in six months, we had to use every second. So we just begged everyone we knew for help. We built a makeshift office in our four-hundred-square-footer with its fussy fax machine and a computer so old you had to kick-start it, and we started making calls. We called journalist friends and asked them how to conduct interviews; we called fund-raiser friends and asked them how to raise money; and most importantly, we called attorney and activist friends and asked them how on earth we could track down the (then) eighty-nine men and women who had been exonerated from death row.

From Jessica's activist experience and from our research, we had some idea of where to look for the major wrongful-conviction organizations. We contacted all the ones who would talk to us, and eventually we started hearing the same refrain: "You have to talk to Larry Marshall at the Center on Wrongful Convictions."

The Center on Wrongful Convictions is a pioneering program that was started at Northwestern University by Larry Marshall, a lawyer and professor of law, and David Protess, a journalism professor. The center has gained national renown through an innovative approach that combines legal and journalistic research with a very hands-on education for Northwestern law and journalism students. One of the biggest obstacles to the successful appeal of wrongful convictions is that often, evidence indicating a defendant's innocence goes uninvestigated simply because of the immense expense and time commitment associated with re-investigating the cases. The Center on Wrongful Convictions addresses this problem by assigning teams of Northwestern University students to do investigative work on possible wrongful-conviction cases. From thousands of applicants, the program carefully evaluates cases and selects the ones with the most glaring evidence of wrongful conviction. From there, the students work on investigations under the guidance of their professors, themselves working attorneys and journalists. Staff of the Center on Wrongful Convictions have been involved in the appeals of nine of the thirteen people who have been exonerated from Illinois's death row since the reinstatement of the death penalty in 1976.

In 1998, the Center on Wrongful Convictions held a historic conference that brought together twenty-eight exonerated death row inmates in one place for the first time. Everyone we spoke to in our search for the exonerated folks remembered that conference and thought that the people who had organized it, if we could win them over, might be of great help to us.

Oddly, Erik remembered that he'd randomly cut out a *New York Times* article about that 1998 conference years before; he'd tucked it in a folder hidden deep in the recesses of his comic book collection. He wasn't the kind of person to stockpile newspaper clippings, but somehow, this one had struck him. "I wonder what it must feel like," he remembered thinking, "to have something like that happen to you."

So we called Larry Marshall's office, armed with a long list of names of individuals they knew who had recommended that we speak to them. After several conversations in which we ticked off all those names repeatedly (and several days when our messages weren't returned, during which, we assume, our credentials were screened and discussed), we were put through to Jamie Alter-Linten, a staff member at the center, who decided that we were more or less harmless and it wouldn't hurt to help us. Jamie had a list of exonerated people who had participated in the conference a few years before. Some of the contact information might not be up-to-date, and we might have to do some more sleuthing, but their list would provide us with enough leads to make some real headway. Jamie also advised us to keep in mind that the list consisted of people who had wanted to speak publicly about their experiences two years before. They might not all feel the same way now.

From that list, and from other leads we'd gotten from various defense attorneys along the way, we located forty of the then eight-nine people who'd been exonerated from death row.

Now we had to call each of them. Cold.

We sat for an hour on the futon in our office/kitchen/living room/dining room, phone in hand, to make the first call. A little excited, but mostly really, really nervous, and a little guilty, too. Here we were, a couple kids in New York City, calling these people who'd been through ordeals beyond anything we could even imagine, to ask them to talk to us—strangers—about the most difficult and painful parts of their lives. We knew we'd sound ridiculous: "Um, hi? You don't know us, but we're actors from New York, and we want to write, um, a play about death row. . . . Would you . . . talk to us?"

Erik was further impeded by his Minnesotan background: Midwesterners don't ask for favors easily. As a kid, Erik once secretly paid for ten boxes of Cub Scout cookies out of his own pocket rather than knock on doors and sell them. So, because Jessica had been raised as a pushy East Coaster, the task of the first phone call fell to her. We looked at the list of names, trying to decide whom to call first. We settled on Shabaka Brown, whose case we'd recently finished reading an article about, because he had a Washington, D.C., address listed and that's where Jessica grew up. Every little bit of familiarity helped.

Shabaka was tough—he'd obviously dealt with more than his share of media vultures—and he asked us a lot of questions. He might consider talking to us, he said, but first we'd have to fax a proposal and some information about ourselves to his office so he could see what we were all about. He'd look at it when he got to work the next day. Fair enough. We faxed the materials to the number he gave us and made the rest of the calls, starting at the beginning of the list.

It took a long time for us to get through to everyone—people weren't home, we figured they wouldn't return long-distance messages from strangers, many of them didn't have answering machines anyway. But when we finally did get through, most of the exonerated folks said, yes, they'd be glad to talk with us. (Shabaka turned out to be one of the few exceptions.) Once a few of them said yes, we started feeling less nervous. It was clear that many of them had told their stories many times to journalists—they were much more at ease with our requests than we were. Lots of them clearly thought it was kind of funny that we were as nervous as we were. Many of them thought it was funny that some artsy theater kids would want to put them in a *play*. And some of them even found it funny that we lived in New York. "Why the heck anyone would want to live someplace like that is beyond me," one person said. "It's dangerous there." Umm . . . hadn't he seen much worse, what with his time on death row and all? "Yeah, but New York is *really* dangerous; heard about what happened to that Louima fellow, I've seen *NYPD Blue*. I just don't know why anyone would want to walk around in the middle of all that." Eventually, after amusing several exonerated people, we started to relax.

We conducted pre-interviews over the phone; from those interviews we were able to gauge people's varying levels of enthusiasm, articulateness (all of them were uniquely so), and eagerness to participate in our project. We also started to file away each of the cases in our imaginations, trying to suss out which ones would fit best in the context of what we were trying to accomplish. We took note of who seemed most interested and began to compile a final list of people we would travel to meet.

Chapter Three

Allan had given us $1,000 in seed money and lent us his theater's nonprofit status; since we were working out of our living room/kitchen/dining room with no assistant, and we could put off paying the long-distance bills for a couple months, we used that seed money to begin our travels across the country.

There wasn't enough to cover plane tickets, so we decided to drive. We bought a road atlas and began mapping our first trip, which would cover the Mid-Atlantic and Midwest, from New York to Minnesota and every conceivable zigzag in between. We calculated the mileage between Erie, Pennsylvania, and Xenia, Ohio; between the South Side of Chicago and the Illinois/Wisconsin border. We budgeted for a rental car (you don't need a license to ride the subway, so we hardly had driver's licenses, much less a car of our own). We tried to find a free dog-sitter for Zooey—with no success. We threw away the perishables in our fridge. Then we called all the exonerated folks in the Mid-Atlantic and Midwest who had agreed to meet with us and started scheduling interviews.

To keep our itinerary straight, we typed everything up—complete with complicated driving directions down labyrinthine country roads that included notes like "If you pass the Dairy Queen beyond the river trestle, turn around—you've gone too far." When we walked out our front door two weeks later, with our backpacks and our bottled water and, yes, the dog, that typed-out itinerary was all we had to lean on. We were going places we'd never gone, to meet people we'd never met, to hear stories we'd never heard. We hoped those directions were good ones.

Our first scheduled interview was with a guy named Neil Ferber. He didn't live too far away—just outside Philly—so we knew we'd arrive at his house after only a few hours on the road. Erik, ever the well-mannered Minnesotan, had offered to bring breakfast over to Neil's from a nearby Denny's (which, we'd been told, if we passed it, we'd know we'd gone too far). Neil seemed to think that us bringing him breakfast was kind of weird, though, and said don't worry about the food, just come on by.

It was a sunny summer morning in eastern Pennsylvania. We spent most of the time in the car double-checking to make sure we still had our itinerary, fighting the dog off the gearshift and back into the backseat, and reviewing the many, many questions we'd written down to ask Neil.

Erik had packed extra batteries, tapes, videotapes, paper towels, vitamins, a copy of *Crime and Punishment*, a secret stash of comic books, dried fruit, legal pads, and a RadioShack car charger into an old wooden fruit crate and dubbed it the portable office. On the side of the crate was a sticker that depicted a 1920s farmer gazing proudly out above a fruited plain. Erik made some *Grapes of Wrath* reference regarding the sticker and then went off on one of his associative tangents, suggesting that maybe there was some poetic parallel there—you know, embarking on a cross-country search for freedom and all—and sarcastically suggested maybe we could explore that when we wrote the book about our trip. Then we both dissolved in peals of laughter. That notion was completely absurd: we'd be lucky if our closest friends were willing to listen to our stories when we got back.

A few weeks earlier, just after Allan had given us our election-night deadline, we'd realized that neither of us had the foggiest idea how to conduct an interview. We called up Leslie Garis (the writer who, with her husband, Arthur, had been dragged along on our first date by Erik) and begged her to let us take her out to lunch and pick her brain. The first thing Leslie told us about interviewing was to keep a jar in our kitchen that we'd fill up with hundreds of questions. We might not use any of them, she said, but it was important to think them up, and to know they were there. We took Leslie's advice, except instead of putting the questions in a jar, we wrote them down in Jessica's journal.

So, in the car on the way to Philly, we sat with the notebook spread open and attempted to *memorize* every one of the over two hundred questions we'd thought up. *Tell us about your case. Did you dream in prison? What food did you miss most when you were inside?*

When did you first know you were going in? When did you first know you were getting out? Who told you? What was that like? Who helped you? Who got in your way? Did you have friends in prison? Enemies? Describe a typical morning. And on and on and on. We figured that if we could remember every single question we'd thought of, nobody would be able to figure out that we had absolutely no clue what we were doing.

We didn't know what to expect from Neil. We'd been unable to find much press about his case, so we knew little about his story, beyond that it involved a frame-up that seemed to have something to do with some higher-ups in Philadelphia politics. We'd spoken to him on the phone and knew he had a classic Philly accent and was gregarious, a big talker, but beyond that he was enigmatic. When we asked about the background of his case, he said, "We can get into alla that when you guys show up." Okay.

One of the few things we did know about Neil was that he was one of the only exonerated death row inmates in the country who'd received any remuneration. It is an almost incomprehensibly unfair fact that, in most states, when innocent people are freed from death row, they receive no compensation from the state that wrongfully convicted them. They are almost always set outside the prison doors with nothing more than a bus ticket home—if that—and expected to start over from scratch, after years with no income or job history. Can you imagine going to a job interview and explaining a twenty-year gap in your work history? Even if you're cleared and released, you still have to check that little box that most of us pass over, the one that asks, "Have you ever been convicted of a felony?" There's no extra sheet provided to write out an explanation, no paper clip to attach an article to that job application, no space for a statement from your lawyers. Even if your conviction was wrong, in the eyes of prospective employers you're marked for life.

But despite this, most states are not financially obligated in any way to the innocent people that they convict. Further, in most places, exonerated people are forbidden by law to sue the state. And even in the few states where exonerated people can bring suit against the government, most often they are required to prove malice: that the prosecution *intentionally* took action for malicious reasons, a difficult proposition given that intentions are conveniently subjective things that tend to exist only inside people's heads.

But Neil's case was different. There was evidence to indicate that Philadelphia higher-ups may intentionally have obscured the facts in Neil's case, and when a newly released Neil brought a lawsuit against the city of Philadelphia, he was awarded a $4.5 million settlement by a jury. When the city appealed the decision, Judge John Herron reportedly said that he was forced to overturn the jury verdict because of technical changes in state liability laws. In his ruling, Judge Herron nonetheless said that he believed Neil's case was a "Kafkaesque nightmare . . . the so-called justice system of a totalitarian state," and that police involved in the case had "tampered with identification evidence and misled judicial officers." Judge Herron, according to the *Philadelphia Inquirer,* also "sent clear signals that Ferber could seek redress in federal court." Soon after that ruling, the city entered into negotiations with Neil. In the deal that resulted from those negotiations, the city admitted no official wrongdoing, but Neil was awarded a substantial settlement.

So, that Neil lived in a quiet suburban neighborhood was no surprise to us, nor was his nice split-level house on a cul-de-sac. We thought that might be a Corvette under the car cover in the driveway, but after three and a half years in prison for a crime he didn't commit, hey, he deserved an indulgence or two.

We put the car in park, cracked the window for the dog, wedged the portable office from the trunk, squeezed each other's hands, and rang the doorbell. The large oak door swung open to reveal Neil, around five feet five, a slimmer Joe Pesci look-alike with slicked-back hair, wearing slippers. He grinned at us and said to come on in. He sat us down in his carpeted living room and offered us something to drink. We said yes just so we could have a moment to fumble with our tape recorders with nobody around to witness our technological ineptitude. By the time Neil came back with orange juice, we'd set up our full-size tape recorder and two mini tape recorders—all courtesy of RadioShack—on the coffee table and attached our borrowed camcorder to its broken tripod with duct tape. Pretty securely. We hoped.

As soon as we pressed RECORD and Neil started talking, we realized that Leslie hadn't been kidding when she said we wouldn't actually *use* the two hundred questions we'd thought up. Our valiant attempts at memorization in the car served no actual purpose beyond soothing our nerves. Questions like *What foods did you miss in prison?* and *What did you dream about?* had little significance next to the incredible things that started coming out of Neil's mouth.

In 1981, Neil told us, he was a furniture salesman in northeast Philadelphia who was going through a divorce. He had some shady friends who he says probably had mob ties, but he didn't know it for a fact; Neil himself was not involved with organized crime and had no known enemies. In May of that year, Neil was arrested out of the blue for the murder of Greek mobster Chelsais "Steve" Bouras and his dinner guest, Jeanette Curro, who were shot one evening while dining at the Meletis Restaurant in South Philadelphia. Neil had an ironclad alibi, he told us—he was at a party all the way across town the entire night; as Neil told us, partygoers testified to this, including several who had no previous relationship to Neil and thus were neutral witnesses. Further, eyewitnesses to Bouras's and Curro's murders described a reddish blond gunman, big and stocky, weighing about two hundred pounds. Neil is wiry, even slight, and had dark, buzz-cut hair at the time. The prosecution, Neil told us, used his social acquaintanceship with low-level mob figures to create suspicion against him at trial, despite Neil's alibi, his total lack of resemblance to the actual killer, and a lack of physical evidence associating him with the crime in any way.

The prosecution also introduced as evidence the testimony of Gerald Jordan, a former cellmate of Neil's at the Philadelphia Detention Center. Gerald Jordan, Neil told us, had spent much of his adult life in jail for petty crimes. In Neil's first trial, Jordan told the jury that Neil had confessed in jail to being one of two gunmen who shot Bouras and Curro. Largely as a result of this testimony, Neil was convicted and sentenced to death. Gerald Jordan later recanted; Neil told us that he'd heard that, in exchange for his testimony, Jordan had been allowed by police to leave jail and spend a (loosely) supervised evening at the house of his girlfriend, with whom he allegedly had sex. Neil told us that it was his understanding that he was wrongly pursued in part because the South Philly police department and judiciary may have been tainted with all manner of alliances. After Neil was freed and reached a settlement with the city, the real gunman was never pursued.

Sprinkled in with this extraordinary story were even more extraordinary details you'd never find in any newspaper—for example, that Neil was so confident that his innocence would eventually come to light that he had suntan lotion brought into the prison and sunbathed in the yard so he'd look good when he got out. That he was making plans to go to Aruba from prison, just to keep his outlook positive. Also, Neil told us, in an active effort to preserve his sanity in solitary confinement, "I usedta rearrange furniture from my store in my mind; I'd rearrange furniture in my house; I'd put some math problems down on paper and try and solve it. I came outta there like Einstein."

Sitting on Neil's beige couches, listening to him talk, it hit us both—really for the first time—that making this play would be possible. Because not only did Neil have an incredible story, he was also an incredible *character.* All the details—his accent, the cadences of his sentences, the metaphors he used, how he used to get mad at the other inmates blaring hip-hop on their radios so he'd blast country western just to piss them off even though he hated country music almost as much as he hated rap—made his story memorable in a way that no newspaper article could ever convey. They made him *human.* And because we work in theater, as soon as we saw him as human in all the details, we could imagine him as a character. We could see an actor playing Neil, adopting his mannerisms, finding his voice (in the first readings of the play, that actor would turn out to be Steve Buscemi). And once we could see that, we could see the first tiny fragment of a play.

Other exonerated folks we'd meet that summer would break our hearts, make us reconsider our assumptions in about 5 billion different ways, educate us philosophically, scare us, reassure us, wake us up. Neil's gift to us, in all his particularities, was to show us that we could do what we had set out to do—we could bring these stories to the stage.

After a few hours, the interview wound down. We'd hardly looked at each other the whole time we'd been in Neil's living room; we were both so blown away by his personality and his story that we knew if we caught each other's eyes, we'd be overcome with the desire to communicate further. We said our thank-yous to Neil, pressed STOP on all the tape recorders, and continued to avoid eye contact with each other. Erik asked Neil what kind of car was under the cover in the driveway; Neil grinned like a proud father and said we could have a look on the way out. He walked us outside to show us the car, which did indeed turn out to be a gorgeous white Corvette.

As we left the air-conditioned cool of Neil's foyer, we were hit with a blast of thick, hot air. While we'd been interviewing Neil, the cool suburban morning had turned to afternoon, and the temperature had risen about fifteen degrees. Zooey was in the car. She was panting far too hard, scrambling all over the backseat; she looked like she was dying. Erik appreciated the Corvette *really quickly* while Jessica, playing into a sexist stereotype for the dog's sake, feigned polite disinterest in automobiles and ran around our rental car to let Zooey out the other side. After Erik spent a few moments with the Corvette, we said our good-byes with Neil, he went inside, and we set to work rehydrating our poor, overheated, lonely dog. She drank all three liters of bottled water we'd brought and demanded that we keep the air-conditioning cranked up full blast practically all the way to Ohio.

We had eight hours to make it to our next interview, just outside Columbus, Ohio. Dale Johnston, the man we were supposed to meet, graciously kept the next morning open for us, too, just in case we got stuck in traffic. Good thing. We drove for hours and hours and hours, hardly seeming to get any closer to the state line. Erik, having three years later experienced this phenomenon repeatedly, graciously calls it "Jessica mileage," explaining that Jessica's positive outlook on the world also extends to her interpretation of maps, and that any long car trip will always take at least two hours longer than Jessica says it will. Jessica counters that Pennsylvania is just a *really big* state. Either way, Pennsylvania was taking a very long time.

We spent most of the drive with our laptop and cell phones plugged into the charger attached to the car's cigarette lighter, tangled up in wires, working. We had three interviews firmly scheduled for this trip—Neil, Dale Johnston, and Gary Gauger in Illinois—and several other potential interviews, people who had agreed to meet with us but who'd been unreachable when we called them back for scheduling. The closest of those, Randall Dale Adams, was in Ohio, and we were hoping to meet with him the next day. (Randall's case was the subject of the acclaimed and chilling Errol Morris documentary *The Thin Blue Line;* we'd both been familiar with his case long before we hatched the idea for the play, so we especially wanted to meet with him.) We were also still trying to set up meetings with a man in Chicago named Perry Cobb, as well as with a former high-school principal in Pennsylvania named Jay Smith, whom we were hoping to meet on our way back. We'd sent a packet to another guy in Chicago named Delbert Tibbs, but he didn't have a phone, so our expectations were low. There was an outside chance we'd be able to meet Rolando Cruz, recently exonerated in Illinois, though we hadn't spoken with him yet. And "Jessica mileage" remained in effect, so we also had to reach Dale Johnston and take him up on his offer to reschedule for the next morning. One of us drove while the other sat in the passenger seat, leaving and checking messages endlessly. And keeping Zooey off the gearshift.

We knew we were nearing Ohio when the mountains flattened out and we began to notice intensely worded antiabortion flyers tacked to all the telephone poles. We looked at each other, feeling our first real twinges of culture shock. Philly was one thing. So were the misty, uninhabited mountains of rural Pennsylvania. And we could handle foraging for *something* vegetarian (Jessica having successfully converted Erik the month before) amongst the McDonald's and gas-station convenience stores. But now for the first time we weren't driving through a city or suburbs or a rural area where we were pretty much alone—but instead through a place full of people who thought very differently from us and didn't much like New Yorkers.

Of course we'd both spent time in places where the prevailing opinions were different from ours. We'd both traveled a lot; we left our little island frequently. But this time felt different, and as we drove through the concrete-and-dried-grass towns of eastern Ohio, we tried to figure out why. We finally realized that when we'd traveled outside our sphere in the past, we'd always been comfortable being outsiders. That's the normal mode of traveling—you leave your home to go somewhere unfamiliar, and you're different from the people there, and you mostly stay out of their world and they stay out of yours, and everyone keeps a respectful distance that enables them to coexist.

But here, we were trying to get inside. We were asking people to invite us into their homes, expecting them to tell us private details of the most intense experiences of their lives. We were asking them to let us in. And so we worried: Would they really want to open up their lives to people who were so different? Much is made of the resentment and judgment that religious conservatives feel toward free-thinking city folks. There was no question that we'd fit someone's definition of sinners—tattooed, unmarried *Nation* subscribers with polymorphous friends and lifestyles way outside the corporate world—and we didn't want to hide our backgrounds, even if we could. So would they still let us in? And was it even our place to ask them to?

We got a resounding yes to both questions when we arrived at Dale Johnston's house the next day. A genteel Caucasian man in his late sixties with immaculately groomed white hair and mustache, Dale greeted us at his door in a blue seersucker suit and immediately explained that his wife had been meaning to bake us a cake, but she got held up working the night shift at the hospital and wanted him to communicate her sincerest apologies. We told him it was, um, really no problem and looked down self-consciously at our scruffy jeans and sneakers, thinking we should've been the ones to bring the cake. Dale led us through their modest, cozy house, pointing out framed family pictures and a beautiful leather-bound Bible along the way. He suggested that since it was such a nice day (cool enough to leave Zooey safely in the car this time), we sit and talk out on the deck. The house, variously decorated with knickknacks and wall hangings quoting Scripture, and seventies-style furniture and pressboard bookshelves, made Erik feel like he'd stepped into his grandparents' Minnesota living room. Another large Bible sat prominently on the coffee table, underlined, written in, dog-eared, friendly.

In the back, we set up our equipment on a brand-new deck that Dale had built with his own hands. Dale was a carpenter in a long line of carpenters and had lived in Ohio all his life, although he joked that he was "a true Southerner," having been "born in the south side of the room, in a house on the south side of the street, on the south side of town, in the southern half of the state." He certainly had the impeccable manners and graceful bearing of a Southerner. Dale had rebuilt his career building houses in the ten years since his release from prison and was now semiretired, as was his new wife, a night nurse at the local hospital. Both were devout Christians; Dale had gained his extensive knowledge of Scripture while spending seven years on Ohio's death row for a crime he didn't commit.

In 1982, Dale told us, he was married to his first wife, Sarah, and lived with Sarah and her two daughters on the outskirts of Logan, Ohio. They had a quiet, mostly peaceful family life; according to Dale, he had had a somewhat turbulent relationship with Sarah's older daughter, Annette, but that was understandable: she was a teenager, itching to marry her fiancé, Todd, and leave home, and he was her stepdad, a relative newcomer to the family who nonetheless held most of the authority. Dale and Sarah had just returned from a vacation to North Carolina; Annette was home with them for the weekend. On October 5, Annette went into town to stay with Todd and his family. Evidently, Dale told us, Annette and Todd had some kind of disagreement, and Annette left his house to walk toward the office where her mother worked. Todd followed, witnesses saw the two of them have a conversation on the sidewalk, and then Annette went back in the other direction with Todd.

Dale told us that he and Sarah received a phone call from Todd's mother that night, around ten thirty, asking if he knew where Annette and Todd were. Dale said no, he didn't; Todd's mother said thank-you, and that was the end of the conversation. Nobody seemed particularly concerned that the two of them were out late; they were teenagers, and teenagers stay out till all hours sometimes. But the next morning, they still weren't back. At first, Dale said, there wasn't a great deal of alarm about their whereabouts; they'd been talking about taking off and getting married, running away together, and everyone figured that was where they'd gone. But then a couple days went by and nobody heard from them, and Dale started bugging the police to get out there and find the kids. The police organized a search party, which went looking in a remote area of Hocking County, Ohio, by the Hocking River. After searching for some time, the party turned up a gruesome discovery: two torsos in the river.

Dale told us that at that point he and Sarah were still somewhat in denial—the police couldn't ID the torsos as belonging to Annette and Todd, and Dale said, "We didn't want to believe it was our kids." But earlier that same year, another couple had been dismembered in a mysterious murder near Columbus, not so far from the Hocking River. So the police stepped up their search, and not long after, in a cornfield, they found the remaining body parts, buried in a circle. From this, they were able to ID the victims as Annette and Todd.

In many rural, highly religious communities, when particularly gruesome murders happen, investigators sometimes jump to the conclusion that the crimes are occult-related, even when little evidence indicates that this is the case. This well-documented phenomenon, sometimes referred to as Satanic Panic, has showed up in connection with many questionable convictions, most notably those of the "West Memphis Three," Arkansas teenagers who came under suspicion for a horrific triple murder in large part because of their interest in heavy-metal music and nature magic. (That case is currently being appealed; for more information, see the HBO documentary *Paradise Lost*, parts one and two, or visit www.wm3.org.)

But this situation was the opposite. In this case, according to Dale, significant evidence suggested that these murders had in fact been related to some sort of ritualized behavior—notably, the dismemberment of the bodies, the painstaking burial of the body parts in a circular formation, and the discovery of another young couple similarly dismembered in a nearby area just a few months before. But this theory was never pursued with any vigor. Instead, Dale told us, investigators focused suspicion on him—and spent a full year making speculative accusations against Dale in the press before ever charging him with anything. In a small town like Logan, this kind of action is known as "tainting the jury pool."

That summer, we would hear of this phenomenon again and again, all over the country. It is responsible for an enormous number of wrongful convictions. Think about it: most of us are at least influenced by what we read in the paper, even if we read it critically. And in most small towns, there are only one or two news sources. So if everyone in the town is getting their news from the same sources, and those sources repeatedly print or broadcast articles in which authority figures express suspicion, no matter how unfounded, toward one person, and most people in the town trust their authority figures—well, after a while, it creates a bias. And when those townspeople make up the entire pool of potential jurors in a case, it becomes quite difficult for any of those jurors to view the evidence as they are required to by law: impartially, and without preconceptions.

Three years after Annette and Todd were murdered, Dale Johnston was brought to trial and convicted of their murder. This despite a lack of any credible physical evidence implicating him, and despite that Dale was at home with his wife and younger stepdaughter the entire night, both of whom, Dale told us, repeatedly testified to this fact under oath.

Dale's conviction was mostly due to two pieces of evidence. The first was the testimony of a witness who claimed to have seen "a man" irately order a couple to get into his car in downtown Logan that night. After undergoing hypnosis nearly three weeks after Annette and Todd's bodies were found, this witness identified Dale as the man in question from a photograph that had been published in a newspaper.

The second piece of evidence was the only physical evidence linking Dale to the crime: the testimony of an anthropologist, Louise Robbins, who claimed to have determined that a bootprint found near the bodies was made by Dale. Louise Robbins had given "expert" testimony regarding footprints at several criminal trials, based on a theory she'd come up with. She claimed that, because the way each person stands and walks is different, everyone's foot will leave a unique impression on any surface, including the inside sole of his or her shoe. Those impressions, she asserted, show up as "wear patterns" on the bottom of every shoe. Louise Robbins's work was later discredited by multiple sources, including the American Bar Association. Melvin Lewis, a law professor who keeps track of over five thousand expert witnesses nationwide, called Robbins's work "complete hogwash . . . it barely rises to the dignity of nonsense," saying, "Her so-called evidence was so grotesquely ridiculous, it's necessary to say to yourself, if that can get in, what can't?" And FBI agent William Bodziak, one of the world's leading footprint experts, is quoted as saying that Louise Robbins's theories had absolutely no foundation.

Robbins's claim that she could identify a bootprint near the crime scene as belonging to Dale was the *only* physical evidence that implicated him in the crime. But jurors in Dale's first trial were not allowed to hear any of the criticisms leveled against Louise Robbins's theories, or even that those theories were controversial at all. Dale was convicted and sentenced to death.

After Dale had spent several years on Ohio's death row, the Court of Appeals vacated his conviction on the grounds that the testimony from the man who'd identified Dale was completely untrustworthy. After his conviction was vacated, Dale's attorneys—who, believing firmly in Dale's innocence, had stuck by him after his initial conviction and filed numerous appeals on his behalf—discovered four witnesses who, independent of each other, had each seen Annette and Todd that night, walking along railroad tracks near the cornfield where their bodies were found. The witnesses also testified that they had each heard gunshots in the area at that time. These four witnesses had seen Annette and Todd near the cornfield at the same time that the hypnotized witness claimed to have seen them being ordered into a car by Dale—in downtown Logan. Based on the testimony of these four individuals, there was no way the couple seen by the hypnotized witness could have been Annette and Todd; and the man ordering them into a car would *not* have been Dale. The authorities had known about these four independent witnesses prior to Dale's first trial, but had not disclosed their existence to Dale's attorneys.

Dale told us that he made it through his years on death row largely through religion, engaging in intensive Bible study during his time in prison. He also devoted himself to making conditions better for his fellow inmates. Most of the guards, he told us, knew about his case and believed in his innocence, so he was treated well. He used this favorable treatment to help improve conditions for everyone. Dale told us:

> When I first got on death row, we was locked in those cages twenty-three hours and thirty-seven minutes a day, except a ten-minute shower, three times a week. Well, the Lord worked through me, and one other inmate down there, to change that. When I left death row, about five years later, the men could be out of their cells up to eight hours a day. We obtained outside recreation, we established a regular library, a law library, had adult basic-education classes, had jobs for the death row inmates to do. When I first got down there, like anybody else, I'm sayin', "Now what? You got kicked in the teeth pretty good this time, what're you gonna do about it?" Said, "Gonna feel sorry for yourself, or gonna make the best of a bad situation?" And I choose the latter. I knew that the state may still have the legal right to kill us. But it does not have the legal right to torture us before doing so, and that's what was being done. So I set out to change that. Set out to put a little bit of the quality back in the life of every man on death row.

Not only did Dale lose a child, he lost just about everything else—his freedom, his contact with his surviving loved ones, his marriage. Sadly, coping with the loss of a child and a prison sentence at once was too much for Dale and Sarah's marriage to bear—even though, as Dale told us, Sarah has always backed him 100 percent, not once doubting his innocence. (We would learn that many, many families don't make it through the separation, the trauma, the twelve-hour drives for one-hour visits once a week; in all our travels that summer, we would encounter only one marriage that had survived death row.) We saw a flicker of how deeply all this had impacted Dale in one moment when we asked him what he'd dreamt about while in prison. He looked us straight on and told us that he'd never dreamt when he was in there—never. And the look in his eye told us that we'd trespassed into some emotional territory that wasn't ours to explore.

Respectfully, we retreated from the subject and let Dale lead us the rest of the way. But that was just a moment, and in the end Dale told us that despite everything—except the death of his stepdaughter, from which he would never recover—he was ultimately able to look at his time on death row as a blessing, because it gave him an opportunity to get serious about religion and to help others.

We were hoping to meet Dale's new wife, whom he'd met through their church just a couple years earlier. It was nine in the morning, and he expected her home from her night shift soon. To pass some time, Dale brought us into the house and showed us his old photo albums from nearly fifty years before, when he'd been stationed in French Morocco as an air force mechanic—the only division of the armed forces that was looking for "technicians, not fighters," as he'd told us earlier. Our politics predisposed us to be critical of an American military that supported colonial powers, and we wondered how the Moroccans in the fifties had felt about the Western presence in their country—a clear example of the ideological differences we'd been so nervous about when we'd first entered Ohio. But we saw the young man in those yellowed photos—strong, tall, almost as poised as the older version here with us—and we thought about all the places he'd been in his life, and in his kitchen, for a moment, we were able to do what we hoped eventually to bring our audiences to do. We looked at someone so entirely unlike us, with beliefs, background, life experiences, so dissimilar from our own—and saw the human being.

Dale shook our hands, looked us in the eyes, and walked onto the front lawn to see us out. As we crossed the street to our car, we heard him say a friendly, warm hello to his neighbor, who was out pulling weeds in the adjoining lawn. We looked back just in time to see Dale's neighbor turn his head away, refusing to return the greeting. Dale quietly looked down, walked back into his home, and closed the door.

Chapter Four

After meeting Dale, it was on to Chicago. Over the cell phone, we'd had a lot of back-and-forth with Randall Dale Adams's defense investigator, who'd been helpful in trying to schedule an interview; but our attempts to meet Randall didn't seem to be panning out. We'd tried hard to meet him; because of *The Thin Blue Line*, Randall's case was one of the most well-known exonerations in recent memory, and we were intrigued. But, we speculated, the same reason we wanted to meet him might be the very reason he wasn't available to talk with us: we imagined that after the film came out, journalists, reporters, and documentarians from all over the world had attempted to contact Randall, seeking comments about his own case and about other people's executions and exonerations. Every few weeks, another interview request. We imagined how frustrating and exhausting that must be: strangers from the TV news calling you up constantly, demanding the details of the hardest moments of your life for little or no compensation. Two hours of talking to strangers for a two-minute segment on the news, and then all the reporters just take off and your life doesn't change one bit. We resigned ourselves to not being able to meet with Randall. And we also resolved something else: if we made this play happen, we would make sure that the people whose stories wound up in it wouldn't be forgotten so easily.

That settled, we left Ohio behind and set out for Illinois. We were tired, having slept just a few hours the previous night on a floor belonging to Erik's old college friend Chris, and then having woken up at 5 a.m. to drive from Columbus to interview Dale. But we'd budgeted for one night only in a motel room, and we were saving that for Chicago. Beyond that, we were sleeping in the car. So we were thankful just to have had a floor to sleep on. And Midwestern convenience stores may not be stocked with vegetarian food, but they do have coffee, so we were doing okay. Or at least a jittery variation on "okay." Erik did most of the driving while Jessica slept entangled in the wires of our portable office, waking only to make zillions of phone calls to Chicago.

We had three still-unscheduled interviews in Chicago—with Rolando Cruz, Perry Cobb, and this guy Delbert, whom we'd only been able to reach by mail. We'd spoken with Perry once but had been unable to reach him again for scheduling, and though we hadn't made any contact with Rolando, the Center on Wrongful Convictions had said they'd try to contact him for us.

We'd been trying to get through to the center for the last two days, with no luck. We were beginning to wonder if it even made sense for us to make the drive to Chicago, given that everything was so up in the air there, and we didn't even have a hotel room. As the day went on and on, we had our first ever real argument (aside from a heated late-night disagreement a month earlier concerning the gender politics of *The Taming of the Shrew*). Jessica was yelling at Erik to drive faster, Erik was yelling at Jessica that she'd underestimated the mileage, and we were both yelling at each other about whether to go to Chicago. Mostly we were just nervous, scared we'd driven all this way and now we'd fail to get the interviews. We knew this was it—we couldn't afford to come to Chicago another time. And some of the most important interviews were in Chicago—after all, these exonerations were the ones that had prompted Governor Ryan to declare a moratorium on Illinois's death penalty, and several of them had been national news. We decided to just keep driving and hope something would come through.

After we'd spent hours leaving messages, wrestling the dog into the backseat, and flipping between various whacked-out AM talk-radio stations, the cell phone *finally* rang. It was Larry Marshall, the attorney who's one of the founders of the Center on Wrongful Convictions. He was sorry he hadn't gotten back to us sooner, but he'd been waiting to hear back from some of the exonerated folks. Rolando Cruz couldn't speak to us, as he had just brought a wrongful-conviction lawsuit against the state and wasn't speaking to the media while the suit was pending. Perry Cobb he hadn't been able to reach, and he had the same number for Perry as we did, so we'd just have to keep trying. And had we had any luck finding Delbert Tibbs? We told Larry that we'd mailed Delbert some information about our project a few weeks earlier and hadn't heard back; we couldn't call to follow up because Delbert didn't have a phone. Larry told us that he didn't have a number for Delbert either, but we should really try to get ahold of him while we were in town. Maybe we knew someone who could go and leave a note on his door? Larry had one piece of surprise good news for us, too: he knew another exonerated man from Chicago named Darby Tillis, who hadn't been on the list of people we'd originally called. Darby lived in Texas these days but happened to be passing through Chicago at the moment. Larry had contacted Darby for us, told him a little about our project, and Darby had agreed to meet with us that night at 9 p.m. at the Golden Nugget Pancake House. Westward ho.

In the meantime, we knew absolutely nothing about Chicago geography and needed to find a motel. Jessica, despite her growing bad reputation for map interpretation, scrutinized the Chicago city map in our road atlas and tried to remember what she'd heard about the different neighborhoods. Around that time, the cell phone rang again. It was Connie, the artist-organizing angel who'd impelled us to write our proposal, calling up to see how things were going.

"Better than they were an hour ago," we told her, explaining that we'd finally at least pinned down one Chicago interview, with Darby Tillis. But we were still trying to reach Perry Cobb, and Delbert was proving elusive. In a moment of the kind of synchronicity that would pop up again and again as we worked on this project, Connie told us that her friend Joann actually knew someone who knew Delbert. Joann is a Chicago theater director who was a casual friend of ours as well; she'd been supportive of the play so far, and Connie gave us Joann's number and told us to give her a call. We called Joann, who told us that she did, in fact, have a photographer friend, named Loren Santow, who'd been working on a series of portraits of exonerated people, and he'd just taken Delbert's portrait. Delbert lived just a few blocks from Loren's studio, and the two men had become friends. Joann gave us Loren's number and suggested we ask Loren to run around the corner and tack a note to Delbert's door. We thanked Joann profusely for her help, and before getting off the phone with her, we also asked which neighborhood in Chicago was which and where we should be looking for a motel. She gave us some good advice that was just the opposite of what Jessica'd guessed from her studies of the map. Thank God we asked a local.

We were able to reach Loren, and he was extremely generous and helpful, especially given that we were a couple kids he'd never met. Not only did Loren track down Delbert for us, he also offered his photography studio as a location for our interview—and told us we could bring the dog.

This was just the first of many synchronicities that would occur during the course of our work on the play. We would hit a wall, there'd be no visible ways around or through it, and then some weird coincidence would crop up that—combined with the generosity and support of loads of people around us (maybe the real miracle)—completely solved the problem.

We were scheduled to meet with Delbert at Loren's studio late that afternoon. We had another meeting scheduled with Darby Tillis later that night. Now we only had to take care of the motel. We'd called about eleven Chicago motels already; all of them were either full or wouldn't take the dog. But something would come up. Right?

We made it into Chicago just before our interview with Delbert was scheduled to begin. Delbert lived in a beautiful historic neighborhood; we got a full tour as we circled it over and over searching for parking. We were already running late, and Delbert had no phone we could call him on to let him know. We'd planned to meet Delbert outside his apartment; then the three of us would walk over to Loren's studio. We were so nervous about making Delbert wait for us, imagining him sitting out on his front steps and wondering if we'd show. We were both anxious, and this endless quest for parking wasn't helping. Turned out we didn't need to worry; Delbert wasn't exactly the kind of guy to get uptight about our being fifteen minutes late. To put it mildly.

After (finally) putting the car in park, we walked up to Delbert's brownstone building to find him sitting on his front steps, smoking a hand-rolled cigarette. A tall, slim African-American man in a worn polo shirt and shorts, Delbert looked like Laurence Fishburne's scruffy bohemian big brother. He must've been sixty, but age didn't really apply; he seemed simultaneously old in soul and young in spirit. Our first thought upon meeting Delbert was that he was organically and effortlessly cooler then anyone we'd ever met. And that was before he even opened his mouth.

Delbert shook our hands and we followed him to Loren's carpeted studio, Zooey in tow. Loren let us in and we watched, embarrassed, as Zooey raced around the studio, frantically sniffing everything and nearly knocking over stacks of expensive and irreplaceable-looking equipment. Finally we managed to corral Zooey and enclose her in the small area where we were sitting. Loren and Delbert were both laid-back about the whole spectacle; Loren poured ginger ale as we untangled all our cords and set up our cameras and tape recorders.

A true storyteller, Delbert started in on his story by setting the stage: "I'm a child of the sixties and the seventies," he began, "so, much of the philosophy that people were motivated by during those times, I was, and continue to be, motivated by. And Martin Luther King had blown my mind; Malcolm was my original hero, but Martin showed me—that even though most of my heroes have been warriors, that peace is superior to war. So in 1972, I went to seminary . . . because I thought that it would afford me a platform from which I could be a force for peace, a force for dialogue, and so forth."

Wow.

We hardly had to ask Delbert any questions; his story just flowed.

He told us that he'd attended seminary for a year and a half, but dropped out when the racism there became too overwhelming. He realized that the seminary leaders were hoping to deal with the racially charged and conflicted atmosphere of early-seventies America by scouting out young black men and women of conscience to, as Delbert put it, "kinda 'put in the gap.' And I was willing to be that, if I could do so without selling myself out or selling my people out . . . but the racism there was so pervasive you could cut it with a knife. And I decided the seminary wasn't going to take me where I wanted to go. So I dropped out of the seminary and started roaming America."

Delbert spent the next two years on a spiritual quest, he said: roaming the country on foot, going where the proverbial wind took him, sleeping under the stars. When he started out, he chose to disregard the fact that, especially down South, there might be white folks who didn't take too kindly to him coming into "their" towns, hitching on "their" highways, and so forth. He told us, "You guys, you've traveled all over the country, and you didn't give it a second thought, because it's your country. Now, it's my country, too, but everybody doesn't *see* it as being my country. I knew that. But in my mind, I decided I was gonna be free in terms of my movements. That I was gonna go wherever I wanted to go in America, in these United States, and if trouble came out of that, then I would deal with it when it came."

For two years, trouble stayed far away. But in 1974, Delbert told us, he was hitchhiking through Florida when, through several twists of fate, he got caught up in a situation he had nothing to do with—but that would in large part determine the next four years of his life. A teenage girl, Cynthia Nadeau, and a male friend had apparently been hitchhiking near Fort Myers, Florida, when they were attacked by a man who picked them up in his truck. Ms. Nadeau was raped, and her friend was murdered. Delbert didn't have a truck—he was traveling on foot—and he hadn't been anywhere in or near Fort Myers at the time the crime occurred. When he was stopped on the highway in Ocala, Florida, by police, Delbert didn't think much of it: it's routine procedure for police officers to stop hitchhikers on the highways, and he'd been stopped several times during his two years on the road. This time was a little different—the police told Delbert that they were investigating a crime that had occurred in southern Florida—but they didn't treat Delbert with suspicion, and apparently Delbert answered their questions to their satisfaction. After snapping a couple Polaroids, Delbert told us, the police officer wrote Delbert what amounted to a note of safe conduct. The note, Delbert recounted, basically said that he had been stopped and questioned, and that the officers were satisfied that he was not the person wanted in connection with the crime. They handed Delbert the note and sent him on his way.

Delbert continued traveling, heading into Mississippi, where he had family. He spent just over a week with them before he got back on the road, headed toward California. Soon after, he told us, he was stopped on the highway by Mississippi police investigating the Fort Myers crime. Delbert showed them the note he'd been given, explaining that he'd already been questioned and ruled out—he wasn't the guy they were looking for. The Mississippi officer said, "in effect, 'Bullshit,' " Delbert told us. "He said, you're Delbert Tibbs; I have a warrant for your arrest." Delbert was cuffed and brought to a Mississippi jail.

What Delbert didn't know at this time, he said, was that during the almost two weeks that had passed, the Fort Myers police had been unable to find the perpetrator, or even to identify any suspects. Hysteria and fear were building in the small town: an armed man was roaming the highways in their area, whom police had been unable to apprehend. Stoking the flames of the small town's fear was the fact that this assailant was a black man, and the two victims had been white. Fort Myers is a Southern, predominantly white town, and at that time racial tensions were still violently potent in small-town Florida. As Delbert reminded us, "This is 1974; black people had only had the right to vote since 1965, and this is a backwater town where it's run sorta like a plantation." Emotions were running high among the town's white residents, and a great deal of pressure was on police to come up with a suspect.

When she reported the crime, Delbert explained, Ms. Nadeau had described her assailant as a black man, about five foot six, very dark complexion, with pockmarked skin and a bush Afro. Delbert is over six foot three, lanky and slim, with light, smooth skin, and no Afro. Clearly, he didn't match the description of the man police were looking for. But he was a black man alone on the highway, and desperate for a suspect, Fort Myers police put out a call for assistance from all the police departments in the area. The Ocala police sent their Polaroids of Delbert to Fort Myers, and against all standard procedure, the photos were used to generate suspicion toward Delbert. The victim was shown the photos until she assented that, yes, this could have been the guy. The police leapt on this, an APB was put out for Delbert, and he was arrested in Mississippi—despite a total lack of physical evidence connecting him to the crime, despite the fact that he was nearly the opposite of the description the victim had given, and despite the fact that police had questioned and ruled him out as a suspect two weeks earlier.

Delbert said he thought this lack of evidence could have saved him at that point if he had treated the police with more suspicion and paranoia. But he'd been on the road for two years, and his interactions with white folks and police had been nearly all positive. He had achieved a sort of "spiritual plateau," as he called it, and was not inclined to be paranoid. Further, police had stopped him in Florida, and Delbert's logic told him that if they really wanted him, they would have brought him in then instead of letting him go. And he knew they didn't have any evidence against him, because there wasn't any—he was innocent. So he waived extradition proceedings.

If Delbert had invoked his right to an extradition hearing, he would probably have been let go by a judge. When an individual chooses to fight extradition, the burden is on the state to produce some kind of tangible evidence implicating that person—not enough to convict, necessarily, but enough to justify the authorities' decision to transfer the individual to another state against his or her will. In Delbert's case, that evidence did not exist. If he had demanded an extradition hearing, Delbert told us, the state of Florida would likely have been unable to meet their burden, and he would have walked free. Instead, he willingly accompanied authorities to Florida.

We would find this to be another common thread in wrongful convictions—that many could likely have been prevented had the accused parties been more paranoid toward police from the outset. Many of the exonerated folks we met had initially cooperated with police. Trusting that their innocence would protect them, and wanting to be helpful to the authorities, they willingly waived their rights—undergoing questioning without an attorney present, waiving extradition hearings, and the like. The results of this cooperation were often later used to wrongfully convict them. We found it incredibly disheartening—if somewhat unsurprising—that these innocent individuals' desire to cooperate wound up leading directly to their convictions.

Delbert spent nine months in Florida jail awaiting trial. During this period, his many friends in the civil rights movement back in Chicago got word of his plight. They all knew Delbert to be a pacifist, a man who, influenced by Dr. King and Gandhi, had planned to be a minister—about the last person on earth capable of such a crime. They started building a movement to help raise money for his defense.

The Delbert Tibbs Defense Committee was able to raise a great deal of awareness, but not so much money. Delbert was forced to rely on the services of an underfunded public defender, he told us, while the prosecution had enormous resources at its disposal.

In our unscientific estimation, this imbalance is the number one cause of wrongful conviction in America. The people we met during our research were different from each other in almost every respect—race, life history, educational background—except for one: each of them had significantly less money to make their case than the prosecution did. In fact, the vast majority had no money at all for their own defense and were forced to rely on public defenders. Before we embarked on this project, we assumed—as do most Americans who haven't had personal contact with the justice system—that a state defense attorney and a state prosecutor are allotted equivalent amounts of money to argue their cases. Not so. In a typical capital murder case, the state provides the prosecution with upward of $75,000—often up to $250,000—while the public defender is *very* lucky to get $12,000. That money doesn't just go to pay the lawyers for their time—it funds investigations, finances trips to search out witnesses police may have overlooked, pays for expert witnesses, and serves any number of additional functions crucial to getting all the evidence into the open and in front of jurors. For example, a well-funded prosecution can hire expert witnesses to testify regarding highly scientific issues related to physical evidence. Even if their testimony is known to be false or controversial, an underfunded defense won't have the ability to hire their own witnesses to refute it. That's information that the jury never gets—and their ability to make a well-informed decision is significantly hampered.

Delbert was represented by a public defender and was convicted by an all-white jury on no physical evidence after what he described as a one-and-a-half-day trial.

Luckily, Delbert had a lot of allies on the outside. The people worked hard, and the movement to free him grew and grew, gaining national attention and attracting the support of political leaders and respected cultural figures. Noted folksinger Pete Seeger gave free concerts to benefit Delbert's defense and even wrote a song about him. And people wrote Delbert letters—stacks and stacks, enough to keep him going through three years of solitary confinement, twenty-three hours a day, seven days a week. Delbert maintained his vegetarianism in prison, even when it meant going on a hunger strike. He refused to watch television, fearing it would make him passive. He maintained a disciplined exercise regimen, and he meditated daily. And he continued to fight as hard for his freedom from the inside as his supporters did from the outside.

Eventually that fight paid off, and Delbert's conviction was reversed by the Florida Supreme Court. The prosecutor, with a vigor that could be interpreted as highly emotional, appealed that decision. The case went all the way to the U.S. Supreme Court. The case heard by the Court did not focus on Delbert's guilt or innocence—instead, like all Supreme Court cases, it was centered around a constitutional issue, in this case that of "double jeopardy." The prosecutor, angry that Delbert's conviction had been overturned, wanted the right to try Delbert again. The defense argued that this violated the Fifth Amendment, which says that an individual cannot be tried twice for the same crime. After hearing the arguments, the Supreme Court ruled in a 4–3 opinion that the prosecutor could, if he chose to, retry Delbert in Florida. The prosecutor's office, citing lack of evidence, failed to do so. After all that effort. By 1977, Delbert Tibbs was finally, officially, a free man.

Of course, Delbert told us, he was a free man when he walked into that prison, and he was a free man during his time inside, too. In his mind, he never let them lock him up, because, he said, "I realized, if I internalized all the hurt, and all the pain, and all the anger, I would destroy myself—they wouldn't even have to execute me."

Delbert, an unlit cigarette dangling precariously from his lip for literally forty-five minutes, then went on to talk with us for two more hours about freedom, philosophy, American history, politics, poetry (he's a gifted writer), and what he thinks we need to do to create a truly just society. He hardly paused when Zooey jumped up on him, when she (yes) knocked over a pile of equipment, when our tape recorder failed. We could've listened to him for hours.

We could quote Delbert for pages and pages and hardly begin to do justice to his eloquence. Delbert is extraordinarily funny, brilliant, articulate, and wise. Whoever locked him up deprived the world of a great human being for those four years; now that he's out, whoever publishes his memoirs will be doing the world a great service.

Sadly, though, we couldn't listen to Delbert for hours—we had another interview to get to that evening, and it was getting dark. Delbert had to get back to his macaroni on the stove. Our minds whirring and our hearts open, we thanked Delbert and Loren both, rounded up the dog, and headed across town to check into our hotel.

Our hotel.

In the car that afternoon, we'd spent two hours calling hotels, motels, anything, hoping the waters would part and we'd find a room for us and the dog. Over and over we were rejected. Fate did not intervene to help. We started to panic—Joann, the only person we knew in Chicago, had a dog allergy, so we had nobody to crash with. We were happy to rough it, glad to take risks, but we were not going to sleep in the car in Chicago. We were stuck. Finally, an overtired, uncompromising, dishonest member of our travel threesome (let's call him Erik) hatched an idea to get us a room.

We got to the last hotel on our list, and the clerk, as all the others had been, was initially resistant to the idea of "dog in hotel." It was against the rules! It said so in the *book*. Erik let the clerk know that *our* dog was special. No dice. So Erik pulled out the big guns: our dog was a *service* dog, he lied, and the hotel was required *by law* to admit us to the hotel. Jessica shot him a look from the passenger seat; Erik shrugged. What were we supposed to do? Erik heard paper shuffling and whispered consultation on the other end. Then a silky, friendly, welcoming voice broke in and said, "I'm the manager; we'd be *honored* to have you and your helper dog reside in our establishment." That's funny, when we'd asked for the manager before, he'd been unavailable. "Service dog," Erik corrected. Reservations were made.

After we interviewed Delbert, we showed up in the lobby of the Ramada Inn, bags in hand. An army of people (all animal lovers, of course) were waiting for us behind the counter. "There you *are!!!*" they chorused. "How can we *assist* you?!?" They were advancing on us like a line of skinny, overly helpful defensive linemen.

Zooey had been either locked in the moving car or tied up in a small photography studio for the last fourteen hours.

Zooey twirled on her leash like a dervish. She spun around three times and jumped six inches off the floor. Then she jumped on Jessica, who was *not* carrying any of our luggage. (Apparently, she required a service dog after all.) Jess was knocked momentarily off-balance, Erik got tangled in the leash and dropped luggage, while yelling, "No *protect!!! Zooey!!!! No protect!!!!!!*" The dog whined, spun, pulled, and almost peed on the floor. The advancing line of grinning concierges stopped. Erik hastily explained that when Jessica, who had epilepsy (actually true) was in danger, Zooey would crawl on top of her and "protect" till help arrived. Now could everyone please step back. They did. And we sweated all the way up the elevator to our room.

Now, we hope the fact that we're fighting a particular policy of an administration and a party that have traditionally *not* been friends to people with disabilities who really need things like affordable housing, job protection, and service dogs takes some of the sting away from our dishonest representation of fact. The enemy of my enemy, etc. Ultimately, all we can really say in our defense is that we were desperate.

We would like to point out, though, that if more prosecutors followed the rule book as stringently as do hotel clerks, there wouldn't be nearly as much of a need to call them to task. Zooey, no protect.

After we got Zooey set up with food, water, and improvised soundproofing in the hotel room, it was off to the Golden Nugget Pancake House to meet Darby Tillis. We had no idea what to expect from Darby; we had never spoken to him before, nor had we read any background information on his case. This interview was sort of a "blind date," set up by Larry Marshall; all Larry had told us was that Darby had been out for several years and was now a street preacher. We were a couple minutes late, but we weren't really nervous; we were still riding high on our interview with Delbert, assimilating all the knowledge he'd thrown at us over those three hours, knowing we'd met a new friend. Also, we had some adrenaline coursing through our veins after pulling off our stunt at the Ramada. So when Darby approached us outside the Golden Nugget—a solidly built bulldog of a man, African-American and in his late fifties, dressed in head-to-toe black with relaxed hair and big gold rings on his fingers—we grinned and shook his hand, stress-free and ready for another adventure. Or so we thought.

The three of us headed inside the old-fashioned diner and ordered coffee and french fries from a beleaguered waitress. Then Erik pulled out the tape recorder and pressed RECORD. Mistake number one.

Darby eyed the tape recorder like it was a loathsome, poisonous snake. Then he slowly raised his gaze to meet ours and quietly, deliberately instructed Erik to turn off that tape recorder. Right now.

We did so with no argument and apologized profusely for turning it on without asking first. However, we admitted to Darby that we were a little confused: Hadn't Larry told Darby what we were doing, that we were interviewing people to create a play from their words? Surely he could understand that we'd assumed that meant it was okay to record him talking. We could understand if he didn't want to be on video, that was fine; but it would be really tough for us to make the play we wanted to make without accurate transcripts of the interviews.

Mistake number two.

Darby leaned forward till his elbows were on our side of the table, and then he fixed us in a gaze that was very focused, very intense, and *very* accusatory. "Plays make money," he told us. "That's what you're doing this for; don't tell me any different. Were you planning just to come in here and record me and then take off? Are you trying to rob me? What are you going to do with all that money?" We were taken aback; we were so incredibly broke, and the proposition that anyone—least of all us—would ever make any money from this play was one that we had literally never even imagined. Hardly anyone ever makes enough money to scrape by on in the theater, let alone enough to turn a profit. We were in debt and sleeping in the car. Our financial considerations regarding this play ranged more toward questions like how to extend our credit limit past $500 so we could rent a car and still make next month's rent than questions of how we would distribute *profit*. (Of course, despite anything we could have imagined, in this case Darby did turn out to be right, and the people whose stories appear in the play receive a substantial share of the profits; accordingly, they've each made more money from the play than we have.)

We tried to explain that actually, plays *don't* usually make money, and that really, that wasn't why we were doing this. We said that on the outside chance that the play ever did make money, then of course the people whose stories it told would be compensated more than fairly—we were doing it for them. But financial reward was the furthest thing from our minds. Playwrights (except for maybe Neil Simon) don't make money—and anyway, we weren't even professional playwrights. We made our modest living from acting and survival jobs like bartending and pool hall cleaning. We'd embarked on this project because we wanted to help get the stories of the wrongly convicted out into the public consciousness, because we thought the American justice system was badly broken and that many people didn't know that and didn't understand how that impacted real people's lives. We believed that theater could make audiences step into other people's shoes, and we wanted to utilize that process to help people understand what it means to be innocent and on death row. We were writing this play because we wanted to help ensure that what had happened to Darby and to so many others never happened to anyone, ever again.

Darby took us in through narrowed eyes, obviously not buying one word. We were at a loss: we'd just explained our motivations, truthfully and from our hearts, and it was clearly not anywhere close to satisfactory. What else could we do? We hadn't predicted this. It's a testament to our profound naïveté that it hadn't once occurred to us that someone might not believe us when we told them why we wanted to talk to them. There was an uncomfortable silence; the waitress came over from the counter to refill our coffee, obviously trying to scope out what Darby was doing sitting at a table with the likes of us. Once she left, Darby leaned back in his seat, fixed us in his gaze, and said, "Let me tell you something."

Okay.

"I've seen evil," he said. "I've seen things the two of you have never even imagined. People do all kinds of things, and there are whole worlds out there that you don't know anything about. You can try to know about them, but you won't. You haven't seen it. You don't know." He continued like this for several minutes, crescendoing in volume, intensity, and anger, beginning to sound like the street preacher he was. The few late-night patrons that dotted the booths of the Golden Nugget looked up from their weak coffee to see what all the fire and brimstone was about. We started to feel like a couple of naive, stupid, young, idealistic white kids—which we were. Babies. What Darby was saying was true: we didn't know what we were talking about. The territory we were asking him to lead us through was territory we'd never even come close to in our own lives. Darby knew way more about all of this than either of us, he was a powerful preacher—and he was *pissed off* at us. And at some other things that were a lot bigger than us, too. He leaned in even further, locking gazes with Erik, eyes blazing. "I've seen evil," he repeated, "and let me tell you, death is nothing next to that. Real evil is a whole lot worse than a man walking you out in the woods and holding a gun to your head." As he made his point, Darby pantomimed a gun with his thumb and forefinger and brought it about half an inch from Erik's nose. Erik blanched several shades at once. Jessica's cheeks went very, very pink.

Darby pulled his hand back from Erik's face and leaned back slightly in his seat, having reached the apex of his sermon. He watched us closely to see what we'd do next, as did all the other patrons of the Golden Nugget Pancake House. There was a very still, very silent moment. Spoons clinked on saucers. Then Erik decided he would try to defend us. "Look, man," Erik said, somewhat frustrated, "we're good people. We don't have bad intentions. Larry told you what we were doing; if you didn't want to talk to us, why didn't you tell him that? We came over here because you said you wanted us to; if you didn't, why'd you waste our time?"

Ground-swallowing-you-up-and-chewing-on-your-bones mistake number three.

This was not going over well with Darby. He'd been around a lot longer than us, he had more fuel, and he had history on his side. Being defensive was *not* the way for us to defuse this situation. He was about to start back in, having preserved enough momentum to pretty much pick up where he'd left off. As she would many times during this project, Jessica laid her hand on Erik's arm, a gentle signal that meant "Please shut up now." Erik complied, reluctantly, and Jessica started in on another tack.

"You're right," Jessica said. "You know more about all of this than we do. Our backgrounds are pretty sheltered; we're not going to disrespect you by pretending anything else. We're not claiming to know anything, or to have any kind of entitlement to ask you questions. If you don't want to talk to us, that's cool. We don't want anyone to do anything they don't want to. It's your life; whatever you want is okay." Jessica didn't know if any of this would have any impact—she was still feeling pretty much like an ineffectual baby—but clearly the right thing for us to do here was listen, and the other right thing was for Darby to decide how he wanted this to go.

Darby said okay, and visibly relaxed. He still wouldn't let us turn on the tape recorder, but he said he'd talk to us a little while we finished up our coffee. Darby didn't get into the details of his case—although we did learn that he'd been both convicted and exonerated with Perry Cobb, the other guy we were supposed to meet up with in Chicago. We didn't ask Darby any questions; we figured he'd tell us what he wanted to, and none of it was going to be usable for the play anyway, since we couldn't record it. We preserved the tentative peace, talked for a few more minutes, drained our coffee cups, and got the check from the waitress, who was still trying to figure out what the hell was going on at our table. It was getting late—eleven or so—and we had to drive upstate for another interview in the morning. We paid the check and headed out into the Chicago dark.

As we were finishing up inside, Darby had told us about the Lincoln he'd recently purchased. On the way out of the Golden Nugget, he said, "Let me show you the car." We followed him to his parking space, duly admiring the Lincoln: large, black, and fitted out with lots of chrome. Erik shook Darby's hand and started to say good-night, apologizing that we'd wasted Darby's time.

Then Darby nodded toward the car and said, "Get in."

There was about a half a second's pause as we tried to determine what the correct response was to this situation. A half hour earlier, Darby had been holding his cocked forefinger to Erik's nose and yelling at us in the middle of a diner loud enough to scare the waitress. Maybe not such a great idea, then, to climb into his car for who knew what reason, headed toward who knew where. But clearly there was no way to decline without being rude—or even offensive. Not to mention that Darby didn't really present it as a choice. It was a challenge—were we two little white kids going to run away, scared, suspicious, and racist, or were we going to come with him? Somehow we both managed to go through all these thoughts during three seconds of hesitation. "Okay," we blurted, hearts pounding in our ears.

What the hell were we doing?

Erik got in the front seat with Darby; Jessica climbed in behind them and leaned into the red leather upholstery, somehow feeling safer tucked in the back. Neither of us asked where we were going. Darby started driving. Wordlessly, he switched on the radio, to a station playing soul music from the seventies. Erik pretended to be immersed in the experience of listening to late-era Motown. Jessica scrunched down in the backseat. Both of us *really* hoped the other knew what he or she was doing. Finally, Erik broke the silence, saying, "You know, this music is okay, but what I really like is the old blues stuff, guys like Little Walter, Brownie McGhee, that kind of thing." Jessica held her breath: Had Erik just insulted Darby's taste in music? Pause.

"Oh, yeah?" Darby asked. "How about Sonny Terry?"

"Yeah, he's great," Erik said. "But my favorites are the harmonica guys. Like James Cotton, too."

"James is the man," said Darby.

And they were off.

Never before had Jessica been so happy to listen to Erik go on and on about musicians she'd never heard of. Apparently, that Erik could talk about the blues completely upended Darby's opinion of us. All earlier hostilities fell away, and Darby and Erik spent the next fifteen minutes immersed in the universal language of music-geek-dom. Darby would throw a musician's name at Erik; Erik would catch it and pitch back another obscure genius. After a while Darby was laughing, slapping Erik's arm as if they were old buddies, and Jessica was leaning up toward the front seat, listening. Darby asked us if we wanted to see a couple of the old Chicago blues clubs; Erik knew all their names already, and Jessica was up for anything as long as everyone stayed happy. Darby drove us past the famous old bars where Chicago blues had been birthed, filling us in on the lore associated with each one.

Then he turned into another neighborhood, pointing out where the crime he'd been wrongly convicted of had taken place. In the seventies, Darby told us, he'd hung out around the neighborhood the crime took place in. But, he told us, he'd been across town when it went down. There was no physical evidence connecting him to the crime, and the only eyewitness who testified for the state admitted on the stand, according to *Cornerstone* magazine, that he "didn't see the faces too well—not well enough to walk up and say, 'He's the man.' " This witness further testified that all blacks looked alike to him in photographs. At Darby's fifth and final trial, prosecutor Michael Falconer testified that the state's star witness, who claimed to have driven a getaway car for Darby and the other alleged perpetrator, Perry Cobb, had admitted to Falconer that her boyfriend had committed the shooting. After five trials and eight years in prison, Darby and Perry were both exonerated; they later received full pardons from the governor.

Darby drove us to the scene of the crime, then to the location of his alibi, pointing out the mileage and telling us stories along the way. We never did get into great detail with Darby about his case, but no matter: we'd dispensed with being interviewers hours before.

Then Darby started talking about God. He'd gotten saved some time ago, been ordained as a minister, and made his living traveling the country, preaching on street corners and at revivals. His wife accompanied him; she was a "good woman," he said, and they were happy. They were based in Texas, but spent most of every year on the road in Darby's Lincoln, saving souls, and people put them up in every town they went to. Just as he was describing this, we rounded a corner and came upon a miniature revival under way in a parking lot.

"Now look at this," Darby said, pointing out the crowd gathered around a flatbed truck, bright lights glaring down on the preacher, who was holding a Bible aloft, working everybody up. A couple tents were in various stages of assembly, and half a stage was up on stilts, but it was clear this wasn't the main event. It looked as if they'd been setting up for an event that would take place tomorrow and the preaching had started spontaneously. Almost a hundred people had gathered, at nearly midnight on a Friday, and were throwing "Amen" 's back at the preacher. "This is how we do it, too," Darby told us. "Sometimes with the truck, like they have, but sometimes we'll just get up there with nothing and start preaching the Word." Darby rolled the Lincoln into the parking lot and stopped. As soon as he stepped out of the car, he was surrounded by people who knew him, clapping him on the back, shaking his hand, calling out, "Hey there! Reverend Tillis!" like he was a beloved kid who'd gone off and got famous, a hometown hero come back from far away. Darby was the king of Chicago at that moment, the crowd clustered around him. We hung behind him, but he introduced us, and everyone smiled and shook our hands, too. Then, just as fast, Darby said good-bye to everyone and guided us by the shoulders back to the car. The evening's tour was over; Darby asked where our hotel was and drove us there, popping in a homemade blues tape for us to listen to on the way.

Erik had our tape recorder in his pocket the whole time. Every few minutes he'd think of it, wondering if he should press RECORD and secretly capture the evening on tape. He'd have his finger on the button, press it halfway down, and then stop each time. We're both glad he did.

Chapter Five

Our wake-up call came at 6 a.m. We'd driven around with Darby till after midnight, and once we got back to the hotel, we couldn't sleep. But neither of us could really talk about the evening, either: our little attempts at explaining it were dwarfed by the experience. So we sat up on the pink-flowered hotel bedspread and just kind of looked at each other, shook our heads, and tried not to raid the minibar till we wound down enough to fall asleep.

Now, we had to get on the road within an hour; we had an interview scheduled for ten thirty up at the Illinois-Wisconsin border, and Chicago rush-hour traffic can take hours. We rubbed our sticky eyes and dragged each other out of bed, reminding ourselves over and over that there was coffee in the lobby. Watery coffee. With creamer, though.

Convincing each other to get out of bed during these trips usually involved one of us shaking the other, "generously" insisting that they take the first shower, then blissfully drifting back to sleep; by the time the extrasleeper got up to take the second shower, it would be almost time to go, and whoever'd taken the first shower would be forced to do the packing. It was only a few months into our relationship, which meant Erik still said yes when Jessica made him get out of bed first *and* pack, every time.

The folks at the front desk, ever the professionals, sent someone up to help us with our bags, seeing as we had the helper dog and all. We felt awful accepting their assistance, but we didn't really know how to turn it down without blowing our cover. As we rode the elevator down to the lobby, we watched Zooey spin around in circles and marveled that we'd successfully passed her off as a highly trained service dog. Zooey jumped up on Jessica, panting, and the porter eyed us sideways. "Zooey, no protect," said Erik. Zooey looked back at Erik blankly, tongue hanging out the side of her mouth.

We made it out of Chicago without incident (the hotel police had decided not to follow us) and headed north. We were going to meet Gary Gauger, an organic farmer who'd been wrongly convicted of the murder of his parents. His story had been in the news more than most: the Center on Wrongful Convictions had been instrumental in winning Gary's exoneration, and his was one of the cases that had spurred Governor Ryan to declare a moratorium on executions in Illinois. Plus, after Gary was exonerated, they'd actually caught the guys who really committed the crime—a rare occurrence. The real murderers had been convicted not too long before our meeting with Gary.

We drove through the flat, grassy landscape of northern Illinois, gradually waking up and wondering what more there could possibly be after Delbert and Darby. In one day, with the two of them, we'd experienced enough to keep us thinking for months. Erik, in a rare burst of biblical references, noted that we'd gotten water from one and fire and brimstone from the other, like talking to Abraham and John back-to-back. One represented an Old Testament god of vengeance; the other held an entirely different kind of word up to the light. Both of them were preachers—whether literally or metaphorically—with opposite approaches to being servants of God. Two sides of the same coin.

And now we were traveling somewhere else, to hear even more. It was the first time we felt really overwhelmed, filled all the way up, knowing there was more on its way but having no idea where in ourselves we could possibly put it. This unfamiliar state of mind would become our normal, everyday mode over the next few months, but right now it was new—the first inkling of how much this play would change us before it was finished with us.

Following Gary's directions, we pulled off the main highway onto a narrow county road. We were in real farm country—flat and green everywhere, nothing but silos to punctuate the landscape. Not too different from the little towns in Minnesota where Erik had grown up. Erik had been raised around farms near his grandma's lake cabin; and his dad's dad still owns five tractors up there in northern Minnesota where the men are men, the women run everything, and John Deere is king. Erik had stepped in enough cow shit, cuddled enough piglets, and been chased by enough enraged mother pigs to feel right at home here in Illinois farm country. Even though he was easily 600 miles from his hometown, Erik had a weird feeling he'd run into someone whose neighbor had joined his grandma's bridge club or something. Better be on his best behavior.

Gary had told us we'd see a sign by the road—this was for his twin sister's rug shop, right next door to his farm. We spotted the sign and drove up a dirt driveway several hundred feet long. On our right was row after symmetrical row of vegetable plants, and in the distance, the rug shop. Eventually, we saw a little house to our left, tucked in a nest of trees. Behind it was a greenhouse; a rusty tractor sat in front of the dilapidated but functional barn.

A friendly beast-mutt came around the car to say hello to us, which of course sent Zooey into hysterics. We cracked the window (it was much cooler here than at Neil's), left her in the car, and headed toward the house.

Gary came around from the back of the house in muddy jeans, T-shirt, and work boots, futilely attempting to wipe his hands on his knees. A white guy in his late forties with a graying ponytail and a big, long beard, Gary looked every bit the hippie farmer, with dirt permanently lodged under his fingernails and a wide grin. He showed us inside to the kitchen and offered us some instant coffee. While the water boiled, Gary went to wash up, and we set up our equipment on the kitchen table.

When he came back in, Gary, used to being interviewed by the likes of CNN, took one look at our little RadioShack cassette recorders and our video camera precariously attached to its tripod with duct tape and had himself a good laugh. "Usually they haul in satellite dishes and trailers," he chuckled. Erik made some ridiculous comment about touring with the Grateful Dead and how much sound equipment the "tapers" tended to lug with them. Gary knew just what Erik was talking about: "The Dead? I saw them in the seventies." Erik's eyes lit up; awed, he managed to croak, "Reaaally?"

Erik had followed the Dead a little during college, and it seems that anyone who's ever been a Deadhead apparently retains the ability to name-drop venues, band members, opening acts, and full on set-lists for hours at a time. When Gary described the Dead shows he'd seen during their heyday in the seventies, Erik got excited enough to run around in circles like Zooey. We were off on a good foot, thanks to Jerry Garcia & Co., and after a few minutes—which to Jessica seemed like hours—we all relaxed in our kitchen chairs as Gary started in on his story.

In 1993, Gary told us, he was living with his parents on the family farm—the same farm where Gary had invited us to meet with him today. Gary's parents ran a motorcycle shop that was known for its selection of vintage motorcycle parts, and they grew a lot of vegetables. Gary helped his dad out in the motorcycle shop fixing bikes, and he also worked the fields. In early April, Gary was moving his plants from the greenhouse to the fields; each morning, Gary would wake up early, head over to his folks' side of the property, and go to work. One morning, Gary came over early and found his folks weren't there. They had mentioned that they might take a trip to a nearby town, so Gary said he figured that must be where they'd gone and got to work. By the time night fell, his parents still weren't back, and Gary started to worry that they might've been in a car accident. He didn't have a way to reach them, though, and knew the cops wouldn't look into anything till his parents had been gone twenty-four hours, so he stayed by the phone till midnight in case somebody called, then went to bed. When he woke up the next morning, Gary's parents still weren't back. He was getting dressed, planning to get on the phone with police and family friends, when a customer came up to the farm, looking for a motorcycle part. Gary accompanied him to the shop, and into a back storage room where he thought the part might be. Which is where they found Gary's father's body, facedown, in a pool of blood.

Gary felt his dad's pulse; he was gone. Gary's first instinct was that his father, who'd been having circulatory problems, had had a stroke, fallen, and hit his head. But his mom was missing, too, and now Gary was starting to really get worried. He rushed to call paramedics, who called the police. Both teams showed up at the farm. Finally, after an hour and a half of searching, they found Gary's mom in a rug trailer, hidden, covered with rugs and pillows. Both Gary's parents' throats had been slashed.

About two and a half hours after Gary found his father's body, Gary told us, the police had him arrested. They locked Gary in a squad car while they combed the property; then they took him to the station.

What happened to Gary after that is something that we had no idea could happen to anyone in America.

Even though police had arrested Gary, he wanted to cooperate, help out; like Delbert, he trusted that his innocence would protect him. So when they brought him into an interrogation room and started asking questions, Gary didn't demand a lawyer. When they refrained from tape-recording any part of the interrogation, Gary still wanted to help. Even when they kept him locked in that room for hours on end; even when they showed him crime-scene pictures of his murdered parents with their heads pulled so far back you could see down their throats; even when, he said, they screamed at him, demanding to know how Gary could have killed the woman who gave birth to him—Gary wanted to help.

Around midnight, they brought in a polygraph examiner to administer a lie-detector test; afterward, according to Gary, the interrogators came back in and told Gary he hadn't passed it. (In fact, the result was inconclusive due to fatigue, but Gary got the impression from the cops that he had failed the test.) They told him they had damning physical evidence: the murder weapon, a bloody fingerprint that matched Gary's, bloody clothes—enough to pinpoint Gary as the killer beyond a shadow of a doubt. They also told Gary that they couldn't lie to him; that if they did, they'd lose their jobs.

In actuality, no physical evidence implicated Gary in any way, and police officers *are* allowed to lie to suspects in the course of an interrogation. But Gary trusted the police. "They seemed very sincere, very believable, and it never once entered my mind that the police would lie about something like this and then take it all the way through trial, lying about it," Gary said. And after nine hours of interrogation, no sleep, hardly any food, and sixteen cups of coffee, not to mention the emotional stress of discovering his parents' murders and then being yelled at over and over that *he* did it, Gary was in a suggestible, vulnerable state of mind—"spaced out," as he put it.

So when the cops suggested that Gary had committed the murder in a blackout state of which he had no memory, Gary was willing to allow for the possibility. And, he told us, when they suggested that he give a "vision statement"—a hypothetical account of what he *would* have done, *if* he had killed his parents, to, he said, "try and jog his memory"—Gary agreed. Around 3 a.m., Gary told us, he allowed his interrogators to lead him through the vision statement. Afterward, Gary said, he told police he had no memory of the events he'd just invented being real in any way, and he wasn't going to sign any sort of confession. Gary was interrogated for three more hours. Around 6 a.m., at the request of his interrogators, Gary repeated the vision statement and again clarified for police that he had no memory of the events he'd described, every single one was hypothetical and imagined, and he wasn't signing a confession.

At trial, Gary's interrogators testified on the stand that he'd confessed.

They claimed, Gary told us, that he was never under arrest; that he was never held forcibly or locked in a room; that he was free to go at any time. They claimed, Gary told us, that he had "voluntarily chatted with them from four o'clock in the afternoon until six o'clock the next morning," and that around five in the morning, Gary suddenly grew quiet and "blurted out facts that only the killer would know." They claimed that the "vision statement" Gary had given was not hypothetical, but instead was a statement of fact. They used the "vision statement" as a confession. And they got a conviction.

This despite the fact that Gary's parents' autopsies later revealed that virtually every detail in the "vision statement" was wrong: Gary's parents could not have been murdered in the way that Gary had described. Despite the fact that there was no tape or video recording of any part of Gary's interrogation or supposed confession—nothing to prove that the police officers' testimony was true. Despite the fact that there was no physical evidence to implicate Gary and no plausible motive—no good explanation of why a son who was close with his parents, who chose to live and work with them, would suddenly turn around and kill them. The prosecution's case hinged on the police officers' testimony that Gary had confessed during his interrogation. Since no part of that interrogation was ever written down or recorded, it was their word against Gary's. And generally speaking, jurors tend to take a police officer's word over that of an accused murderer. Based on the officers' testimony that Gary had confessed, and additional testimony from a jailhouse snitch who claimed that Gary had confessed to him in jail (and received a lesser sentence in exchange for his testimony)—and no other substantial evidence whatsoever—the jury deliberated for less than three hours before convicting Gary.

Gary was one of the few exonerated people we met who'd actually had enough money to hire an attorney from the start. Unfortunately, the attorney Gary hired had never argued a capital case and was later said to have told Gary's twin sister, Ginger, that "death penalty cases are won on appeal"—implying that it was somewhat pointless to even try to win death penalty cases at the trial level. Gary would go back to jail after each day in court and make exhaustive lists of all the inconsistencies and mistakes in the prosecution's case that day. But, Gary told us, his lawyer didn't put the lists to use aggressively, and Gary's family had given the attorney everything they had as a retainer. They didn't have any money left to hire someone new.

While Gary was trying to simultaneously adjust to death row and cope with the death of his parents, his twin sister, Ginger—along with several friends—was fighting for him on the outside. Ginger knew her brother, and their parents, better than anyone else, and she never doubted Gary's innocence. In winter of 1994, Ginger heard about a lawyer named Larry Marshall, who, with the help of his students at Northwestern University, had just won an exoneration in a high-profile capital case. Larry was going to speak in Chicago, and Ginger and a group of friends, including an old family friend named Sue—who would later become Gary's wife—drove down there in a blinding snowstorm to try to talk to Larry about Gary's situation.

Not too long after that, Larry took on Gary's case. Larry showed up at the prison to meet Gary, telling him through the glass, "Look, this isn't going to cost you anything. There might be expenses down the line, and it might take four to six years to get you out, but for now, we're just going to move forward; you don't need to worry about the cost." Gary, who by that time was totally mistrustful of lawyers, wondered what Larry's angle was. But Larry kept coming to the prison to meet with Gary and kept preparing briefs, and he wasn't sending any bills. That's when Gary started to realize he had a very special lawyer on his side—as well as about sixty of Larry's students, all working on Gary's case. "Right action is actually a real concept for Larry,"

Gary told us. "To do something because it's the right thing to do, rather than the most career-rewarding or whatever. It's amazing how rare that is."

In early 1996, Larry filed a motion to overturn Gary's conviction, and in March Larry won Gary a new trial. Unbeknownst to either Larry or Gary, at the same time the Bureau of Alcohol, Tobacco, and Firearms (ATF) had been running a sting operation on a Milwaukee biker gang called the Outlaws. In their investigation, the ATF procured an audiotape of two Outlaws talking at length about having killed Gary's parents. Apparently Gary's folks, who were well-known in the biker community for their motorcycle shop, had been targeted by the gang: a couple of bikers had allegedly killed Gary's parents while committing a robbery. According to Gary, authorities had this information as early as 1995. But they fought Gary's appeal in early 1996, publicly affirmed their belief in Gary's guilt as they were doing so, and applied to the Illinois Supreme Court to overturn the decision that had granted Gary a new trial. All without acknowledging the information they had concerning the Outlaws. Prosecutors did, however, acknowledge that without Gary's "confession"—which had by then been ruled inadmissible—they didn't have enough evidence to retry him. To the media, they maintained their belief that Gary was the guilty party and implied that Gary would be released because of what they referred to as a "technicality." Gary was released in August 1996. Eight months later, the evidence concerning the Outlaws became public, exonerating Gary.

Prosecutors and police almost never pursue other suspects after someone is exonerated, because to do so would be to fully acknowledge that they had convicted the wrong person—a potentially career-ending admission. Instead, prosecutors and police usually maintain that the people in question were wrongly freed: a judge made a mistake; a jury handed down the wrong decision; and so on. But here, they were forced to try the real suspects. The two Outlaws had been picked up on tape discussing the murder, and one of them pled guilty. Shortly before we met with Gary, the two men had been convicted.

Gary also made public statements requesting that the two Outlaws not be given the death penalty. "Why would I want them to die?" he said. "It's not gonna bring my parents back. No good's gonna come from it."

Gary'd gotten this far in his story when his wife, Sue, returned from selling vegetables at the farmers' market. A warm Midwestern woman in sweatshirt and jeans, Sue had the earthy, solid bearing of a farmer, too. She greeted us and we chatted for a couple minutes before Gary asked how her day had gone at the market; Sue got a few sentences into her answer before she burst into tears. Right away, we turned off our tape recorders. Sue wiped her cheeks, apologized, and explained: She'd been approached at the market by a customer who wanted beets. He'd asked her where she farmed, and she told him; the customer responded with a knowing "*Oh*. You farm with that guy who got in all that trouble," he said. Sue responded that, yes, Gary was her husband, and did the customer know that two other guys had just confessed and been convicted of the crime. The ill-informed customer replied, "Yeah, but Gauger confessed too. The paper said," and then went on to cast further aspersions on Gary. "I know I shouldn't get so upset," Sue said to us, but we thought she had every right.

Gary comforted Sue, reminding her, "There's gonna be idiots"; he seemed able to let it roll off his back. But we were disgusted by the customer's behavior toward Sue and Gary. It's hard enough to lose your parents to a brutal murder; harder still to be imprisoned for it when you're innocent and then be forced by the state to face death yourself. It takes even more determination to find yourself a good lawyer who'll work for you pro bono, and to struggle your way through the process of overturning a jury conviction. It is almost unimaginably difficult to get a capital conviction overturned, even with glaring evidence of one's innocence. Obstacle after obstacle stands in the way: courts often refuse to admit new evidence that wasn't introduced at the first trial; jurors believe the system doesn't make mistakes; sometimes, the same judge that heard the first trial is assigned to hear appeals. People almost never—if ever—get freed from death row on "technicalities." So, after all that, that an innocent person would be forced to contend with continued rumors, suspicion, and gossipmongering from their own community seems ridiculously unfair.

And it's not just their community—exonerated folks are often treated by authorities like they got away with something. This suspicion turns the exonerated folks into "permanent suspects." Many prosecutors, likely covering their own tracks, maintain a public belief that the exonerated folks must've had "something" to do with the crimes. In fact, even after his exoneration, some officials in Illinois publicly raised doubts about Gary's guilt—even though the real murderers, whom Gary never met in his life, had been convicted of the crime.

The people we interviewed should be able to come home and move on. But strangers like that customer, insistent on the truth of their suspicious, uninformed judgments, make that impossible.

As the conversation about the customer was finishing up, there came a knock on the door. Gary went to answer, and there was Larry Marshall—who'd previously been sort of a mysterious, semimythologized presence to us—now, here in person. He'd come out to talk to Gary about some legal matters (and, we suspected, to check out these obnoxious kids who kept calling him, asking for his help finding exonerated individuals). Larry sat down with us around the kitchen table, and the five of us talked for a while. Larry asked whom we'd met so far, who was still on our list, and we traded stories. He also gave us a beginning education about the lack of resources exonerated folks have upon their release. "If you let someone out on parole for a crime they did do," Larry told us, "they're provided some support and some segue, job counseling, at least fifty bucks to get a suit. But the guys who are exonerated, who never did anything in the first place, basically, the system opens the door and says, 'Scat.' Like a cat that's being let out of the home." We'd known that exonerated folks weren't given any financial compensation for the time they'd spent in prison. But we'd had no idea that there weren't even any structural supports for them—no job training, no readjustment counseling, no assistance finding work, nothing. We'd see the consequences of this in stark relief as we continued our travels.

Fortunately, Gary didn't have to contend with this as much as some others did—he had his family farm to live on, and a livelihood working the land. We wrapped up the conversation as Gary showed us around his greenhouse, pointing out varieties of heirloom tomatoes, purple potatoes, onions. He gave us stalks of garlic to take home and plant in our little fire-escape garden back in New York. It's still growing there; it comes back every year.

After our interview with Gary, it was on to the family section of the trip. Erik's beloved great-aunt had recently passed away, and her funeral was the next day, in a little town in northern Minnesota called Detroit Lakes. Up at the Wisconsin-Illinois border, we were almost to Minnesota already; another day's drive and we'd be in Detroit Lakes. Erik thought it would be a good opportunity for Jessica to meet his extended family, since most of the aunts, uncles, and cousins from his mom's side would be gathered. We'd been dating almost five months by now, so Erik figured Jessica should be ready for full immersion in his enormous Scandinavian clan. That night we'd stay outside Minneapolis with Erik's mom, stepdad Dave, and brother Douglas; the next morning we'd get up early and visit with his dad and stepmom Sue for a bit on the way to Detroit Lakes. Jessica agreed, on the one condition that they stop in Minneapolis first to have lunch at her old favorite vegetarian collective restaurant with Jason, one of her best friends. No Scandinavian cousins allowed.

We had an argument on the way over how long to spend in Minneapolis: Erik was saying an hour and a half, and Jessica was insisting on at least two hours. She may have been trying to postpone the deluge of cousins and the ensuing festival of high-stakes name-memorization. Due to emotional overstimulation and sleep deprivation, we yelled a little, which excited the dog. But eventually we decided we'd compromise on an hour and forty-five minutes (duh).

We got to Minneapolis on time, and then we also got to the suburbs on time to meet Erik's mom, Nellie (Erik had taken over the mileage estimating by now). We and Zooey were attacked upon entry by Buddy, the family's psychotic terrier; after Buddy was pried off our legs and shut in a room, Nellie asked, "So how's the trip going?" We paused, each trying to figure out where to begin. We looked at each other for a minute, realizing that there was no way we could explain what we'd gone through in the last few days. "Great," we both said. "Let's have dinner." After dinner the family all agreed that they liked Jessica much more than the last woman Erik had brought home, about whom there were apparently several horror stories. Jessica hadn't been aware any comparison was going on, but she was glad she'd passed muster with Mom's side of the family.

The next morning we woke up early to make the four-hour drive north to Detroit Lakes. We'd scheduled a two-hour stop to visit Erik's dad, Steve, and stepmom, Sue, in central Minnesota. When we arrived at their place, they had a whole breakfast spread out on their kitchen counter. We went straight for the coffee. After about a half hour, Erik and Sue were ensconced in conversation, and Steve sat his six-foot-four frame down next to Jessica on the couch. "You know, I want to tell you something," he said in his Minnesota accent. "When Erik was in high school, he was so artsy, and not just with the theater; he used to stay up all night making collages and painting on the walls and things, with the loud music playing. And we loved how creative he always was, but we worried a little bit about him. He was so unique, you know. Kinda weird. We were a little worried he wouldn't ever find anyone like him. And just talking to you for a half hour here, I'm just so relieved Erik's found somebody else who's artsy like he is, who's also kinda weird." Jessica grinned ear to ear. It was a great welcome to the family. Plus it gave her ammunition to make fun of Erik later.

Then Steve and Sue, too, brought up the horror stories about the last woman Erik had brought home. The first time she'd come for dinner with the family, the story went, asparagus had been served, covered in butter. Apparently she took one look at the asparagus and demanded, "Don't you have any hollandaise sauce?" In the incredibly polite and gracious world of Minnesota Nice, this was a big, big no-no. The family still discussed it at *every single* visit. The first thing Erik's splintered family had agreed on in years was hating Ms. Hollandaise; the second thing was that Jessica was very kind to take Erik in, considering his checkered past. Steve gazed on Jessica, admiring her act of charity. Erik gaped at his father. "Oh, no! They like Jessica more than they like *me*," he realized suddenly. "You know, we like her more than we like you," said Dad, beaming. "We sure do," said Sue.

After a bit, we got back on the road to Detroit Lakes, a little town way, way north. Detroit Lakes gets down to forty below in the winter, but in June the only problem's the mosquitoes—everything else is beautiful, lots of open, grassy plains and pine trees and lakes. We were running late, but we sped on the open, flat highways and pulled into the cemetery literally five seconds before the funeral started. We managed to keep Zooey calm and she sat next to us on her leash as we stood in a circle with Erik's mom's family and said good-bye to his aunt Mibs. Mibs and her husband had raised Erik to love dogs, pets, and animals in general. It seemed fitting that Zooey had come along to pay tribute by whimpering a little and wagging her tail a lot.

Afterward everyone gathered in the basement of the Congregational church that Erik had attended as a little kid, to remember Mibs and eat ham sandwiches. A church well-known—in the Midwest anyway—for a deep mistrust of the concentration of power in the hands of few people, the Congregational church values decentralized authority. Coffee cake detail is usually decided by consensus. There was a paucity of vegetarian food here—as in the rest of the rural Midwest—but we'd adjusted by now, and we just ate a lot of cookies and celery with ketchup. Northern Minnesota was a culture shock for Jessica, as much as Ohio had been—except here it was even more crucial she fit in, since this was Erik's family. She stood amongst the Lutheran brethren, surrounded by casseroles, checkered tablecloths, and accents so Minnesotan they were almost Canadian, and hoped she didn't get anyone's name wrong. If she did, they were too polite to mention it. Of course they were—they were *Minnesotans*.

Afterward, we headed up to Erik's grandma's lake cabin, where we'd rest a day or two before turning around and heading back to New York. Erik's grandma Joyce is an extraordinary woman, tough and self-sufficient enough to build her own canoes and head out in them to fish for her own food; she'd even gone to Alaska a few years back with a tour group to pan for gold. She'd had this cabin since long before Erik was born, and he'd grown up there summers; it was his favorite place in the world. We had a beautiful couple days there, as Zooey raced through the woods on the property chasing rabbits and jumping into the water for no reason. Things felt very familial. Comfortable. We started thinking maybe we should integrate into each other's families in a more enduring way.

Chapter Six

Finally, though, it was time to head back to New York. We had a lot more work ahead of us. Before we'd left, we'd managed to find three interns from NYU to work with us on the project. Bonnie, Maria, and Jen. If there is a heaven, interns get to boss everyone else around beyond the pearly gates. We'd FedEx-ed the interview tapes to them from the road to be transcribed; now there were pages and pages of text at home, waiting for us to weed through them.

We also had one more interview pending, in Pennsylvania, with Jay Smith. Jay was a former high-school principal who'd been wrongly convicted of the murder of a teacher, along with her two kids. He'd been freed several years ago; now he lived a quiet life with his wife in the mountains of rural Pennsylvania. We'd talked with him from Chicago and he'd said to give him a call when we were a few hours away so we could come on up.

With that settled, and the rest of this trip's interviews finished, we had a lot of time in the car to talk. We went over and over the impressions we'd carried away from those first interviews. We talked a lot about the threads we were already beginning to trace through all the cases: shoddy or overworked (usually seriously underpaid) representation; defendants' waiving their rights due to a desire to cooperate with police; "jailhouse snitches" who received reduced sentences in exchange for testimony; overzealous prosecutors; media firestorms that created immense public bias against the defendants long before trials even began. As we talked, it started sinking in how widespread these factors were, and how identifiable. If *we* could see the problems, and potential solutions for many of them, surely the people who made the laws would be able to see them, too—and fix them. As we cataloged the common factors in the wrongful convictions we'd encountered, we became more and more angry that they were allowed to go on happening.

At the same time, we talked about how, when you traced the chain of events, you could see how the jurors could hand down the wrong verdict. One thing can lead to another: a suspect's trust in the police and in his own innocence can put him in a vulnerable position where officers, acting aggressively to apprehend someone they see as dangerous, collect information that can be used to make him appear guilty. And if the suspect has any prior criminal record whatsoever—a bar fight, possession of a controlled substance, check forgery, shoplifting, theft—it raises the stakes considerably.

To a reasonable outside observer, it's clear that those kinds of charges don't necessarily indicate that a suspect is capable of *murder*. But if a suspect's history is presented to the public in a particular way, a story of a "dangerous" person emerges. We began to realize that *narrative* is just as important in a criminal investigation and trial as it is in a play. Only in a criminal investigation, the stakes are much higher—for both sides. And real-life narratives are never clean or simple, and hardly ever easy to follow.

But people like narratives that they can follow. And news programs need viewers to tune in, and newspapers need readers to pick up the paper every day. So, often, the media presents the story in a way that will attract the public: simple and sensationalistic. Often, local media repeatedly present stories that portray the suspect as shady, dangerous, an "alleged murderer." In a small town, these stories can reach and poison the whole population—the entire potential jury pool.

The prosecution and the defense are well aware of this phenomenon. It's our belief that the number of wrongful convictions has likely shot up considerably from the practice of trying cases in the "court of public opinion." With all the technology now available, a few keystrokes can easily corrupt the functioning of a system that looks pretty fair on paper. People start believing the stories they're told—by a media that is supposed to be objective—and the presumption of innocence dissolves.

In many places the authorities also literally control the press's access to information about the case. It isn't supposed to work that way, of course—but, particularly in small towns, the authorities hold a lot of sway. Reporters need good relationships with cops, prosecutors, judges: every week, journalists have to approach those authorities for the answers to their questions. And if a journalist writes a story that's particularly critical, well, maybe that journalist doesn't get called on at the next press conference. Or maybe her phone calls for comment don't get returned so fast. Her sources start to dry up, and all of a sudden she finds herself unable to do her job so well. So there's a strong individual motivation for reporters to stay on the right side of the authorities. This phenomenon is most pronounced in small towns, where *everybody* knows each other, but it occurs all the way up to the national level. In this country, we have an idealized picture of the press as being objective and disinterested, separate enough from the workings of the system to tell the people the truth. But, like everything else, the press operates through human relationships. And often, the nature of those relationships precludes objectivity.

Next, the case goes to trial, and an underfunded public defender (in most cases) lacks the resources to pursue leads that would produce evidence proving her client's innocence. Further, the police control the investigation, and therefore all the evidence. They then turn over that body of evidence to prosecutors, with whom they have a cooperative relationship. The prosecutors are required by law to present the evidence they've received from police to the defense during the discovery process—but prosecutors, understandably, want to win their cases. And few safeguards prevent an overzealous prosecutor from withholding potentially exculpatory evidence from a defense attorney during discovery. Not to mention that prosecutors are allotted investigative resources that public defenders almost never receive, enabling them to dig up new evidence, interview reluctant witnesses, analyze forensic materials, and the like. All of these factors can combine to create a situation in which jurors (already potentially influenced against the defendant by media coverage) hear all the prosecution's evidence, but never learn about evidence that would prove the defendant's innocence. So those jurors come back with a wrong verdict—thinking they're doing the right thing. And further, the law states that a juror has to support the death penalty in order to sit on a jury at a capital trial—and statistically, pro-death-penalty jurors are more likely to convict, and to impose the death penalty, than anti-death-penalty jurors.

Many other factors can intervene, too, and many other things can go wrong. This was just the beginning of what we would learn about how the system can malfunction, and what can happen to the people who get caught up in it. But even the rudimentary knowledge we'd gained thus far was enough to show us how dangerous it is that the state is allowed to punish people in the most irreversible of ways when the potential for error is so large, and so systemic.

We were also realizing how crucial it is that the few safeguards that do exist be allowed to function properly. The most familiar and extensive of those safeguards exist within the judicial branch and are known as the appeals process. But the framers of our Constitution laid out a system of checks and balances with the intention that if one branch of government fails in its duty or overreaches in its power, it will be corrected by another. That's why, in capital cases, a defendant has recourse through the executive branch. In case the judicial branch fails, a governor has the power to grant stays of execution in questionable capital cases, and even full pardons. These laws were created in an attempt to ensure that the state corrects its mistakes when someone's life is at stake. One of a governor's duties is to carry out this function with a great deal of caution and thought: the governor is the last resort, the final safety net for the wrongly convicted, and it is crucial that he or she take that responsibility extremely seriously. (There has been some public conversation recently about limiting or ending a governor's ability to use this power. By this point, we were well aware of just how dangerous that would be.)

Which led to our next big topic of car conversation. It was the summer of 2000, and George W.'s presidential campaign was in full swing, all over the headlines of *USA Today*, which was the only newspaper available in most of the towns on our way home. Even in

USA Today, people were talking about the record number of executions that had taken place during W.'s tenure as governor of Texas. In just three years, under the governorship of George W. Bush, Texas executed more people than any other state in America had executed in the last *two decades combined*. Now, a few years later, America has other concerns on its mind, and many people have forgotten how controversial and extreme Governor George W. Bush's record on the death penalty was. But that summer, it was on a lot of people's minds, including ours. And after meeting five innocent people who had narrowly escaped being killed, we started to see how shocking those Texas statistics really were.

Now that we'd met and begun to form relationships with people who'd been intimately affected by all these previously abstract-seeming policies and politics and facts, that adage "the personal is the political" started to become literally true for us. Our emotional lives were connecting with our political ideas in a way that was stronger than either of us had anticipated. It felt integrated, and right, but it was also scary. It's much more manageable to go through the world when the injustices that don't affect you directly are an abstraction. The world becomes a more emotionally overwhelming place when you look at those injustices, whether they touch your life or not, and see the human face.

Having begun to get a glimpse of how emotionally charged this issue is, we began to talk about the ways in which emotion plays into the phenomenon of wrongful conviction as well. In the car, we realized how the likelihood of wrongful conviction is further increased by the ubiquity of television images of grieving spouses, siblings, and parents—and the near-total lack of images of the real people on the other side. It's a difficult problem, because the victims' families deserve enormous compassion and understanding, and it is crucial that we comprehend the extent of their pain. These families—who could be our neighbors, or us—have suffered an unimaginable loss; and when we see them on television, we see their real faces, hear their real words, and our hearts go out to them. This kind of compassion is what keeps us strong as a society. But, unfortunately, the human sides of these kinds of stories are often presented in a seriously imbalanced way. Often, the victims' families are the only ones we see; we don't see footage of the families of the wrongly convicted. And even more unfortunately, the media often exploits the images of grieving victims because it makes for "good television." The media, which are supposed to objectively present both (or all) sides of any given story, are often heavily weighted to one side, and heavily emotionalized. And when that combination of imbalance and emotionalization enters into court proceedings, it becomes dangerous. The law, ideally, is supposed to protect us from one-sided emotionality. The law is not supposed to be driven by passion. Nor are verdicts. It's a tough ideal to realize, but it's tough for a reason.

As we realized this, we also realized that it was important for us to maintain objectivity—while retaining our compassion—in the process of creating this project. Yes, we were writing a play, and the idea for that play had been triggered by a powerful emotional experience. And we were having incredibly moving experiences in people's living rooms. But as we proceeded, we knew that the play would be most powerful—and our understandings of the stories most complete—if we maintained some objectivity in our approach. Our job as playwrights would be to present these stories—and the people who were telling them—as they presented themselves to us; not to comment on them, focus on our feelings about them, or "make them our own." Our job as playwrights would be to illuminate the stories without layering our own emotions and opinions on top of them.

* * *

Regardless of our intentions for the play, though, our present experience was pretty intense, and the stories we were hearing just kept opening us up further and further. Going through this emotional experience together wasn't just affecting us individually; it was also affecting our relationship. We'd been together six months by then, but the intensity of what we were doing had accelerated things substantially. In the car on the way back to New York, we started talking about getting married. (Zooey overheard us and got jealous, communicating her attachment to Erik with a lot of misbehavior. But she finally came around and stopped licking herself obsessively when Jessica fed her an *entire* ice cream cone at an Ohio DQ.)

We had plenty of time on the road to hash out how we felt about "the institution" and all its associated mythologies, prejudices, and cultural assumptions, which both of us had real questions about. Why codify a human relationship within a legal framework? Wouldn't that mean defining the very thing—love—that was most undefinable? Didn't the institution of marriage begin back in the days when women were considered property, and hadn't marriage originated as a way to transfer ownership of that property from a father to a husband? Did that history leave a stain that couldn't be scrubbed out? And what did it mean that we were thinking of participating in an institution that many of our best friends were prohibited by law from participating in? We'd never join a country club that excluded black people; why were we considering joining a more metaphorical club that excluded all our queer friends? On the other hand, though, would our boycotting the institution really make it more available to others, or could we find other, more effective ways of helping make that happen? Did getting married mean accepting all the heterocentric, patriarchal conventions associated with traditional marriage, or was it possible for us to make a new model, to do it in a new, progressive—even radical—way? We went back and forth and back and forth, trying to figure out how to discard the ugly parts of the institution while keeping—and expanding—the beautiful parts. The questions we were asking each other were very real to us, and we spent hours and hours hashing them out. Okay, fighting about them. Even though we already agreed about them.

But we each felt like we had found an equal partner, and in the end it came down to that. Nothing was missing: we could even make art together and were already doing it. We both intuitively felt that we'd be with each other forever, whether we got married or not. And even though we both have extreme theatrical proclivities (in other words, we're drama queens), in this instance, we just sort of calmly *knew.* So somewhere on some freeway between Illinois and Pennsylvania, we got engaged.

Soon after, we reached the western Pennsylvania mountains and pulled over to call Jay Smith. He told us he was sorry, but he'd spoken with his family about it again and really felt that it was time to just put this history behind him. He'd been talking to the media about his case for years and he was tired. He didn't want any more attention, he said; he wanted to move on. He hoped he hadn't put us out of our way. We assured him that he hadn't, told him we understood, and got back on the highway to New York.

On all our trips, we rarely stopped for the night. Once in a while we would, if we had a friend's floor to crash on (like at Erik's old friend Chris's place in Ohio), or if our interview schedule demanded it (like in Chicago). But most of the time, one of us would drive while the other slept; we'd trade off shifts, drink a lot of coffee, turn the air conditioner up when our eyelids got too heavy. We didn't speed, though: the last thing in the world we wanted was to be pulled over by cops with our backseat full of information about wrongful conviction. Not that you can get a ticket for that . . . yet. So carefully observing the speed limit, we made it back to the city in a day and a half.

When we walked back into our apartment, we were greeted by an insanely blinking answering machine, a gazillion unread emails, and pages and pages of interview transcripts waiting to be turned into something an audience could follow. When we started reading those transcripts, we were daunted. We'd remembered the flow of each conversation, the details, individual sentences so striking and distilled we knew they'd work perfectly in a play. What we didn't really understand till we saw it on paper was that in real life, people don't talk in anything even remotely approximating dramatic language. They go off on tangents, loop around, say *um* a hell of a lot, offer you coffee, change the subject. Those transcripts had a lot of ellipses: interruptions, digressions, detours, pauses. On paper, nothing was linear; the stories were totally convoluted. It seemed impossible: we were *never* going to be able to distill this into something that made sense, much less something that had a dramatic story arc.

We had another problem, too: we were out of money. And to stay on schedule, we needed to be on the road down South no more than a couple weeks from now. Our fund-raising "plan" had been to raise money by the seat of our pants—just enough at a time to reach the next stage. Now, we'd just about exhausted those first few stages, and we didn't have a bridge to the next.

We had a little money left, but not anywhere near enough to fly down South and hit the road for over a week. And besides, in the meantime, two weeks of office supplies and intern expenses (we did pay them a little) would eat up most of what we had. So we looked at our bank account. Ugh. We would've happily dipped into our own money at that point, if such a thing as "our own money" existed. But we'd spent our limited reserves on the project already, and Jessica had quit her bartending job to work on the play full-time. Erik got a few residuals from DreamWorks, Jessica did a quick commercial for hair regrowing solutions for women; but those checks were few and far between. Jessica's hair was not going to pay the rent. We were living off ramen noodles and coffee, frustrating the phone company and selling more books to the used-book store.

We were stuck.

We were too busy working to stop and worry about it, though. Before we'd left, Erik had landed a role in a movie; when we came back, Jessica got a part in it, too. So we had a shooting schedule to contend with, transcripts to start editing—and travel plans to make. We just kept on going as if we had the money to go down South: reserved the plane tickets, made appointments for the interviews, rented the car. Somehow we managed to convince the bank to increase our credit limit—then promptly maxed out the Visa.

In the midst of all this, one evening an old friend of Jessica's, her high school sweetheart, called from San Francisco. Andrew and Jessica had lost touch over the last year or so; he was calling to catch up. He told Jessica about Olivia, the new woman he'd just met: how wonderful she was, smart and talented and dynamic. Jessica told Andrew about the project we were working on, everything we'd learned so far—and that we'd now hit a serious financial brick wall. And he said, "That's funny, Olivia's father runs a foundation, and he was just saying the other day that they want to start funding theater." After we hung up, Andrew called Colin Greer, Olivia's father, who runs the New World Foundation—and thanks to Andrew's help and Colin's generosity, within a week we had $7,500 in our hands, enough to fund our trip through the South.

This was the second time that we'd hit a major brick wall only to have a window appear in front of our faces. It sounds clichéd, but at that point it became clear to both of us that this project wanted to happen. So many people, more than we could ever have imagined, were willing to selflessly put in time, money, and energy to help us make this play a reality. And *something* was bringing all those people into contact with us at the very moments their help mattered most. Up till we found Colin Greer and the New World Foundation—or, more accurately, until they found us—we'd been able to ascribe this phenomenon to our dogged outreach, plus a lot of luck. But it was too much to believe that only luck had made Andrew call *that week* after he hadn't in nearly a year, *and* to have just started dating someone whose father ran a progressive political foundation, *and* for that foundation to have just decided to start funding theater, *and* for the foundation to have the flexibility to grant us $7,500 (they chose the amount), which just *happened* to be exactly the amount of money we needed to finish our travels. If it were just that one instance, okay. We would have accepted it as a major lucky coincidence. But when we looked at it together with Allan's immediate receptivity, and Connie's strange and coincidental ability to put us in touch with Delbert, and that Darby (who didn't have a phone and lived in Texas) had happened to be in Chicago *and* happened to call up Larry Marshall the exact day we were coming into town—not to mention all the other little incidences of synchronicity that had accumulated over the last few months—we had to accept that something else was at work here. Call it God, the universe, or just a play that was willing itself into being. Whatever it was, we weren't in control of this anymore.

It's good we had that realization at that point. The first trip was a big brand-new adventure, and we'd been so busy trying to figure out how to do what we were doing that we didn't notice how exhausted we were. But our workload would increase exponentially over the summer—and so would the number of obstacles. There were several points at which, without something strong to carry us through, we might have given up in the face of those obstacles or collapsed from exhaustion. Neither of us had ever done anything remotely as hard as this before. If we'd had only our prior experience and our belief in the project to go on, we might not have made it. Once we accepted that something bigger than us was helping the play along, it helped us along, too. We were just the conduits, and if it took sixteen-hour days seven days a week for five months plus resources we didn't even know we had, then so be it.

That's not to say we were tranquil and easygoing in the face of our newfound faith. Sometimes the stress took its toll on our brand-new relationship, and sometimes the six cups of coffee a day and no sleep made us cranky. The stories themselves got under our skins; the details haunted our dreams. We were becoming a mental and emotional clearinghouse for the death penalty: it was draining to incorporate all the new things we were learning about how unjust our system is, and how deeply that scars real people in real ways. We got pretty pissed off at times, and now and then we took it out on each other—we didn't always have time to process all our new emotions, since there was so much work to do. But if things really got tense, we'd look at each other and ask, "Is this really as bad as being on death row for something you didn't do?" Kind of puts things in perspective. We kept going.

Chapter Seven

We stepped off the plane in Atlanta, early morning, bleary-eyed, and headed right for the rental counter. We'd made a weeklong reservation, and we were looking forward to squeezing into our economy-class box-on-wheels and getting on the road to Colbert, Georgia. Our intern Bonnie had agreed to dog-sit Zooey, so the drive would be almost luxurious without a frantic ball of fur clambering up in the front seat every two minutes. We'd even packed some road food from the health-food store, having learned our lesson from the Midwestern 7-Elevens. We were all set.

Until we got to the bright yellow rental counter. No, no, not Hertz. Hertz is an upstanding company with a reputation for dependability and professional flexibility. The name of the rental company that we had reserved a car with was—let's call it Nertz. Short for "Not Hertz."

They took one look at us scraggly (possibly drug-running, gun-toting, God-hating?) New Yorkers and decided they'd need to run our credit card again. Okay, no problem.

Of course, there could be no problems. We'd been careful. We had *planned ahead*. We'd made our reservation just after the bank increased our credit limit, and there was, for the first time ever, plenty of room on our card. Then a voice broke through our illusion of fiscal responsibility: "There's a problem." Our shoulders slumped. The boulder we'd rolled all the way to Georgia was going to roll back and crush us; and not even on the highway or in the middle of an interview, but *at the airport*.

We still had enough to rent the car—we'd made sure of that—but apparently Nertz required $500 available credit as a deposit, and it looked as if this was definitely not going to happen.

"I'm sorry," the extremely bored woman behind the counter said as the fluorescent lights shone down, illuminating the circles beneath her eyes. "I'm going to have to cancel your reservation."

We had an interview scheduled in two and a half hours. We had a two-hour-and-fifteen-minute drive in front of us. Our entire trip was timed out to the minute—if we got behind now, we'd be behind the whole week. We'd already been waiting longer than we'd planned for. Every other rental car counter in the airport was mobbed with better-dressed, more-experienced renters. They were being handed golden steering wheels and we were stuck with our thumbs up our butts in the Atlanta airport—with no visible options.

We waited in line at Nertz for another twenty minutes while the bored lady disappeared into the Krispy Kreme Room, a little break area somewhere behind a mirrored wall: a netherworld where time moved slow as grits and customers got ignored, overlooked, and forgotten. After ten minutes of waiting, Erik started muttering, wishing he could pick his nose and wipe it under the counter, wishing he could come up with an act of revenge a little more creative and tasteful than that, spinning off into fantasy, imagining what he'd do if he were Lou Reed. "Lou Reed wouldn't stand for this," Erik leaned over and told Jessica, who, having not been privy to the thought patterns that had led up to it, was both alarmed and amused by this statement. "He'd say something devastatingly cool and sexy, and Bored Lady'd get distraught and turned on all at the same time, and she'd melt into a puddle of confusion and obsequiousness and"—louder now—"we'd be driving away from the fucking Atlanta airport on the road to talk to another guy from death fucking row!" The 'death row' part of that seemed to freak out the couple behind us just a little. Or maybe it was the Lou Reed part. Regardless, they stepped back, whispered to each other, and moved over to the Nenterprise rental counter across the way.

While we waited for Bored Lady to return, we called the credit card company on our cell phone—but apparently, someone at good old Nertz had unsuccessfully tried to run our card, twice, minutes before the credit increase was about to register. This created a perfect credit storm that we are still trying to untangle, and a series of security measures made it impossible to increase our tender credit any further for forty-eight hours. "Policy," the Visa lady cooed.

Then Bored Lady came back from the Krispy Kreme Room, licking her fingers and towing along a manager who looked suspiciously like G. Gordon Liddy. Liddy, arms folded, eyes narrowed, glowered behind Bored Lady like rent-a-car muscle as she politely explained to Erik the three-page policy that Erik became convinced Nertz had developed expressly to deal with *him*. Having given up on any hope of acting like Lou Reed, Erik tried to reason with Bored Lady: "That can't be possible," he told her. "They took the reservation on the phone, everything cleared; nobody told us we had to have five hundred dollars extra on the card." No dice.

"I'm sorry," Bored Lady repeated, "I'm going to have to cancel the reservation."

Now, to Nertz's credit, Bored Lady *was* polite. Bored, devastatingly patronizing, pedantic, repetitive, and curt. But polite. In Bored Lady, we recognized our first manifestation of "Southern hospitality," which is real, and beautiful—and takes twenty minutes longer than New York hospitality, which lasts thirty seconds and is considered successful if one walks away with one "Fuck you" instead of a hailstorm of them.

Just as Erik was about to introduce New York hospitality into the mix, Jessica noticed the steam leaking from Erik's ears, laid her hand gently on his arm (again, the universal signal for "please shut up now"), and stepped forward into battle. Jessica has logged many, many hours doing conflict resolution, mediating disputes in hippie collectives, and being raised by two communicative, therapy-oriented parents; all that usually pays off when she is trying to get something she wants from a bureaucrat. So with the mysteriously expanding staff of the Atlanta airport Nertz (Liddy and Bored had by now been joined by a David Spade look-alike and a guy shaped like a side of beef), Jessica followed all the rules: first she sweetly asked to speak to a manager. Then, when Mr. Liddy, the previously mute manager, finally stepped forward, she told him how much she understood Nertz's point of view.

Of course they needed some kind of deposit on the car. Maybe we could find a solution to this, together. We had a debit card: Could they take an imprint of that and hold on to it? No. Okay. We could write them a check for $500, and they could keep it till we came back? No. Even if they called our bank to confirm that the check would clear? Nope. Okay, fine. We'd go get $500 from an ATM and they could keep that till we returned the car.

No.

"I'm sorry," Jessica said to Mr. Manager, "I don't understand why five hundred dollars cash isn't as good as five hundred dollars credit. Could you explain that to me?"

Mr. Manager's explanation was "It's policy." Ah. And furthermore: "It's standard; all the other rental places have that exact same policy."

Jessica tried again: "And you have no leeway in the way you implement your policies?"

"Sorry," he grumped, "it's policy."

Mr. Liddy didn't get any further than that, because by now the volume of steam coming from Erik's ears had increased substantially and the "please shut up now" arm touch wasn't working anymore. So, ever the East Village gentleman, Erik stepped back up to the counter and started yelling. When Erik (who is working hard on this) sees any level of injustice going on because of "policy," he starts yelling. Even, unfortunately, if it's just about a rental car. But he had a point: what he was saying, in between the swearing, was that it was prejudicial of Nertz to require that their customers use a specific form of payment: you have to have a lot of money to have a lot of credit. Nertz's demand that we pay for the car and the deposit on a credit card was unfair to people without a lot of money, who could pay for the rental but just didn't have a gold card. Goddamnit.

Everything Erik *said* was reasonable and true, but unfortunately he said it at a decibel level designed to break through the indestructible concrete wall of "policy" with sheer volume. So the entire staff of the Atlanta airport Nertz asked us to leave their counter. Now. In a Southern accent, the tone that precedes "Would you like us to call security?" really does sound like an invitation to share lemonade on the porch. But we could tell what they were harboring behind it: it's in the eyes.

So, with everyone within a three-hundred-foot radius staring, we dragged our huge duffel bags full of equipment out into the atrium and surveyed our options. If what Mr. Manager had said was true—that all the other rental places shared their policy—then we were stuck in Atlanta, Georgia, with no way to get to any of our interviews. Even if we could wire money to our credit card, it would still take a day to go through, and by the time we got on the road and made up the lost driving time, we'd have to cancel at least three interviews. And we couldn't afford a hotel in Atlanta; we'd been planning to sleep in the car. We were screwed.

But we stubbornly refused to take Mr. Liddy's word for anything, so we lugged our bags around to all the rental counters to find out for ourselves. Turned out all but one shared Nertz's policy; we were faithful Alamo customers the rest of our time on the road.

Nertz, maybe next time you should offer us a doughnut while we're waiting: since then, in working on the play, we've spent literally thousands of dollars on rental cars—and none of it's gone to you. Probably, it would've been smarter of us to just go ahead and buy a damn car. But that would go against our East Village "policy." Hmm. What would Lou Reed do?

Just a half hour behind schedule, we got on the highway headed toward Colbert, Georgia, a tiny town outside Athens, to meet a guy named Henry Drake. We had the a/c cranked up high—Georgia was *hot*—and Jessica read articles about Henry's case out loud as Erik drove. We stopped on the outskirts of Athens to pick up some Krispy Kremes for Henry, then continued on; the semirural Wal-

Mart–Arby's–McDonald's sprawl gave way to rolling green fields full of strange giant-marshmallow-looking things that we eventually realized were bales of hay wrapped in white plastic. Highway turned to county road and rusted-out cars dotted the yards of the occasional ramshackle houses. So this was what Georgia looked like.

Reading the articles about Henry's case, we were both blown away by the injustice of what had happened to him—and the random luck involved in his release. The crime Henry was accused of occurred at Colbert's town barbershop in December of 1975. The seventy-five-year-old barber, Mr. C. E. Eberhart, had run the shop for decades and was well-known and loved. One afternoon, William "Pop" Campbell dropped by his shop. By the time Campbell left, Eberhart had been beaten to death with a hammer and Campbell had $400 in his pocket. When Campbell was caught, he said nothing—but later, thinking that his friend Henry had turned him in, he claimed that Henry had killed Mr. Eberhart. At trial, Campbell tried to portray Henry as the lone killer, but enough evidence implicated Campbell so that both men were prosecuted. Campbell was tried and convicted first; he then served as the prosecution's star witness against Henry. Henry, dirt-poor, was convicted and sentenced to death despite a lack of any physical evidence implicating him, despite the fact that he had an alibi, and despite the medical examiner's testimony that Mr. Eberhart could not have been killed by more than one person.

Campbell and Henry were held at the same prison and had occasional contact with each other. Not long after their convictions, Campbell, who was in poor health, told Henry that he had confessed to a visiting minister, and that the minister had then convinced him to sign an affidavit admitting he had lied in his testimony against Henry. In the affidavit, Campbell wrote, "I lied at this trial. I said Henry was the one who killed the barber, Mr. Eberhart. I was the one who killed Mr. Eberhart. Henry wasn't even there. He didn't have anything to do with it."

After signing the affidavit, however, Campbell handed it over to his attorney, Pat Beall, who, citing attorney-client privilege, refused to release the affidavit or the information it contained—for years. In prison, Campbell, not a young man, was getting more and more ill; after a while, it became clear his days were numbered. Besides, he'd been sentenced to death, too—he didn't exactly have a lot to lose. Campbell repeatedly admitted privately that he had lied at trial and that he knew Henry was innocent. But Pat Beall, Campbell's attorney, was trying to get Campbell's sentence reduced, and he advised his client not to repeat those admissions in court. Henry, younger than Campbell and in good health, tried to convince Campbell to come forward with the truth. But Henry's powers of persuasion were not so strong; Campbell and his attorney refused.

In 1982, three years after Henry's state appeals had been exhausted, Campbell died in his cell. Now that Campbell had died, Pat Beall finally felt that he could come forward and testify that his client had, repeatedly and in writing, confessed to being the sole murderer. After being presented with Campbell's affidavit, the Federal Court of Appeals for the Eleventh Circuit accepted Henry's habeas corpus petition and ordered a new trial. In 1986, Henry's sentence was commuted to life in prison. Six months later—after Henry had spent nearly ten years on death row—the parole board released him on the grounds that he was actually innocent.

A note about habeas corpus: in basic, nonlegalistic terms, habeas corpus (which in Latin means "bring out the body") gives convicted persons an opportunity to introduce to federal appeals court new evidence that was not available at the time of their initial trial. It is a crucial constitutional protection, precisely because of situations like Henry's. It ensures that an innocent person always has the opportunity to bring before the courts new evidence that would prove his innocence.

In 1995, in the wake of the Oklahoma City bombing, Congress passed a bill entitled the Effective Death Penalty and Anti-Terrorism Act of 1995. One of the provisions of this bill was to seriously limit habeas corpus appeals in capital cases. Before 1995, there were no time limits on the introduction of new, potentially exculpatory evidence; now, typically, a defendant has only 180 days after state appeals are exhausted to introduce new evidence. At the very most, under the 1995 law, a defendant has a year to bring new evidence before the courts.

That Pop Campbell died in prison, freeing his lawyer from attorney-client confidentiality and making Campbell's confession available, was a fluke in itself; under today's laws, that fluke would have had to occur within a year of the end of Henry's state appeals for a federal court even to accept the evidence. Because of the Effective Death Penalty Act, if evidence comes in past an arbitrarily chosen time limit, juries never get to hear it—even if it proves the defendant's innocence beyond a shadow of a doubt. If this law had been in place when Henry was on death row, Henry—an innocent man—would be dead right now.

In the car, we tried to imagine what it must feel like to languish on death row for a decade while the real killer sits beside you in prison—and you know his confession would free you, if only he'd come forward. It actually seemed so absurd that we couldn't figure out why it had taken ten years for Henry to convince the courts of his innocence. It looked so obvious.

But the descriptions of Henry in the newspaper stories also made us a little nervous to meet him—partly because he'd had a record before he was wrongly convicted, mostly because of our own prejudices about the South and the white folks who lived there. We kept a journal during part of our time on the road, and Jessica wrote in it on the way to Henry's:

> We're in Atlanta, driving through a heat that makes the highways look like water, toward Colbert, Georgia. We're going to talk with Henry Drake, a fiftysomething guy kept on death row for over ten years for a murder another guy confessed to. I'm nervous, and to be honest, I know that some of that comes from my own prejudices—here we are driving through the only part of the U.S. either of us has never spent a lot of time in, a place full of stereotypes and heavy, heavy history. I know from our research that Henry is a white guy who lives way out in the middle of nowhere, Georgia, in a totally isolated trailer; a guy who had a record before he went in of robbery, theft, abandonment. I've got prejudices in my head about that, which is something I don't really want to admit. I haven't made up my mind that I have a negative opinion of him, and from the evidence in his case, it's clear that he's innocent—without a doubt. But I'm a little nervous.

Our nervousness couldn't have been more unnecessary. We pulled up to Henry's trailer, folded into a little grove of trees, with four cats wandering around and several rusty cars in the yard, a couple of which were cool-looking vintage numbers. Henry came out to greet us in a powder-blue T-shirt and green polyester shorts, around five feet nine, slight, with white buzz-cut hair, blue eyes, and the gentlest soul you could ever imagine. It appeared to us that he was at least somewhat mentally challenged, and he spoke with a deep, slow drawl—but his welcoming, mild intentions came through right away.

He pointed out his mom's trailer, right next door, and invited us into his living room to sit down. Inside, his trailer was spacious and homey, with burgundy carpets, lots of framed photos of Mom, Bibles and crosses everywhere, and more cats. We all had a Krispy Kreme—Henry insisted—and then sat down to talk.

Perhaps most tragic about what had happened to Henry—more than being fingered by a friend, more than knowing a piece of paper existed that could free him, if only the courts would accept it—is that he seemed never to have understood all the details of his case. That went a long way toward explaining why it had taken so long for Henry to convince the courts of his innocence—it takes a lot of persistence and ingenuity to get anyone to listen to you once you're convicted, and that was clearly even more difficult for Henry. None of the newspaper articles we'd read had mentioned this.

We'd thought some of the other folks we'd met were put in extraordinarily vulnerable positions, what with not being able to afford decent representation, having no access to resources, and the like. Now, talking to Henry, we imagined what it would be like to be accused of a crime you didn't commit, to be assigned a lawyer who didn't prove your innocence effectively, to know the real killer could exonerate you in a minute if he wanted, to have nowhere to go for help—*and* to simultaneously be unable to fully understand what's happening to you. Not only do you have nobody really fighting for you on the outside—you're not even able to fight for yourself.

We don't know exactly what Henry's IQ is, so we're not sure whether he's "mentally retarded" according to the law. But after speaking with him for just ten minutes, it was clear that his intelligence was too low for him to be able to describe the twists and turns of his case. We tried to ask him about them, and his answers were confused, consisting mostly of impressions, feelings, and images mixed in with randomly placed facts. After a while, we gave up trying to talk to him about his case and asked him instead about his feelings; when we did, the conversation became much clearer. He told us about his religion: how much he loved Jesus, how he read the Bible in prison and it got him through. He told us all about his mom: how he loved her, too, and she was eighty-six years old. And he talked a lot about animals: how he couldn't even swat a bug on his arm, and he could never understand how people hunt, since deer are so beautiful; he could stand there and just look at their eyes forever. He also told us that he'd forgiven everyone involved in his wrongful conviction, because what are you going to do, stay angry?

We couldn't imagine how anyone could ever convict this man of murder.

Our meeting with Henry was the first time we understood the degree to which our criminal justice system can prey on the most vulnerable members of our society. We had begun to get a sense of how the system pursues and prosecutes the most economically disadvantaged among us—but we didn't get the full picture until we realized that it's not just the poor, it's children and the mentally retarded, too. You hear things—from Amnesty International, Human Rights Watch, organizations like that—about how execution of children and the mentally retarded violates international human rights standards, how countries all over the world band together to ban the practice. But you don't really understand why that is until you're sitting in a trailer in Colbert, Georgia, with a man who was swept up in a situation he never had full comprehension of, fingered by the real killer, with no money to hire a good attorney to protect him, nobody to explain to him what was happening, unable to follow his own trial let alone understand the law, who was almost strapped to a chair to have twenty-five hundred volts of electricity run through his body for a crime he never knew a thing about. You don't really understand what the word *defenseless* means till you see that.

Erik's father, Steve, has made his career working with mentally retarded adults, running group homes, and helping the people who live there move toward self-sufficiency and independence. When Erik was growing up, he spent lots of time with the remarkable people his dad managed; many of the folks who lived there became his friends. He'd learned to respect them for what they could teach us; he'd also come to understand the way most of our society locks them away like so much human trash. Henry's IQ was a little higher than those of the people Erik had known as a kid; Henry did okay living on his own, as long as his family was nearby to look after him. But meeting Henry, Erik realized that the "slower" people who get caught up in the gears of the criminal justice system are not so different from the ones he grew up with.

Henry's situation wasn't unique—it is extremely common for innocent mentally retarded people to be fingered by more intelligent criminals who know how defenseless they are, and then to suffer heavy sentences because of their inability to navigate the justice system. Human Rights Watch, in its official report on mental retardation and the death penalty, writes:

> By virtue of their disability, people with mental retardation are less likely than other defendants to be able to protect their legal rights and to secure a fair trial. For example, one attribute of mental retardation is the inability to comprehend abstract concepts—including the most basic concepts relevant to criminal proceedings. Robert Wayne Sawyer—an offender with mental retardation executed in 1993—was asked by a psychiatrist to define evidence. "It's what lawyers put on a yellow pad like the one you're using" was the best definition Sawyer could offer.

> Miranda warnings are written at a seventh-grade level of difficulty; many people with mental retardation function at a lower intellectual level and are unable to understand the language and meanings of the warning. Eddie Mitchell, a retarded man on death row in Louisiana, waived all his rights during his interrogation. But when an attorney asked him if he had understood what "waiving his rights" meant, Mitchell raised his right hand and waved.

Mentally retarded people are especially vulnerable to the system in a myriad of other ways: for example, mentally retarded adults are often eager to please the cops, to tell police what they want to hear, so, when prodded by police, they often give false confessions—with no inkling that this will result in their conviction and, sometimes, death. The same is true for children. (As of this writing the United States is one of five countries that allow the execution of children who were under eighteen at the time of their crimes. The other countries are the Democratic Republic of the Congo, Iran, Nigeria, and Saudi Arabia.) In a society that supposedly values compassion, it is unfathomable that the state has historically been allowed to exercise its immense power to punish upon the most vulnerable among us, the very people who have the least ability to defend themselves.

In 2002, perhaps taking this into account, the Supreme Court ruled in *Atkins v. Virginia* that execution of the mentally retarded is unconstitutional. This was a watershed event, bringing our justice system closer in one crucial way to meeting international human rights standards. *Atkins*'s importance should not be underestimated: at the time of the *Atkins* decision, 2,455 persons were under death sentence in the twenty states whose laws permit the execution of the mentally retarded; an estimated 5 percent of those may be mentally retarded, which means the *Atkins* decision could affect over a hundred lives. But many, many mentally retarded people had been sent to their deaths in America in the time between the reinstatement of the death penalty in 1976 and *Atkins* in 2002. In that period, at least thirty-five people with mental retardation were executed in the United States—and possibly many more than that, given that IQ tests for death row defendants are in no way automatic. In Texas, when George W. Bush was governor, he approved the execution of a mentally retarded inmate named Mario Marquez, a brain-damaged man with an IQ of 60 whose verbal and reasoning skills were comparable to those of a seven-year-old child. A few hours before his death, Marquez told his attorney that he "want[ed] to be God's gardener and take care of the animals." Bush also approved the execution of Oliver David Cruz, a man who was either mentally retarded or a few IQ points above that definition. And he repeatedly refused to take inmates' mental capacity into account when approving last-minute requests for review. All this while campaigning on a platform of "compassion."

And even given the *Atkins* decision, many of our society's most vulnerable are still susceptible to the death penalty. According to the Supreme Court, to be defined as "mentally retarded," a defendant must have an IQ under 70 and have been identified as retarded before the age of eighteen. If a defendant was not subjected to testing in his youth, or if his IQ is just a few points above 70—as Henry's may be—the death penalty can still be imposed, no matter whether the defendant actually understands his case, his rights, or the justice system.

As we sat talking with Henry, we knew there was no way his story could make it into the play. We were fashioning the play based on people's own words, and Henry's weren't cohesive enough for an audience to understand. As a character he would be heartbreaking. But as a "first person account" there wouldn't be enough understandable narrative to establish a context for what the character was saying. We were unhappy with that, though, because we wanted to communicate to our audiences what we'd learned from meeting Henry. Many people in America think the death penalty is reserved for the most vicious killers, the truly dangerous among us. And in some cases, that's true. But in the case of children and the mentally retarded, death sentences can be handed down to the most defenseless, most vulnerable members of our society. Even when they're innocent.

After Henry stood with us in the front yard and proudly showed us his brand-new litter of kittens, we made our way back to the highway. We were both quieted by the realizations we'd had meeting Henry. All of the interviews we'd done so far had been moving and disturbing, but at least the other folks we'd met had been able to draw on their own intelligence and creativity to help get themselves out. Henry's was a different story. If Campbell hadn't confessed—and if his confession weren't finally made available—Henry would be gone right now.

We wove silently through the giant-marshmallow-covered hills on the way back to Athens. On this trip, too, we had just enough money to spend one night in a motel. We were blowing it the first night because we had an early wake-up call, a long drive, and two interviews in front of us tomorrow. We pulled into a motel outside Athens with pink, chipped paint and a nonworking whirlpool in the room, paid our forty bucks, ordered a pizza, and crashed.

Chapter Eight

At four the next morning, the phone buzzed loudly four times, apparently our wake-up call. We stumbled toward the sink and got ready as quickly as our half-asleep bodies could manage; we were both eager to get on the road to Birmingham.

Neither of us had traveled much through the Deep South. We'd each spent some time in North and South Carolina, Kentucky, places like that; but Alabama, Mississippi, northern Florida—those were a different story. Though we knew there was more to it, that South to us was black-and-white film reels of Selma, or clips of a Ken Burns documentary. It was films like *In the Heat of the Night*, the legacies of racism and the civil rights movement. Our images were abstracted by distance and history, wrapped in a thick web of emotional, cultural, and political associations. Birmingham was sort of mythical to us. We'd both learned so much about what had happened in that city, and yet neither of us had ever even been in the state that contained it. We were anxious to see what would happen when our mythology met up with reality.

We made our way to the highway and drove through the half-light, watching out the windows as the sun crept through the dark blue sky and turned it pink. In the last miles of Georgia, we discovered Waffle House, a diner chain specific to the South that would prove to be our main food source for the rest of our Southern trip, with its cheap, weak coffee and abundant carbohydrates. In Georgia by the Alabama border, we walked beneath the bright yellow sign into the fluorescent lights of Waffle House, and the patrons peered at us over their *USA Today*s as if we were brand-new arrivals from a faraway planet. As the waitress pulled shrink-wrap off a hard, gray piece of meat she graveled, "You're not from around here are you?"

Erik: No, can't say as we are.

Waitress: Where you from, honey?

Erik: New York City.

Waitress *(visibly disturbed)*: New York, huh? What's that like?

Erik: You know, big, noisy, lots of people—

Waitress *(interrupting)*: We figured you were from somewhere else. *(Referring to the tattoo on the back of Jessica's neck)* What's that tattoo mean?

Jessica: Um, it's a tree of life? Religious symbol, you know.

Waitress *(again, disturbed)*: Well . . . that's different.

Long pause.

Erik *(jumping in)*: That a John Deere out back?

Waitress: You bet your ass, son.

Erik: Uh . . . My grandfather was a farmer, you know; taught me how to fix one of those with a ball-peen hammer and a can of WD-40.

Waitress: Oh, really? *(No longer disturbed, now flirting)* Buy you a coffee?

This was not a unique conversation. Everywhere we went there was a Waffle House, and at every Waffle House the skeptical locals viewed us as suspicious characters. Big-city people on the make? Grifters? Carpetbaggers. Hillary! We got the general idea that they wanted us to get the hell out. Of the Waffle House, and the state, too, if possible. Had the Bored Lady put out an APB on us?

It got a little ridiculous after a while. But as we continued, we learned how to answer the locals' questions properly, picked up a little Southern hospitality, and after a short grilling on tattoo and attire, our Waffle House visits turned out okay. All ideology was set aside, the only religion steak and eggs with lots of butter. We tried not to mention we were vegetarians. *That* probably would've gotten us kicked out.

We did have a lot of silent, curious people sitting next to us, though. So, just for fun, sometimes we'd occasionally throw things into the conversation for their benefit: ". . . and that was *after* I stopped working at the brothel . . . I know, it's ridiculous, but Wayne Newton and I were about to go down to South America to smuggle back some cows for the bovine porn cartel . . ." Between Georgia and Mississippi there are probably a dozen people who ran home from the Waffle House with amazing stories about those two weird Yankee drifters they had had breakfast with.

* * *

After Waffle House, it was always back to work. We got back in the car and started sifting through our files for the few articles we had about the man we were going to meet in Birmingham, Bo Cochran. Our meeting with Bo was another last-minute gift from a lawyer, this time Birmingham defense attorney Richard Jaffe. We'd gotten to know Richard in setting up an interview with another exonerated client of his, a guy named Randal Padgett. Randal had requested that we schedule our interview with him through his attorney's office; when we called Richard's office, we struck up a rapport with him.

Richard Jaffe is a firebrand of a Southern defense attorney. He's been in Birmingham for over twenty years, alternately working as a public defender and taking on high-profile paid cases; last year, he won his third death row exoneration. He has the charisma and razor-sharp mind of a big-city superstar lawyer, and given his personality and style, he might make more sense on one of the coasts; but he's chosen to stay in Birmingham, out of dedication to the people of Alabama. We're sure lots of folks are grateful to him for that—not least of all Randal Padgett and Bo Cochran, two men whose lives Richard helped save.

As soon as we told Richard about our project, he and his assistant, Meredith, were extremely helpful. They arranged for us to meet with Randal in Guntersville, Alabama; then, a couple days before we left for the South, Richard called up and asked if we'd also like to meet Bo Cochran, another innocent man he'd helped free from death row. So now we were on our way to meet with Bo in Birmingham.

Richard had set up this interview just a couple days before, so we didn't have a lot of time to research Bo's case; also, there wasn't a lot of press on it. We'd found out that Bo was a black steelworker who'd been accused of killing a white convenience store clerk in a 1976 robbery; we'd have to wait to hear the rest of it from Bo himself.

When we crossed the state line into Alabama, we saw the typical interstate "Welcome to . . ." sign, with lovely flowers surrounding the state's name written in loopy cursive. Immediately after that, we saw another sign advertising a rest stop. Once again, we'd had too much coffee at Waffle House, so we gratefully pulled off, parked, and walked through the RV-filled lot to the Alabama Welcome Center. The Alabama Welcome Center was built to look like a big old house, except instead of rooms and furniture it had open spaces inside that held vending machines and racks of tourist pamphlets. The grounds were immaculately manicured, ringed with beds of hot-pink and white impatiens. It was probably the prettiest rest stop either of us had ever been to. Manicured. Spotless. To the right was a flagpole, which flew the American flag, the state flag, and the Confederate flag. In front of the doors, planted smack in the middle of the concrete, was a big rock; affixed to the rock was a huge plaque that said, "Alabama: We Dare Defend Our Rights." We wondered who the "We" referred to, and whose rights they were defending. Particularly since we had just read in the car that Alabama is the only state in America that—despite that the U.S. Constitution guarantees all citizens the right to an attorney—neither guarantees a lawyer to inmates after their initial convictions nor funds an office to help death row inmates find lawyers to represent them. And if you've been unlucky enough to be convicted of a felony in Alabama (with or without proper counsel), guess what? You lose your right to vote. "Whose rights," indeed.

After rushing to the bathrooms, we decided to explore this Alabama Welcome Center a little. In the back of the building, in keeping with the big-old-house theme, was a charming wraparound wooden porch that looked out on a lawn and woods. Pots of carefully tended flowers dotted its edge, and beautiful old rocking chairs were lined up all along the porch. At first glance—with the flowers, the rocking chairs, the manicured lawn, the chirping birds—it looked to us like the classic genteel Southern setting. The only thing missing were the mint juleps. Until we looked again—and saw that the rocking chairs were literally chained to the porch, locked down with padlocks and big steel links that looked not entirely unlike shackles. The image expressed the underbelly of that genteel world so perfectly. Maybe it was a classic Southern scene in more ways than one.

Alone with the unintended symbolism on the porch, we took a couple pictures, then headed back out front to the "We Dare Defend Our Rights" rock. As we bent down to take a photo, a group of locals came up behind us, white folks, the men in baseball caps and white sneakers and the women in gold jewelry and Aqua Net. Most of them continued on toward the vending machines, but one woman hung back. In her forties, she wore a big blond bouffant hairdo, enormous round glasses, and a loud paisley polyester shirt. She stood behind us, watching our little photo shoot with her arms crossed. Finally, in a loud drawl, she said accusingly, "Why don't y'all take a picture of the No Pets sign while you're at it?" Without giving us a chance to explain why the No Pets sign lacked the rock's historical baggage (at least as far as we could figure out), she lifted her chin up to the sky and huffed in toward the bathroom. Unsure whether to feel righteous or embarrassed, we slid our camera back in its case and headed half-proud, half-sheepish toward the car.

We hit the tail end of rush hour on our way into Birmingham; we'd been hoping to get to drive around the city a little before we met up with Bo, but the traffic foiled our plans. Bo had asked us to meet him in a city park at eleven; he'd given us directions and said for sure he'd be able to pick us out in the parking lot. We pulled in about fifteen minutes late—to see that our car was the only one in the lot. We panicked, embarrassed at our lateness—had Bo already come, waited for us, and left? An argument started brewing there in the deserted parking lot, as each of us blamed the other for not calling Bo to let him know we were running late. Eventually, though, we decided maybe it'd be a good idea to just *call* Bo instead of standing there blaming each other for not calling him.

Bo answered the phone, and we told him where we were; he let out a big laugh and said, "Oh, y'all are on Georgia time." We'd neglected to notice that the time had changed somewhere near the Alabama Welcome Center. We weren't late, we were early. Bo chuckled at us and said he'd be right over.

Five minutes later, he pulled up in his big maroon car, a black man in his sixties with a warm, weathered, deeply lined face and an Alabama drawl so deep it almost sounded like another language. He shook our hands heartily, still amused by our confusion. We all headed through the grass to a little sheltered picnic area, where we set up the tape recorders.

At first, we didn't ask a lot of questions; it took us a while to familiarize ourselves with Bo's dialect. Luckily he was gregarious and *loved* to talk, so we just listened closely as he told us about his childhood, growing up in the forties and fifties in a poor household outside Birmingham, led by a tough, hard father who never showed him much love. Bo was scuffling with the law by the time he was a teenager, often in the wrong place with the wrong people at the wrong time. Work wasn't always plentiful, but Bo worked hard when he could find it: sometimes construction, sometimes in fields, sometimes in factories. He had some brushes with the law; there were robbery arrests, and Bo spent a stretch of time in jail. But these were the pre-civil-rights days, and the all-white police force didn't always stay entirely inside the law, especially with young black men. Bo was beaten repeatedly by police, sometimes when he'd been arrested, sometimes not.

In 1976, an A&P in Homewood, Alabama, was robbed. Bo told us that he'd been at the scene of the crime; he was leaving the A&P when the cops showed up. They surrounded the store and shined their lights on him, he said, and out of instinct—having been beaten and threatened so many times by cops—he ran. Bo was still running—around half a mile away—when he heard a gunshot. Just minutes later, the cops caught up with Bo and hauled him into the station.

After questioning him for some time, Bo told us, they brought him to another room and locked the door. The detectives told him to strip; he took off his jacket, Bo said, and handed it to one of the cops. Bo then bent down to untie his shoes; when he heard the cop say, "Look what I found [in the jacket]," Bo looked up. The cop was holding a wad of bills—reportedly, about $250—wrapped in an A&P rubber band. Strangely, Bo had been searched three times previously that night and the only money they'd found on him during those searches was thirty-two cents. But, Bo told us, after the detective discovered the bills on their fourth search, Bo wasn't surprised when they charged him with robbery.

But then they told Bo they were charging him with murder, too—and his jaw dropped. He'd heard that gunshot, but figured the cops were firing in the air to try to apprehend him. He had no idea someone had died.

The cops told Bo that the white A&P manager, Steven Ganey, had been killed just after the robbery, and that Bo was the only suspect. Bo—represented by a public defender who was allotted $1,000 to try the case—was brought to trial and quickly convicted of capital murder, on no physical or eyewitness evidence, by a jury of eleven whites and one black.

When he first got to death row, Bo told us, he was deeply depressed: he wouldn't talk, wouldn't eat. Things looked hopeless for him. But on Alabama's death row, unlike most death rows, inmates aren't isolated from each other twenty-three hours a day—they actually get to interact, and this, Bo said, is what saved his life. The other guys kept talking to him; they wouldn't let him isolate himself. Finally Bo started talking—and then, he said with a laugh, "I talked so much they were after me to shut up!" The other guys lifted him up, Bo said, and he started hanging out with them in the law library—and then started using that time in the library to teach himself the law.

Bo was one of the victims of Alabama's unique policy of not guaranteeing inmates lawyers after their initial trials. Like the vast majority of people on death row, Bo was extremely poor and had zero access to an attorney after the state quit providing him a public defender. Even though the law guaranteed Bo several more appeals, he had nobody to argue them. His knowledge of the law was improving—but not enough to argue his own case against the DA. He started writing letters to anyone who might possibly be able to help him find a lawyer. He wrote the ACLU, the NAACP, everyone—but Bo looked guilty, and nobody would help.

Bo knew he didn't kill Steven Ganey, though, and he didn't give up. He told us that he kept on studying law, writing letters—and keeping up with Supreme Court decisions. In 1986, the Supreme Court handed down a decision in *Batson v. Kentucky*, ruling that it was unconstitutional for attorneys to use peremptory challenges to exclude prospective jurors on the basis of race. (In a trial, each side has a limited number of opportunities to rule out potential jurors without stating a reason for it—these are called peremptory challenges. Historically, these have often been used by prosecutors to exclude black jurors in cases involving black defendants. The *Batson* decision made this practice illegal.) Bo believed that the prosecution in his case had excluded several black jurors this way; he'd watched it happen. He started thinking this new decision might help convince a lawyer to take him on.

In 1986, Bo wrote to Bryan Stevenson, a whip-smart and dedicated attorney who runs a critically important Alabama organization called the Equal Justice Initiative. The Equal Justice Initiative is virtually the only in-state resource for Alabama inmates; it receives no state funding, surviving solely on private donations and public-speaking fees earned by its five-attorney staff. Currently, the Equal Justice Initiative is working on appeals for about 100 of the 190 death row inmates in Alabama. Bryan saw something in Bo's case, and he recruited a team of pro bono attorneys from a Philadelphia firm to work on it. Not long after, Richard Jaffe came on board.

When they started working on the case, not only did they find clear-cut *Batson* violations—a former prosecutor who worked in the DA's office around the time of Bo's trial would later testify that the philosophy of his office was, in his own words, "that prospective black jurors at that time were antipolice, antiestablishment, and should not be left on juries"—but they also turned up significant evidence that Bo was innocent of murder. The victim's body had been found hidden beneath a trailer in a trailer park some distance from the A&P. Given the distance between Bo and the victim when the gunshot was heard, and that Bo was being rapidly chased by police right up until they detained him, it is difficult to imagine that Bo could have shot the victim, dragged the body all the way to the trailer park, and carefully hidden it before the cops caught him. Not to mention that Bo's clothing showed no trace of gunpowder residue. *And*, according to Bo's counsel, the gun Bo owned was not the same caliber as the one used to kill Steven Ganey. This evidence clearly indicated Bo couldn't have killed Ganey—but it was still difficult to understand how, in the chaos of that night, Ganey had wound up dead. When Bo's lawyers found an eyewitness whose testimony about what he saw and heard on the night of the murder indicated that a police officer may accidentally have shot the victim, though, a clearer picture emerged.

In 1996, after hearing this evidence at a federal appeal, a jury of seven blacks and five whites acquitted Bo Cochran of murder. They upheld the robbery conviction, but by then, Bo had already spent almost fifteen years on death row; not long after, he was released on time served.

Interspersed with the story of his case, Bo told us about his recent wedding, his family, the new house they were building; he told us about religion, how he (like so many others) had found God on death row. He teared up when he told us about the buddies he'd had in prison; many of the guys in there were guilty, sure, but many of them were not. And he talked a lot about his firsthand experience with the insidious ways in which racism infects the Alabama justice system. It was worse before the civil rights movement; back then it was fairly accepted practice for white cops to beat and threaten black suspects, and it was legal for prosecutors to rule out jurors just because they were black. Now, those practices are illegal and less widespread, but they still go on. And things are still horribly imbalanced: in a state where the black population is just 26 percent of the total (according to the 2000 U.S. Census), black people make up 46 percent of Alabama's death row inmates. Of the twenty-seven people executed in Alabama since 1976, 39 percent were white and 61 percent were black. And it's not just Alabama: nationwide, blacks make up 42 percent of death row inmates, even though they make up only 12 percent of the U.S. population. The overwhelming majority of district attorneys, who decide in which cases to seek the death penalty, are white: according to Amnesty International, in 1998, of the 1,838 such officials in states with the death penalty, 22 were black, and 22 were Latino; 1,794 were white. And although blacks and whites are victims of murder in almost equal numbers, 82 percent of prisoners executed since 1977 were convicted of the murder of a white person. Maybe that Southern scene we'd seen at the state line—rocking chairs locked up and chained down—isn't so different from the rest of America.

Bo was incredibly warm with us, even jovial; he greeted us laughing, and while much of the interview was dead serious, by the end of it—after a long talk about weddings—we were laughing together again. We said our good-byes, thanked him heartily, and headed back toward the highway. We had an hour and a half to get to Guntersville, still in Alabama but way upstate and off the beaten path. We were going to meet Randal Padgett and his then-girlfriend (now wife), Brenda Massingill.

The abstractions, associations, and sometimes inaccurate assumptions we'd carried with us to the South didn't only have to do with racism—as urbane, bohemian East Coasters we had also stoked some elaborate preconceived notions about white, Southern fundamentalist Christians.

When we arrived, Randal and Brenda invited us into Brenda's cozy blue home, tucked into the woods way, way outside of town on a winding country road. Brenda—an attractive woman in her forties, snappily dressed and outgoing, with quite a twang in her voice—was a consummate hostess, with cold drinks and snack trays prepared well in advance of our arrival. The house was furnished country-romantic, lots of calico and ribbons and warmth. And there were religious reminders everywhere: framed psalms, verses about Jesus on the end tables, by the couch, on the walls. Brenda greeted us with loads of energy: immediately it was clear she was quite a presence. Randal was more the shy, sweet type; his six-foot-three, two-hundred-some-pound frame contrasted with his soft-spoken, gentle manner. We pulled up chairs and they settled down on the couch across from us;

Brenda sat up straight and clasped Randal's hand in both of her own as he started in on his story.

In 1990, Randal told us, he was a chicken farmer, living in the small town of Arab. He and his wife, Cathy, had recently become estranged—Randal was having an affair with a married neighbor and it had just come out into the open. Randal and Cathy continued to share responsibility for their two children, though, and Randal was watching the kids the night before he and his girlfriend were scheduled to take a trip to Destin, Florida, for the weekend. Early in the morning, the kids' aunt picked them up, and Randal and his girlfriend left for Destin. That day, the kids and their aunt went over to Cathy Padgett's house to pick up some things. The children, at that time six and eleven years old, walked into their mother's bedroom and discovered her brutally murdered body.

Cathy Padgett had been stabbed over forty times, and it appeared that she had been raped. Despite that Randal had no criminal record, nobody had ever heard him so much as raise his voice to his wife, and he did not stand to profit from her death financially or otherwise, people immediately started pointing fingers at him. Randal's affair was a known thing, and in the small, conservative town of Arab, that alone was enough to invite suspicion. Police ran DNA tests on the semen found inside Cathy's body. It matched Randal's.

Randal was stunned. He knew he hadn't killed Cathy; he figured the DNA test had to be wrong. Other forensic tests were ordered, including tests on blood found at the scene. The results of the blood test indicated that the blood was neither Cathy's nor Randal's—it had to have come from someone else—but Randal's court-appointed attorney didn't bring this out into the open effectively at trial. There was no other solid physical evidence against Randal, but the affair seemed to provide a plausible motive, and the DNA evidence was damning. Randal was convicted and sentenced to death.

In prison, Randal was terrified. He'd never been in trouble with the law, never fought; he was a quiet, gentle guy who'd always believed in the system and thought dangerous criminals were the only ones who ever got locked up. He'd never guessed that the system could send an innocent man to death row—until he wound up there.

Randal's kids had been with him the night of the murder, so, he told us, "They didn't never have any question about whether their daddy killed their momma or not." But Randal's in-laws shunned him, apparently believing he'd killed their daughter. It was five and a half hours each way from Arab to the prison; not many people were willing to make the trip to bring Randal's kids to visit him. He didn't have many people left to help him out. But an acquaintance of Randal's, Brenda Massingill, kept writing him letters. They'd been coworkers for a brief period and were friendly from town; they didn't know each other much more than that. But Brenda had a gut feeling about Randal: she knew he was innocent. And Brenda worked with Randal's now ex-girlfriend—whom she had a different kind of gut feeling about.

Brenda kept writing to Randal and eventually persuaded him to let her visit. Randal was hesitant—why was she being so nice to him? She had friends who were cops; were they sending her down to try to ensnare him in something? Finally Brenda convinced Randal that this wasn't the case, and their friendship blossomed.

Brenda started visiting more and more regularly, she told us, and the more she learned about the case, the more she became convinced of Randal's innocence. Brenda was hearing lots of other things, too—that the girlfriend had been bragging around the plant about weird stuff—like that she and her husband had saved the husband's semen in jars. Brenda and several other workers had also said they'd noticed the girlfriend reading *Presumed Innocent* around the time of the murder—a novel that features a murder and a fake rape staged to hide the identity of the (female) murderer.

By this time, Richard Jaffe had decided to take on Randal's case. When Richard looked at the forensics of the "rape," Randal and Brenda told us, he knew something wasn't right. Cathy had been found naked from the waist down, and semen was inside her—both of which would indicate that she had, in fact, been raped. But on closer inspection, it wasn't so clear this was the case. Cathy was found with one of her legs propped up in an awkward position—as if someone had posed her to suggest she'd been raped—but, as Randal and Richard both told us, it was actually physically impossible for her to have been raped in that position. And more importantly, none of the physical trauma associated with rape was present. Cathy had been stabbed dozens of times, but the vaginal area was completely free of injury. A close examination of the physical evidence indicated that despite initial appearances, Cathy had almost certainly not been raped—more likely, someone wanted it to *look* as if she had been.

Other aspects of the physical evidence indicated that someone other than Randal had committed the crime. First, there was the blood found at the scene that belonged to neither Cathy nor Randal. And second, Cathy had many defensive wounds—indicating she'd put up a serious fight, for quite some time. Cathy was small; Randal was over six feet and two hundred pounds, a strong guy. If he'd wanted to overpower someone that small, it wouldn't have been too hard; they wouldn't have been evenly matched enough for there to have been a real fight. Cathy's defensive wounds were actually more characteristic of crimes in which the attacker is the same size—and possibly gender—as the victim.

Then there was the letter that had been sent to the police shortly after Randal's arrest. The letter had a strange, questionable return address and was signed "Phil." Phil claimed to be a drifter; in the letter, he confessed in detail to the murder of Cathy Padgett. The letter contained specifics that would have been unknown to anyone but the killer. But there were inconsistencies in the letter: words misspelled on purpose, other facts wrong. Some people suspected that Phil wasn't a real person, but rather a persona invented by the real killer to simultaneously protect himself or herself and Randal.

In 1997, Randal's case came up for appeal. Richard presented the ample physical evidence—the blood tests, the evidence indicating that the "rape" had been staged, the evidence that Cathy could not have been killed by a man of Randal's size—and then offered an alternative theory of the crime: that Randal's former lover had murdered Cathy and planted Randal's semen, staging a rape to deflect suspicion from herself. Richard called the girlfriend as a witness at Randal's second trial; when he asked her on the stand where the semen could have come from if it hadn't come from Randal, the girlfriend, backed into a corner, replied, "I guess it would have had to have come from me." Randal was acquitted and freed.

When Randal got out, he told us, life on the outside had changed. His son had been eleven when Randal went in—now he was eighteen, just about ready to go off to college. His daughter, six at the time of Randal's conviction, was now thirteen, almost a young woman. When Randal was arrested, he had been reading his daughter a chapter book each night before bed—when he got out, she brought him the book, opened it to the page they'd stopped at, and asked him to start reading to her again. Slowly, Randal started the hard work of rebuilding his relationship with his children.

Everything was hard work for Randal when he first got out—even basic things like driving. Randal's depth perception had been affected by years spent in a five-by-eight-foot cell; he told us that the first time he tried to drive again, he pulled into a parking space—and drove right into a building. He also faced the tough task of finding work again, trying to pay off the enormous debt he'd racked up in lawyers' fees. And he neither wanted to nor was able to leave the tiny town in which he'd been convicted—so he was always coming face-to-face with those who'd had a hand in his conviction, reopening old wounds. Randal told us a story about a time just after he was released, when he was at a baseball game in town. Someone who'd helped convict Randal—and who still publicly claimed that Randal was guilty—was there, shaking hands, kissing babies, and handing out flyers promoting his reelection campaign. He approached Randal and handed him a flyer. Then, perhaps thinking better of it, he explained, "I know you're probably not going to vote for me—but it's got the football schedule on the back." This guy had called Randal a monster, had argued hard to have him killed—and almost succeeded. And now he was asking for his vote? It was experiences like this, Randal told us, that made it difficult for him to get past what he'd been through.

But Brenda helped—and so did religion. It was clear that evangelical Christianity held the central place in Brenda and Randal's lives and identities. Everything was filtered through the lens of Jesus, whether they were talking about the character of a prosecutor or how they'd supported each other emotionally when Randal was in prison. Brenda was more outspoken about it, but that was just the difference in their personalities—Brenda is, in her own words, "big on taking stands," while Randal is shier, more soft-spoken. But it was obvious that for both of them, religion wasn't just about going to church, or even about personal belief; it structured how they spent their time and lived their lives. Brenda spent hundreds of hours ministering at the women's prison, and both Brenda and Randal saw prayer as a direct cause of Randal's release. And it was clear that they believed Jesus was coming back in a literal way in the near future.

Before meeting Randal and Brenda, we both would probably have guessed that we'd feel a little weird sitting in an Alabama living room, being talked to at length about Jesus by fundamentalist Christians. We'd both always conflated Southern evangelical Christianity with the religious right, with a set of beliefs motivated more by rigid ideology, judgmental Bible literalism, and antigay, antifeminist prejudice than by spiritual faith as we'd define it. But Randal and Brenda didn't seem to hold any of those prejudices. They were as critical of hypocrisy and rigid ideology as we were. They didn't believe they had a direct, exclusive line to the truth, and they didn't believe they had the right to stand in judgment of other human beings. Their faith was flexible and inclusive, and it manifested all the best human values: forgiveness, nonjudgment, love, and openheartedness. In talking with Randal and Brenda, we found that their evangelical Southern Christianity had a lot more in common with our progressive, urban neo-Buddhist beliefs than we would ever have thought—and that maybe *we'd* been the ones carrying around judgments and ideological preconceptions. We emerged from that interview moved by Randal and Brenda's story, their faith, and their love—and with another set of assumptions about the South, and the people who live there, overturned.

Chapter Nine

Many of the cultural assumptions we'd brought with us down South had been turned upside down—for example, that evangelical Christians were all rigid and right-wing, or that white guys with criminal records who lived alone in Georgia trailers wouldn't raise kittens, forgive their enemies, or take care of deer (instead of shooting them and hanging them over the rear end of a rusted-out pickup). But one set of assumptions we'd had about the South did, unfortunately, keep being confirmed: the ones having to do with race.

We recognize, of course, that we're a couple of Yankees; that makes us outsiders to the intricacies of social organization and history in the South, and we freely admit that sometimes that blurred our perception. But sometimes, it also made it clearer. There's that old saw about most car accidents happening within two miles of the driver's home: sometimes when we're close to something, our perception isn't nearly as careful. The biggest mistakes, accidents, and atrocities can happen in the most familiar setting. When you've gone down one road many times, you can start to take that road for granted. But for us, it was all brand-new; we had our eyes wide open and our blinders off, watching the signs.

And we saw that some of the mythology we'd brought with us about race was turning out to be not too far from the truth. The Alabama Welcome Center still sported the Confederate flag and displayed that rock; the neighborhoods we drove through still seemed 100 percent segregated; and the stories Bo had told us suggested that racism still had a regrettable choke hold on the Alabama justice system. The ark built from phrases like "Well, that was back in the old days," "Nobody lynched him, did they?" "Things have changed," was leaking.

Most of the images we carried around about racism in the South came from history class, where we'd learned about what it was like before the civil rights movement: we remembered the film stock of segregated lunch counters, demonstrators being beaten and hosed, and the kind of poverty that isn't supposed to exist in America anymore. As we drove, we saw that kind of poverty still exists with a vengeance, and that it's still primarily black neighborhoods that suffer the most. In Mississippi, when you leave the interstate and its nearby clusters of fast-food joints, convenience stores, and condos, and you drive down the roads that show up as faint lines in the road atlas, you can see it: neighborhoods of crumbing shacks, many with no running water, kids scuttling around shoeless, rusted-out cars and none that run. And then you cross the train tracks—literally—into the white neighborhoods, with their colonial brick houses, clean streets, brand-new, bustling schools. Segregation is so deeply institutionalized in many parts of the South that even though it's been illegal over thirty years, it persists almost as strongly in economic form. The evidence was scattered by the roadside. In front of houses were ramshackle mailboxes, scratched with last names like Washington, Jefferson, Black, White.

We watched it from the car as we crossed from Alabama to Mississippi. We left Guntersville in the late evening and drove through most of the night, on our way to Canton, Mississippi, to meet Robert Earl Hayes. We were starting to get tired, but the world out the windows kept us up, and when it was too dark to see, we kept each other awake talking, hands clasped on the gearshift, squeezing each other's fingers when we got sleepy.

After the sun rose, we stopped at Waffle House for breakfast; for the first time in our travels (not counting our meeting with Bo) we were early, and we had time to sit and read the local paper over coffee. We were amazed at how little real national and international information it contained; *USA Today* was the only other paper available, and all its articles were pretty much condensed in sound-bite form. And cable news, like a lot of AM radio, rarely goes into any depth without degenerating into a bunch of yelling and screaming. We realized the lack of alternative or in-depth news sources down here. No place for people to get any national information beyond the most basic facts. Beyond that, people had to dig for news on the internet—and lots of folks don't have the time or resources to do that. We'd thought before about how information deprivation can create a political climate that's seriously skewed—but, obvious as it seems, we'd never thought much about how widespread, and dangerous, that problem is in America. (To our shame, we might add.)

After breakfast, we drove the last forty miles or so to Canton,

Mississippi, where we were scheduled to meet with Robert and his wife, Georgia. We exited the highway into one of those fancy brick-colonial white neighborhoods, then kept going into the next one, full of broken-down houses and chain-link fences. Everyone's head swiveled to check out the two weird white kids in the rental car; we were quite a sight in this neighborhood. Obviously white folks who weren't cops didn't come around here too often, let alone white folks who looked like us. Erik was sporting a pretty thick beard around this time, so unless Jesus had come back and decided it was a good idea to take a spin around a predominantly black neighborhood as a hippie cracker, there was no immediate explanation for our presence. The kids in their yards were staring; we waved as we made our way toward Robert and Georgia's yard.

Robert and Georgia came out into the yard to greet us. They looked fabulous: the two of them had dressed up in their Sunday best for the interview, Georgia in a royal blue suit with rhinestone buttons, Robert in slacks and tie. Robert was built like a farmer, short and strong, a soft-spoken black man in his thirties with a shaved head and a compact body. Georgia was half a head taller than Robert, a big woman with a lovely face, a loud voice, and a head full of ringlets. They were the youngest couple we'd met so far; Robert was only around ten years older than us. We knew he'd been on death row for seven years, and out for three—which meant he'd been convicted when he was about our age. That realization brought things close to home in a whole new way.

They invited us into their house and showed us around. Their house was tiny; the paint was peeling and the structure wasn't sound, but they'd made a home out of it, cozy and pretty and sweet. Little tchotchkes were everywhere, flowery picture frames and ceramic figurines, potpourri, and posters. They'd only been married a couple years, and their house, however humble, was a romantic first nest. We sat down in the living room to begin the interview.

Robert and Georgia were formal with us at first; not only were we likely the first noncop white people in their neighborhood, we were probably the first white folks who'd been inside their living room. Instead of tiptoeing around trying to break the ice, though, we started right in on the subject of racism. It had been on our minds ever since we'd gotten down South; it was probably on theirs, too. We figured we might as well just talk about it. As soon as we said the word *racism*, Robert and Georgia started trading stories about Mississippi cops. Robert's brother had been shot in the neck and killed by police in a marijuana bust. And Georgia talked to us about her friend, a mother who had called the cops for help when a bully came into her house chasing her daughter; the white cops showed up and threatened to arrest the mother, who'd only been trying to protect her kid. And just the other night, Robert had been stopped by police as he was riding a friend's horse; even though nobody in the area had reported a horse stolen, the cops accused Robert of stealing it. With no probable cause, they detained him; Robert repeatedly asked them to write him a citation if he had violated the law in any way; they refused. Finally they let him go, but Robert was quite shaken up.

After gauging our reaction to these stories, Robert and Georgia seemed to figure out that we were sympathetic, and they visibly relaxed. Robert started telling us the story of how he wound up wrongly convicted on death row, and how, after seven years, he came to get out. Robert adores horses; in 1990, he told us, he was a horse groom working the racetrack circuit. A group of workers followed the races, from Ohio to Fort Lauderdale, Florida, to places in between; it was kind of like a traveling carnival, a nomadic lifestyle with lots of drinking, gossip, and intrigue—and a lot of tension and drama between the blacks and the whites who worked the tracks. Almost all the workers were single, and everyone was thrown together in close, temporary quarters, like summer camp—including a lot of white folks who weren't used to intermingling so closely with black people. For some, it wasn't an issue at all—Robert took pains to make us understand that he knew lots of white folks who weren't racist. On the racetracks, some of the whites and blacks hung out together socially, dated, and slept together; and some folks were just fine with that. But for other white track workers, the intermingling triggered a lot of ugly behavior.

At the tracks, Robert sometimes dated white women. This immediately made him a target for gossip, rumors, and hostility. He also participated in the rowdy social culture of the racetrack—one that sometimes included fistfights—and he was a little guy, so he was pretty scrappy. And he was not known to back down from a fight. Not even with white people. In the eyes of some of the whites who hung on to outmoded and hateful attitudes about race, this made him "uppity." This perception would prove dangerous to Robert.

When a white female groom, Pamela Alberson, was found murdered in her dorm room at the Fort Lauderdale track, people started pointing fingers at Robert. Pamela and Robert had dated, he told us; people had seen the two of them talking the night of her murder. Never mind that the workers all lived together in dorms and everyone was always talking to everyone else. Never mind that everyone dated everyone else at the track, too. Police zeroed in on Robert immediately.

They took depositions from nearly everyone who worked with Robert at the racetrack. None of the workers were eyewitnesses to anything that would directly and positively implicate Robert in the crime, and several people stated under oath that they had seen him far away from Pamela's room at the time of the murder. But other workers, swept up in the drama of the investigation, wanted to "help" the police—and gave depositions full of gossip and uncorroborated suspicion, things they'd "heard around," "hunches," and "feelings." Using these depositions, the police began to build a case against Robert—never mind that just about everything contained in them was hearsay.

Then there was the physical evidence in the case. The crime scene was a mess. Evidence was lost, mishandled, contaminated—and investigated incorrectly. A year later, examining Robert's case file down in Broward County, we would find sworn testimony from one of the investigators at the scene that they had been instructed to look only for "Negro hairs." And through this disregard, as well as a series of other omissions, the police ignored what was arguably the most concrete, important, and damning piece of physical evidence in the case—a fistful of sixteen-inch-long Caucasian hair that Pamela was found clutching in her hand. The hair had clearly been ripped out of someone's head during the attack. But, for all purposes, it was ignored by investigators; the police and prosecutors never had it tested.

Robert, represented by a public defender, was brought to trial and hastily convicted by a jury of eleven whites and one black. He was sentenced to die by the state of Florida and sent to the third-largest death row in America, behind only those of California and Texas.

While Robert was in prison, he told us, he lost nearly everything. Because Robert's a little guy, he was targeted in prison, forced to fight hard. Cockroaches and rats filled the cells on death row. And, Robert said, the guards harassed him, throwing him out of his cell and sometimes threatening him physically. His parents had passed away a few years earlier, and his remaining immediate family members deserted him—all but one, his eighty-year-old grandmother, Big Mama.

Another important person stuck by Robert's side, too—his public defender, Barbara Heyer. Many defendants are actually guilty, and their attorneys know it. But this case was different. From the evidence, Barbara was convinced of Robert's innocence, and it lit a fire under her. Unlike a lot of other underpaid, overworked, beleaguered public defenders, Barbara worked tirelessly on Robert's case. In 1997, after seven years of hard work, she finally won him a new trial.

In the intervening years, she'd discovered evidence concerning a man named Scott, a white racetrack worker who had worked the same circuit as Pamela and Robert. Scott gave a deposition in the initial investigation, as someone who had worked with them on the track. Back then, he didn't seem to have anything too significant to say. But after Robert's conviction, Scott was locked up for a similar rape-murder at an Ohio racetrack. The Ohio victim was a white woman who was said to have been dating black men; Scott had allegedly pestered her to go out with him, and she'd apparently rebuffed his advances. Barbara found out that the same scenario had allegedly occurred between Scott and Pamela Alberson. According to witnesses, Scott had apparently repeatedly expressed anger that Pamela dated black guys; he also, they said, kept asking her out, and she kept saying no. Evidence indicated that she'd rebuffed him again, and he'd grown angry about it, on the day of the murder.

Barbara tracked Scott down, had him sent in from an Ohio prison, and put him on the stand. In her arguments, Barbara had already brought up the fistful of long, reddish brown hair that had been found in the victim's hand and ignored by authorities. (The prosecution's explanation for the hair, Robert told us, was that when the victim was struggling with her attacker, she "reached up and grabbed her own hair." Never mind that that seems to us like a highly illogical thing to do—according to court testimony, the hair found in the victim's hand didn't even appear to be consistent with Pamela's.) When Barbara called Scott to testify, Robert said, Scott had short, salt-and-pepper hair. When she asked Scott what his hair had looked like back in 1990, he testified that it was the same length and color back then, too. But then, Robert told us, Barbara pulled out a copy of an ID photograph taken of Scott at the track in 1990. In the photo, Scott had long, reddish brown hair. Robert was freed.

After spending seven years on death row for a crime he didn't commit, Robert was sent home without so much as a bus ticket. He had to get from the southern tip of Florida back home to Mississippi; he was broke. His attorney paid his way. When Robert settled in back home, his main goal was to get a job working with horses again. He loved horses, and before he went to prison, he'd worked with them for years. Robert told us that after he got out, he applied for his horse trainer's license; on the application, they asked if he had ever been convicted of a crime. Robert answered no, because his conviction had been overturned. According to Robert, they wrote back, telling him he had lied, denying him the license and the opportunity to carry on with his livelihood.

This part of Robert's story illustrated a problem that haunts many innocent people who are released from prison. When you're exonerated, the initial conviction isn't wiped from your record—it's just supplemented by a statement that the conviction was overturned. This wouldn't seem to be such a big deal, until you think about the question that shows up on every job application: "Have you ever been convicted of a felony?" If your record says you have, you're required by law to say yes—and most prospective employers won't keep reading past that yes to read about the conviction's being overturned. It's already extraordinarily difficult to find work after spending time in prison—technology changes rapidly, and many people are released into a work world very different from the one they left, not to mention that it's tough to explain a seven-year gap in your work experience. Added to those factors, that mark on the record often ensures that exonerated folks will be forced to remain unemployed for years after their release. Just another way they're being punished for something they didn't do.

After a long search, Robert had finally found work, and with Georgia, he was beginning a new life. Robert and Georgia had first met the year after Robert's release. They told us the story: Just after they were introduced, Georgia had fallen ill and had to spend time in the hospital. Even though they barely knew each other, Robert patiently stayed by her side, supervised her doctors, and stuck with her till she was well. Two months later, they were married. Georgia told us it had been tough at first: before she moved in, she hadn't realized how much of a mark those seven years in prison had left on Robert. Whenever she came in the house, even if Robert was sleeping, he'd startle and jump; other nights he'd be awake till dawn, pacing, unable to get to sleep. Not unlike someone who'd just come home from a war. Georgia learned to knock on the door before she entered a room; she learned how to bring him back when he'd drift off into memory. Robert told us, "I was in there seven and a half years, and it ain't never gonna go away. Lost my relaxation. Lotta other things, too." Robert would never get back the time his wrongful conviction took from him. But at least, with Georgia's help, he could begin to build something new.

As the interview wound down, we went out front to snap a picture. Robert stood on the front step, while Georgia stood on the ground beside him, low enough that his arm rested comfortably on her shoulders and he stood half a head taller than she did. They were quite the happy young couple, in their Sunday best, standing up tall under the Mississippi sun in front of their brick home. All the kids in the surrounding yards stared at us like space aliens again. But Robert and Georgia yelled out hellos to all of them, and they all grinned and waved back.

As we pulled out, we drove past sidewalks lined with falling-apart front porches, over roads full of years-old potholes. Robert and Georgia's neighborhood was full of families, folks doing their best to make homes from what they had, kids playing in yards, moms with babies on their hips, neighbors talking to each other. Just as we were about to cross over to the next neighborhood—the rich white one with lawns too carefully manicured for kids to play in them—we saw a big billboard by the road, obviously meant to be seen by Robert and his neighbors as they drove to work each day. Smiling down from the billboard was Trent Lott's enormous airbrushed visage; he was giving a giant thumbs-up. The slogan by the photograph was something like "Trent Lott, working hard for Mississippi." It probably wasn't lost on Robert or his neighbors—as they bumped over their potholes that had gone unfixed for years, onto the smooth streets of the next neighborhood over—which finger ol' Trent was *really* holding up.

Next, it was on to Quincy, Florida, just outside Tallahassee, to meet David Keaton. Northern Florida—the part that's not a peninsula—is sometimes nicknamed Southern Alabama; its culture is less like that of Miami or Fort Lauderdale and more like that of Mobile. We left central Mississippi, and for hours we drove south, and south, and south. The foliage around us got more green and lush; the concrete thinned out; the air outside the car turned thick and almost tropical.

As we got close to the Gulf, the human climate changed, too. We'd felt like outsiders almost everywhere we'd traveled so far, except maybe Philly and parts of Chicago, but up until now we'd always been the ones who were uptight about it. We were always nervous we'd offend someone, conscious we were being stared at, tiptoeing around other people's territory. Everyone else—except maybe the bouffant lady at the Alabama Welcome Center—didn't seem seriously bugged by us, just curious. But down by the Gulf coast, that started to change. The stares we got through the windows weren't curious: they seemed hostile. We were way off the interstate by now, and when we stopped for gas at a tiny, run-down road stop outside Mobile, two dented pickups pulled up near us, both of them with big old gun racks on the back. Their drivers glared and trailed us inside with their eyes, unblinking. When we went to pay for our gas and get some coffee, the people at the counter looked us up and down; they glared, too. Without saying a word, everyone there let us know loud and clear that we weren't welcome. We weren't wearing political buttons or bumper stickers, we were dressed pretty plainly, and we'd picked up some Southern manners already. It wasn't racial tension: all the people giving us dirty looks were white. We didn't have money; we weren't lording around in a fancy car. We couldn't find any explanation for the hostility besides that we obviously came from somewhere else. The towns we were driving through were tiny enough that unfamiliarity is rare, and anyone unfamiliar is not to be trusted. If this point of view permeated a place's culture so intensely, it would probably inform the local justice system, too. With all that mistrust heaped on us just for coming here from out of town, it was easy for us to see how innocent people could come under suspicion for reasons that had nothing to do with guilt or innocence.

The tank full, we got back in the car, vowing not to leave it again till we got to David Keaton's house. We drove through back roads, under hills, through the sunset into dark. We were due at David's house around nine; we'd promised to bring takeout. Outside Quincy, we stopped at a Burger King drive-through and broke our ban on buying meat to get dinner for David.

David had given us another set of "if you pass the river trestle, you've gone too far" directions. After we got off the county road, we were supposed to cross the train tracks, take a left at the Texaco, then a quick right at the red house, then three blocks to a green house on the corner, where we'd probably see a white truck parked outside, which is where we should take another left. Et cetera. On the phone, they'd sounded like directions we could follow, but now it was dark, and most of the streets weren't marked. We made the left turn at the Texaco; after that, it was hopeless. We circled around and around David's neighborhood, another one full of folks who were clearly unused to seeing white people there who hadn't come to give them some variety of hard time. The streets were unlit. We squinted at the few street signs; none of them sounded like the ones David had named. We took a turn onto a narrow road that led way, way out into the middle of nowhere. The Burger King in the backseat was getting cold, we were late, it was dark, and given the vibes everyone had been throwing at us for the last several hours, we were starting to get nervous. Finally we decided to go back to the Texaco and start over from there. Then lights flipped on behind us. A red sports car was tailing us. We turned left, they turned left. We turned right, they turned right. Jessica started to get a little freaked-out. This was a really rough neighborhood. No matter who was in that car, we'd probably be in trouble. If they were locals, they were probably following us because they didn't want us in their neighborhood. If they were cops, they were probably following us because they thought we were there to buy drugs. If they were cops who pulled us over and saw the transcripts and videos in the back of our car, we'd definitely be in trouble. Then the car backed off and flipped its brights off. Our pulses slowed; we turned right and doubled back to the Texaco once again. We debated calling David to apologize and then just getting the hell out of Quincy, but decided to try one last time to follow the looping directions. The red car had disappeared.

On our way back, passing a block we'd driven by three times, we saw a figure in front of one of the houses, waving his arms and yelling. We slowed down and saw he was yelling at us. We couldn't make out what he was saying. Gingerly, we rolled down the window; of course, it was David, trying to show us where his house was. Apparently in the twenty minutes we'd been lost, word had gotten around the neighborhood about the white kids who kept driving around the block over and over, and David knew it had to be us. Embarrassed, we parked the car, grabbed the food, and followed David into his house.

David shook our hands inside the door, a lanky, long-limbed black man with a gentle manner and huge soft liquid eyes. His right hand was damaged from a work mishap. He didn't so much shake as haul his hand up to you and set it there. We knew from articles that he was pushing fifty, but he looked closer to forty, with clear skin, a shaved head, and a beard. He showed us around his clapboard abode, the floors made of particleboard, the couch ripped up; his grandfather had built the house, and it had clearly once been a labor of love, passed down through generations, but now it had fallen into disrepair. On top of the TV was the only photo in the place, a framed eight-by-ten, black-and-white shot of David back in 1970, a high school football star. In the photo, David clutched a football, ready to spring forward; he had a big grin on his face, his wide eyes full of possibility. Just months later, something would happen to David that would take that look away from him forever.

In 1970, David was a senior in high school when a local grocery called Luke's was robbed by three young black men. The thieves held everyone in the store hostage while they robbed it. Two police officers were among the hostages, and they confronted the robbers, attempting to stop them. In the ensuing chaos, both police officers were shot at, and one was killed. The robbers absconded with the money before anyone could stop them.

The tiny town was up in arms. The local police force was under enormous pressure to produce the culprits; supposedly, they questioned just about every young black man in town. One night, David was out with some friends; on their way home, David said, they saw a "big commotion" around his grandmother's house and ran the rest of the way there, wondering what was going on. When he got close to the house, he found police shining flashlights in the windows; the police asked David and his friends if any of them knew David Keaton, and David, knowing he hadn't done anything wrong and wanting to help, immediately identified himself.

The police immediately cuffed David and hauled him in to the station. Despite the fact that, David told us, he had never even been to Luke's, and despite that no hard evidence connected him to the crime, they interrogated David literally for days, without granting him access to an attorney or allowing him to call his mother. (This, of course, is illegal—every citizen has the right to have an attorney present during questioning.) Over and over, David told us, he asked to call his mother so she could obtain an attorney for him; over and over he was put off. David was held and questioned for nearly a *week* before he was brought before a judge or allowed access to counsel. And by the time David was brought before a judge, it was too late.

"This was just after the sixties," David told us; he was afraid. "They would bring you in, beat you up, mess you up, hang you up; nobody'd ever hear nothing else about you." David said that for days, he was deprived of sleep, moved from facility to facility, questioned for hours on end—and allegedly threatened. "They said they was going to kill me," David told us. "They said I could die right there. Or they'd put me in prison so far I'd never get out." David was just eighteen years old, still in high school. This was just after the civil rights movement—racial tensions ran very, very high in the tiny, deep Southern town of Quincy, and black folks were regularly subjected to violence from white folks, including police. After a couple days of isolation and interrogation, with no access to the outside world, David started taking their threats seriously. Maybe they really *were* going to kill him. The only way out, they told him, was to confess to the crime.

At first, David told us, he refused. He hadn't done anything; why would he confess to a crime he hadn't committed? But they kept the pressure on him, unrelenting, David said; they told him they'd never let him go. After a while, David started thinking. They'd told him enough about the crime that he knew there had been eyewitnesses. Surely when those witnesses got a look at him, they'd know he wasn't one of the guys who robbed the store. So maybe, David thought, the best way to keep himself safe was to confess now, do what they told him, say everything they were telling him to say. Then the police wouldn't hurt—or kill—him; he'd be safe, and everything could get straightened out when the witnesses saw David in court. They'd testify that David wasn't the robber they'd seen; David would explain that he'd given a false confession because he was scared; then they'd throw out the confession and find the real guys.

If you think about it, David's logic made sense. Except that his solution was based on a faulty assumption, one that many people make—that eyewitness identification is infallible. In fact, eyewitness identification is one of the least reliable forms of evidence, and the potential for human error is vast. According to a paper released by the

Michigan State Appellate Defender's Office, "Many continue to believe that eyewitness identifications and testimony are generally reliable and persuasive forms of evidence, and that any inaccuracies are readily detectable by the layperson. However, recent scientific studies show that eyewitness accuracy is affected by numerous factors, including identification procedures commonly used by police." And Deborah Davis and William C. Follette, in an article published by the *Southern Methodist University Law Review*, write "A very large literature in the eyewitness identification area has repeatedly shown that witnesses asked to identify the perpetrator of staged crimes or to describe other witnessed events do so confidently, although the event itself provided little opportunity to observe clearly . . . research has shown that as the complexity of a criminal event increases (e.g., more bystanders, more perpetrators, the use of weapons, other events occurring simultaneously with the crime, a more complex environment), descriptions of and memory for any given detail, including the perpetrator, will decrease in detail and accuracy." Many factors—including trauma, difficulty identifying cross-racial facial characteristics, and memory distortion—combine to make eyewitness identification one of the more fallible and controversial forms of evidence—although most people assume it's watertight. This mistaken assumption on the part of jurors is a major contributor to wrongful conviction. Professor Marc Green, a visual identification and perception expert, writes that "a recent study (Wells et al., 1998) examined the first forty cases where DNA exonerated wrongfully convicted people. In 90 percent of the cases, mistaken eyewitness identification played a major role. In one case, five separate witnesses identified the defendant. Huff (1987) studied five hundred wrongful convictions and concluded that mistaken eyewitness identification occurred in 60 percent. This is an amazingly high number considering that eyewitness identification is an important factor in only 5 percent of all trials."

The day after David "confessed" to his interrogators—after being illegally held in custody for nearly a week—he was finally brought before a judge, charged, and assigned an attorney. Not long after, he was brought to trial. Many of the "facts" in David's "confession" were way off base—not least of all his claim that there had been five armed robbers, when most everyone at the scene, including the cops, saw only three. But the eyewitnesses were virtually all white, none of them had regular personal contact with black people; even the sheriff made comments to the effect that all black folks looked alike to him. When asked if the perpetrators had sounded like local people or if they were from out of state, he stated, "Nah, they just sounded like regular niggers to me."

The witnesses bucked David's expectations; none of them came forward at trial to say that David hadn't been the guy. David refuted his confession on the stand, but without the witnesses to back him up, it was tough for David to convince the jury that the confession had been false. Despite any physical evidence against him, he was convicted and sentenced to death by an all-white jury.

At age eighteen, David was sent to death row. David was a gentle soul—not to mention only a kid—and prison was hard on him. His whole life, David told us, he had always looked forward to Christmas and Thanksgiving; he was close with his family, and holidays meant a lot to him. But after a couple of those holidays spent isolated in a cell, David said, it hurt too much, and he had to condition himself not to feel that Christmas spirit anymore. Same thing with books: he used to love to read—philosophy, history, anything he could get his hands on. After a little while in prison, without access to books, the desire just left him.

One thing didn't leave David in prison, though: his contact with God. David had always been religious; even as a kid, he felt called to the ministry, dreamed of healing the sick, had mystical experiences.

In prison, as David was kept in solitary and quiet twenty-three hours a day, those mystical encounters increased. During most of our conversation with David, he carried a deep, heavy melancholy—except when he told us about his spiritual experiences. Then he would lean forward, his eyes widening, lit up from the inside. We could see that the call to the ministry hadn't just been present during David's childhood; he still had it, even now.

Unfortunately, David told us, his time in prison had scarred him, and he wasn't able to answer the call. Too much of his energy was spent struggling with a deep depression and the habits it triggered: alcohol and drugs. Just after finishing a story about a profound mystical experience he'd had in prison, David told us, "But now, a perfect day to me would be just to get plastered, you know—to forget." He'd been too young, too vulnerable, when he went into prison to emerge with his faith intact. Now, it was all he could do to keep his everyday life together. David was intensely open with us emotionally, and as he described his life to us, we were struck by how much of it seemed to be spent engaged in a continual, active struggle between hope and despair. David would describe beautiful dreams he had, ideas, religious experiences—but then he'd rush to tell us all that was lost to him. To us, it was obvious that it wasn't entirely gone—his longing for his old self was palpable, he could almost touch it, it was in him still—but his access to it was blocked. David was only on death row for two years before he was exonerated, but prison had hurt David too much, and too young, for him to be able to recover.

We spoke with David late into the night; the dim lights glowed against the dark outdoors, illuminating the rough, torn edges of David's house, the places where the carpet didn't meet the walls. We talked until we all got quiet. A tiny fraction of the weight on David's shoulders touched our own, and we imagined what it must be to feel such a palpable longing for something deep inside yourself—that someone had taken, long ago, and placed just beyond your reach.

As we drove off, we were silent, gazing out our respective windows into blackness. We'd circled David's neighborhood so many times before that now we were able to find our way out without the map, and we stayed quiet as we snaked back to the main roads, thinking about how even the strongest souls can be so fragile when shoved up against force and bars and concrete. We'd met enough exonerated folks by now that we were beginning to make connections among them; as conversation started up again, we talked about Delbert and David, two such spiritual men, their roots not too far apart, who'd wound up in such incredibly different places. If David had some of the resources, community, and experience that had seen Delbert through, he might be up in Chicago instead of in Quincy, solid in his faith instead of feeling forced to question it. We talked about what it is that allows some people to come out the other side of such experiences, while others get trapped inside them forever. And we wondered, if it were us, which category we'd fall into.

We also talked about what we'd observed as we traveled through the South. Honestly, we had hoped to come down here and find that our assumptions were wrong—to find that the racial politics of the South had completely changed since the bad old days. And certainly, we found that the heroes of the civil rights movement had caused significant, undeniable, and beautiful progress. But old habits die hard: we saw the poverty and harassment that plagued many of the black folks we met, and we also found a strong resistance to change among some of the white folks—a desire to *keep things the same*, as if keeping things the same would keep them safe. It's probably no accident that the towns where the white folks are struggling hardest to hold on to old "traditions" are also the ones with the highest unemployment rates in the country. It's easier to blame an unknown Other—or a whole race of them—than it is to take apart the policies and mind-sets that cause poverty and injustice. Easier to just decide a group of people are different from and worse than you, and blame them for your problems. And once you've done that, it's not so hard to take the next step of believing those folks are violent criminals—whether they actually are or not—and locking them up. We were starting to see that this pattern was still all too common.

As we talked, we realized that it's not just the South: this same pattern informs how people treat each other throughout the entire country. It's as if the Bill of Rights stops at the railroad tracks and wraps itself warmly around only one side of town. And it's not even exclusively a racial division; more than anything, the dividing line is based on class. So many of the people we'd met seemed to have been unjustly villainized, locked up, thrown into unimaginably horrific circumstances—basically by virtue of being poor. And the rest of us were busy pretending the problem didn't exist. Were we so busy shielding our eyes from the big scary truth about the system that we couldn't stop to care about the human beings who get caught up in it? What had happened to our collective outrage? Had we grown too big to care about one story?

Wrapped up in our joint reverie, we didn't notice we'd taken a wrong turn until we were two hundred yards down a dark, winding road leading away from the highway. We looked up, interrupting ourselves, and had to shield our eyes against the flood of white light that came down from above us. Squinting, we peered through our fingers to see rows and rows of razor wire. Apparently, we'd taken a turn into the employee parking lot of the local prison. Enormous signs were bolted to the chain-link, warning us that trespassing on prison grounds was against the law.

It was just too much, to be this close to a prison by accident, after all the stories we'd been hearing. We knew nobody was more serious about their "no trespassing" policy than prison authorities. Ours was the only car around, and the back seat was full of tapes of interviews with the wrongly convicted. We had absolutely no excuse for being there. But we *had* to take a picture. Pulling up as close as we could to the fence, we jumped out and snapped one; out of the corners of our eyes, we thought we saw a big beam of light swing in our direction as we slammed the doors and hightailed it out of north Florida.

Chapter Ten

Back on the highway, we scanned the exits for convenience stores that might have coffee. It wasn't too long until we found one, and good thing, too, because we had to drive the whole night through, and we hadn't slept well since Georgia.

A couple days before, we'd gotten a phone call that caused a minor logistical upheaval. Okay, it caused the third fight of our still-young relationship. When artistically inclined (Erik's dad would say "reality-challenged") people like us get in a fight, it's like reason left the building with Elvis and OD'd in a motel bathroom. There are fireworks, mortar rounds, buckets of tears, and stupid, stupid, stupid reactions to the smallest comments. From the outside, it's actually kind of funny. The people at the rest stop seemed to think so, anyway.

The problem was that Erik had a lead in the movie we'd both been acting in the month before, and they'd called him back at the last minute to reshoot some scenes. Normally the extra money would have been welcome, no question, but we still had two more interviews scheduled, both in southern Florida. We didn't have the cash to fly back down South again later—we had to do the interviews while we were already down here. And we couldn't ditch the interviews—every last one was important. But actors don't get to argue with their shooting schedules. Erik was going . . . period.

Jessica could probably have done the last leg of the trip on her own, but it would've been tough. It was a *lot* of driving, and little time to sleep. And probably not the safest thing—who knew where the interviews were, in what neighborhoods, with what people around. Everything had gone great so far, but we'd been relying on each other a lot—it would be a very different experience for one person. We decided to enlist Jessica's best friend, Nick, a musician in New York, to come down and help with the last three days.

Jess and Nick had traveled a lot together, and we were only talking about three days, so Nick was game; we even managed to find a discount last-minute plane ticket for him. Only thing was, at the end of the trip Jessica had to return the rental car and fly out of the Atlanta airport. Which meant Nick would have to fly in and out of Atlanta, too. Which meant we'd have to go pick him up there. We were in northern Florida, and the rest of our interviews were down around Miami—Atlanta was a pretty big detour. But it was the only way to work it out. We made the arrangements: changed Erik's ticket so he flew home from Atlanta to New York three days early, and got Nick a round-trip ticket from NYC to Atlanta. We drove like hell all night from Quincy, Florida, to make it to Atlanta in time to get Erik on his

7 a.m. flight; Nick's flight got in at seven thirty. We had some precarious exhausted road-hypnosis moments on the way, and around sunrise we got worried—we were still really far away, and we were afraid we wouldn't make it. But by the time the sky had turned from pink to blue and the beginnings of rush hour were thickening the traffic, we were there. Erik had to run to his gate—once again attracting attention at the Atlanta airport—but he made it onto his flight, and Nick stepped off his just minutes later. Nick and Jess hustled to the car and got on the road—all the way to West Palm Beach.

After thirteen hours of driving and half a dozen calls from Erik, Nick and Jessica were down in picture-postcard Florida, the Disney World Florida everyone imagines, with the palm trees and the waterfront high-rises and the beach. Jessica and Nick were on their way to meet Brad and April Scott, who lived in a condo in West Palm. The Scotts' development was just off the highway; Jess and Nick pulled into the driveway and rang the bell. Brad answered the door, a muscular white guy in his late forties with tattoos, short dark hair, and a mustache—he looked like he might've been an ex-biker. April, his wife, was short and strong, with long, platinum blond hair, tight jeans, and a demeanor simultaneously sweet and tough-as-nails. Their place was modest but suburban and nice, with new carpets. Jessica introduced Nick (who everyone had thought was Erik), set up the equipment on the kitchen table, and started the interview.

Brad had been wrongly accused of about the worst crime imaginable—the murder of a child. Years before, in 1978, a young girl had been murdered in the town of Port Charlotte, Florida. The investigation was sweeping. Virtually every adult male in the area was questioned, including Brad. Brad had been nowhere near the scene of the crime: he had an alibi, which he proved to the police with receipts and testimony from several people, and so the police quickly released Brad and continued with their investigation.

For eight years, the murder went unsolved. Every year, on the anniversary of the crime, the town held a candlelight vigil. Meanwhile, police ruled out suspect after suspect; they couldn't crack the case. Brad was sympathetic toward the victim and her family, but it didn't preoccupy him; he went on with his life, moved to another town, married April, had kids.

Their daughter was a year and a half old and their son was two days old when the police came to arrest Brad. They picked him up outside his home; then they went to his house and hauled in April, who'd just come home from the maternity ward. April said the cops told her that Brad had confessed—a lie—in hopes of eliciting incriminating statements from her. She didn't make any, though—her husband was innocent.

Brad was held in the county jail for two years while the prosecution built a case against him. Even with two years to work on it, they didn't come up with much—but they went ahead and tried him anyway. No matter that no physical evidence incriminated Brad. No matter that police had investigated Brad years earlier and let him go. Brad had lost the proof of his alibi years before—witnesses had died, and Brad had thrown away the receipts that provided hard evidence that he couldn't have committed the crime. After a rushed trial (Brad said several jurors wrote him letters saying they'd been pressured to arrive at a guilty verdict quickly, despite their doubts), Brad was convicted and sentenced to death.

Brad talked a lot about the terrible conditions on Florida's death row. The facilities were old, he said, practically unchanged since the fifties: concrete and rats and what felt like three-hundred-degree heat. The guards were cruel—to him, yes, but especially to the black inmates. Brad talked a lot about the racism he'd witnessed in prison, how black guys got much harsher sentences, how they were spit on and regularly brutalized by white guards. The guards might've been nicer to Brad, since he was white, except that Brad stood up to them when he saw them act racist toward black inmates. So he was tagged a troublemaker, subject to brutality and mistreatment as well.

Brad also talked at length about how dehumanizing death row was, no matter what one's race. The attitude of the authorities, Brad said, was "this person did a terrible crime, so why treat 'em humane? Go ahead and torture 'em before you kill 'em." Inmates were paraded through the halls on the way to the showers, Brad said, naked, shackled at the wrists and ankles; they were strip-searched, beaten, subject to constant verbal humiliation. Once prison dentists pulled one of Brad's teeth while it was infected, Brad told us, which caused the infection to spread; they responded to the worsening infection by pulling twenty-one of Brad's teeth in one day, all while he was shackled, strapped down, and cuffed. Afterward, he told us, he was kept chained in a tiny Plexiglas cage for three hours while the guards stood around drinking coffee, as he waited for them to take him back to his cell.

Brad said that he probably wouldn't have made it through the humiliation and dehumanization of prison if it weren't for his family. Brad was the only person we encountered in our travels who was married when he was wrongly accused and still married to the same woman when he was exonerated. Most marriages don't survive death row. Prison visiting conditions are extremely limiting and difficult—the travel alone can cost hundreds of dollars a month—and the state provides no support for the spouses and children of the incarcerated. Brad's wife said, "They make everyone who cares about a prisoner suffer. Even if someone's not innocent like Brad was, even if someone really is a murderer, he's still got a mom, and his mom's still gonna love him; why punish *her?*"

But Brad and April's marriage survived, against all odds, thanks in no small part to April's unfailing dedication to keeping the family intact. Formerly a stay-at-home mom, April put herself through college and found full-time work to support their family for the five years Brad was locked up. And although the prison was an eight-hour drive each way, nearly every week she brought the kids up to see their dad. Brad and April talked at length about how difficult prison conditions made it for them to keep their family together. Families of prisoners had to drive for hours, stand in long lines in punishing heat—and subject their children to things that kids should never have to be exposed to. Brad was innocent, but some of the guys on death row weren't; there was no way for Brad's kids to see their dad without also coming into contact with some dangerous guys in the visiting room. Apparently, Ted Bundy once leaned over and told April that their daughter, seven at the time, was "real pretty." The guards, April told us, didn't bat an eye. And when she finally found out—after five and a half years—that her husband's conviction had been overturned and that he would be released, she said, prison authorities refused to let her speak to Brad and give him the news.

April told us that Brad finally found out from his lawyer, two days later; three months after that, the paperwork was finally done, and Brad was released. He came home to a son who'd never known him outside of the prison visiting room, and to a daughter whose only images of having a dad in the house dated back to when she was a toddler. Brad said he plunged back into family life wholeheartedly, but his kids took a long time to accept his presence. It was tough. Nine years later, they said, Brad and April were still working hard to repair the damage the system had done to their family. They were also still grappling with a stigma that followed and haunted them: Brad had been wrongly accused of killing a child, and both he and April spoke about the unique burden that came along with that. Friends wouldn't let their kids come over and play; acquaintances looked at Brad like some kind of monster. For a kindhearted, family-oriented guy who loved children, that was maybe the hardest part.

Brad and April's tenacious commitment to their family in the face of such extraordinary difficulty was quite moving. Both Brad and April had grown fierce, forced to fight harder than most of us could ever imagine just to keep Brad alive and their family intact. Being an innocent person on death row was hard enough—trying to be a husband and a father at the same time was almost inconceivable. And April had presented a whole other dimension of the story—her story—one we hadn't heard yet. The system didn't just send an innocent man to prison—for all intents and purposes, it put his whole family on death row for those five years. Jessica left Brad and April's house incredibly impressed with Brad and April's strength; and wishing Erik had been there to hear about it.

Jessica and Nick drove into Miami that night and circled the city to find a motel. The next morning, it was up at dawn again, to go interview Freddie Pitts, a black man who'd been wrongly convicted in 1963 of the murder of two white service station attendants in the Florida Panhandle. He'd been convicted and exonerated in conjunction with another black man, Wilbert Lee, and their case was somewhat famous; the real murderer had turned out to be a white guy, and the case became well-known within the then brand-new civil rights movement.

Before the trip, we had spoken with Freddie on the phone; he'd agreed to meet with us at his home in Miami. We'd also been trying to get in touch with Wilbert Lee; we'd hoped to interview the two of them together. Wilbert didn't give his number out, Freddie told us, but he'd give Wilbert a call and see if he was interested. We didn't hear back from Freddie again after that, so we figured Wilbert didn't want to talk to us. But one of them was certainly better than neither.

Jessica and Nick pulled up in the driveway of Freddie's Miami home, a low, stucco, Spanish-style house with a landscaped lawn in a somewhat swanky neighborhood. Freddie answered the door, a black man in his sixties, medium height, with the build, bearing, and voice of James Earl Jones. Immediately he pulled out a cell phone, made a quick call, and within minutes Wilbert showed up. Apparently Freddie had been able to get through to Wilbert after all.

Wilbert was Freddie's opposite in both physicality and demeanor: where Freddie was barrel-chested, with a deep, slow voice, almost regal, Wilbert was tall and lanky, warm and vivacious, a mile-a-minute talker. Freddie chose his words carefully; Wilbert was an effusive storyteller, full of jokes. But they shared the same history: they had been convicted of the same crime, spent nearly thirteen years together in prison, and were finally exonerated together in 1976. Both later moved to Miami, where they'd remained close friends ever since.

We'd heard lots of stories already about racism and the death penalty down South, some contemporary, some dating back to the seventies. But we hadn't heard any stories from before the successes of the civil rights movement. Freddie and Wilbert's story brought those old history-class film-stock images to life.

In 1963, they began, Freddie and Wilbert were young men living in Florida, acquaintances through family but not good friends. Freddie was in the army, and Wilbert was working. They met at a party at Lee's house one night and, along with a couple young women, went to run an errand. The ladies had to use the bathroom, so the four stopped at the town's gas station. Freddie and Wilbert stayed outside; the women went inside. Apparently a small argument ensued when the gas station attendants told the women that the bathroom was for white folks only and that they'd have to go out in the bushes behind the station. But the argument died down quickly; the women exited the station, met Freddie and Wilbert outside, and they left.

The next day, Wilbert and Freddie were hauled in for questioning. The night before, the service station had apparently been robbed and the attendants murdered; a receipt and witnesses placed Freddie and Wilbert at the station sometime that night. In 1963 small-town northern Florida, that was enough. The cops thought they had their men.

The first day, Freddie and Wilbert were questioned briefly and sent home. But the next morning, police showed up at Wilbert's house at 5 a.m., rousing him from bed. They brought him to the station, where, Wilbert said, the officer told him, "Nigger, get on upstairs and sit down; I'm lockin' your ass up for first-degree murder." Freddie was already in the station, being "questioned" in another room. Freddie and Wilbert were interrogated for hours and hours without benefit of counsel; they were given primitive lie-detector tests; they were threatened; and they were beaten. That night, a deputy came in, Wilbert said, and told the officers, "Get this nigger out of here, 'cause the mob crowd is coming." They paraded Wilbert downstairs, telling him to keep his eyes fixed straight ahead. Out of his peripheral vision, Wilbert said, he saw an enormous horde of angry white men brandishing shotguns and rifles. The cops ducked Wilbert into the squad car just in time, driving him miles and miles to the jail, where they locked him in a cell.

Wilbert was held for a couple days, he said; released for a day, and then brought in again. This time, Wilbert said, they brought his ex-wife in, crying. Wilbert told us that they told him if he didn't confess, they were going to shave her head and execute her. Army lawyers and investigators were trying to get to Freddie—he was one of their own—but the local cops, Freddie said, wouldn't let them in. Finally, through what Freddie and Wilbert told us were threats and violence, the cops elicited "confessions" from both of them. Not long after, they were brought to trial—represented, Freddie said, by a public defender who was the family attorney of one of the victims. Their trial—which, Freddie said, "wasn't really a trial, it was a penalty hearing"—lasted a day. They were convicted by an all-white jury and sentenced to death on August 28, 1963—the same day as Martin Luther King's March on Washington.

They arrived at a death row that, like everything else those days, was segregated. There was a white side and a black side, with an empty cell between them. Freddie and Wilbert were put next to each other; Freddie told Wilbert not to worry, that he was writing a letter to the FBI. When the FBI guy came, Freddie said, they found out he was the sheriff's best friend. Wilbert said, "They sat back and laughed at the two niggers on death row."

In 1966, Freddie and Wilbert said, a deputy from another county told the sheriff that he had some information about the murder of two service station attendants. They recalled that the sheriff's response was something to the effect of "I don't want to hear anything you have to say because I have two niggers on death row to burn for that." But not long after, they said, the sheriff was up for reelection, and his opponent accused him of a cover-up in the case. The debate escalated, until finally a reward was offered for information in the case; at that point, it came out that the "information" the deputy had procured was actually a confession by the real murderer, a white man.

The confession was amazingly accurate, down to details such as objects that had been missing from the store, unlike Freddie's and Wilbert's "confessions," which were full of gross inconsistencies—among other things, they stated that one of the attendants had been bludgeoned when he had, in fact, only been shot. Still, it took several more years for the evidence to come through the court system and for Wilbert and Freddie to be freed. In 1976, they finally were.

Eventually, unlike most exonerated folks, both received full pardons and were awarded some money by the state legislature. Because of this—along with a great deal of support from their communities and families—both were able to put their lives back together fairly quickly and began advocating for other wrongly convicted folks. Delbert was on the same death row as Wilbert and Freddie—he came in just as they were being released—and they worked hard on his case, becoming part of the movement that helped to free him.

Over the years, Freddie and Wilbert advocated for and helped free several other innocents. By 2000, both were happily married, with kids and grandkids, living comfortably. Freddie worked part-time as a consultant and advocate, and Wilbert worked—believe it or not—for the Department of Corrections, counseling juvenile offenders.

When Wilbert had to leave for work, Freddie kept going, talking about what had changed since the sixties and what was just the same, what was wrong with the system and how he'd fix it, where the country was twenty years ago and where he thought it was going in another twenty years. Freddie has sacrificed more than enough time to his society—he deserves to retire as much as just about anyone you can think of. But it's too bad, because if people like Freddie occupied all our public offices, we'd be living in a stronger, fairer—and very different—country.

Freddie and Wilbert, their very sentences full of history lessons, were the perfect ending to the Southern trip. Elder statesmen who'd borne witness to four decades of the Southern justice system—they'd been there before, during, and after the civil rights movement—they were uniquely qualified to talk about where injustice comes from; the myriad ways people have fought to fix it; and which battles have been won, which have been lost, and which still hang in the balance. The interview with them provided a historical perspective and an overview we hadn't found anywhere else.

When we first came down South, our heads were full of film reels and disembodied history lessons; by the time we left, those history lessons were brought to life, made human, real, and complicated. We saw just how much progress had been made since the sixties—a lot—and just how real, material, and important that progress was in the lives of the ones who'd lived it. At the same time, we saw that the underlying patterns, the human causes of injustice, linger. Many people down South still treat strangers with a suspicion strong enough to be threatening; hatred, racism, and mistrust still infect parts of the culture and most of the system, even if they are no longer codified. The South has its own legacy, its own specific problems. But what we learned as we traveled through it was that these days, those problems aren't so very different from those anywhere else. The South's problems are the country's problems, and the country's problems are human problems. Racism infects the system in Illinois as well as in Alabama; we open-minded New Yorkers stereotyped white, Southern evangelicals as much as they stereotyped us. We could no longer make ourselves feel more comfortable about injustice by thinking that it happened in some other place, "down there" and far away, carried out by other people who were nothing like us. The roots of it are in all of us, no matter where we live; and so is the ability to change it.

Chapter Eleven

Jessica and Nick landed safely in New York; Nick went back to his music, and Jessica and Erik started back in on the morning-to-midnight phone calls: to exonerated people, to donors, to our actors, and probably a couple to God (we reversed the charges). By this time, we were exhausted. Our trip through the South had been so emotionally full, so logistically complicated, and so physically draining. We'd traveled thousands of miles. Neither of us had gotten a full night's sleep in weeks; we were each up to seven cups of coffee a day, and the caffeine was proving less and less effective. Our emotions and thoughts had been stretched and pulled like taffy by the experiences we'd been having. We didn't think we could take much more, but we had to go to Texas.

There's just no way to understand the death penalty in America without visiting the state that leads the nation in executions, a state where capital punishment is so much a part of the culture—and enjoys such wide support—that a wide majority of Texans support the death penalty, despite that 69 percent of those sampled say they believe an innocent person has been executed in their state. "Collateral damage," it's sometimes called. We had to go down there to see just how deep that damage went—and we wanted to know what kind of collateral Texans were exchanging for all that damage.

When we started scheduling our Texas interviews, we discovered, to our surprise, that the trip there would be quick. Texas carries out more executions than any other state—but has few exonerated people. This is because, on average, it takes an innocent person eight years to go through the necessary appeals to get off death row—and in Texas, most inmates are executed before they hit that eight-year mark. One can extrapolate from this that there would be many more exonerated people in Texas if they were allowed to live long enough for the truth to come out.

At first, we'd only been able to find one exonerated death row inmate in all of Texas, a man named Clarence Brandley. After we returned from the South, we spent several days calling all the lawyers and organizations we knew, looking for others. But no luck. Two exonerated Texans we found out about had died shortly after being released; another didn't talk to the press. We came across several cases where a great deal of evidence indicated innocence, but the inmates were executed before that evidence could come out in court. (In all fifty states, after someone is executed, all the evidence in his case is destroyed and the case is closed forever—so there's no way to officially exonerate someone after he's been executed.) Clarence was the only innocent man we could find who'd seen Texas's death row and lived to tell about it. We scheduled our interview with Clarence and booked a flight to Houston.

Two days before we were to fly down there, we got a call from Clarence's lawyer, Paul Nugent. He'd heard we were coming down to interview Clarence, and he wanted to tell us there was someone else we had to meet. He had another client, Kerry Max Cook, who'd just been exonerated that year. "What happened to him is the most extraordinary story you'll ever hear," Paul told us. We'd heard some pretty amazing stories that summer, so we didn't give the superlatives much thought—but we were curious to meet Kerry, so we extended our trip by a day so we could visit him in his home outside Dallas.

When we arrived at the George Bush Intercontinental Airport in Houston, the first thing we saw was a bronze statue of George the Elder. The sculptor intended it to look as if Bush were midstride, staring defiantly into the future with a sport coat flapping in the breeze behind him, but it looked more like someone had stapled a deformed bronze manta ray to his shoulder. After pausing for a picture, we continued on through the airport, taking in the murals, the monuments, the ads for oil companies. Neither of us had been in Texas since we were little kids. The South might've been an unfamiliar part of America loaded with cultural mythology, but Texas was its very own country.

Texas is *really* hot and *really* muggy in the summer. Even hotter than Georgia: that day, it was 105 degrees. We piled into our rental car, cranked the air-conditioning up high, and headed toward Clarence Brandley's home outside Houston. We had two hours to get there, and Clarence was only about forty-five minutes away, so we decided to stop on the way for something to eat.

We'd returned from the South less than a week earlier and hadn't had any opportunity to make up the sleep we'd lost on the road, not to mention to recover from the jet lag. We were a little delirious. We had not had any fun in almost a month and were starting to talk constantly in legalese. For some reason (deliriousness), we thought it would be funny to bring "disguises" with us to Texas—Erik had procured huge aviator sunglasses and a fake mustache, a big old trucker hat, the works; Jessica had brought enormous movie-star shades and a platinum blond wig. On the highway outside the airport, we donned our disguises, goofing around. We each thought the other looked so ridiculous that, in a moment of impromptu public theater, we decided to wear them into the strip-mall Mexican place where we stopped for lunch.

We were quite a sight as we strolled into the restaurant filled with red-and-white checkered tablecloths and Kmart piñatas. It was barely lunchtime; only a few senior citizens, a couple of bouffanted housewives, and a kid or two occupied the place. They all, of course, fixed their eyes on us as we opened the door and the bells on the handle jingled loudly. We made our way to a wobbly table; soon after, our waitress tentatively approached. We didn't do anything to change our image as total weirdo freaks by loudly asking if the refried beans were vegetarian.

The grown-ups around us were trying not to stare; the chubby kids were gawking unabashedly. Erik turned to one of the kids, a crew-cut seven-year-old, and raised his eyebrows over his sunglasses; Jessica gave the kid an exaggerated wink. The seven-year-old turned beet red and quickly snapped his gaze back to his tacos. We were having a ball.

Then the door-handle bells jingled, and we looked up to see whom we'd get to play with next. Two huge Texas cops strode in, in full highway-patrol uniform; their aviator glasses were even bigger than Erik's. Of course, they sat down at the table right next to ours. We'd been made sufficiently paranoid by the experiences of the last few months that we started entertaining all manner of ridiculous fantasies about the danger we might be in. People just didn't wear absurd clothes for no reason in Texas—at least, not outside Austin. And they certainly didn't wear sunglasses indoors. The cops might think we had donned our disguises for sinister or dishonest purposes—maybe they'd mistake us for fugitives, some kind of bizarro Bonnie and Clyde. Maybe they'd stop us after they finished their enchiladas, start asking questions. The sweat on Erik's upper lip was making his mustache droop. (Or maybe it was the enchilada.) But we couldn't take it all off, not in the middle of the restaurant, just because two cops had walked in—that would look even weirder. Suddenly we became docile, got quiet, started acting less like guerrilla-theater performers and more like mimes. Our burritos came, and we sat there, next to the highway patrolmen, in our sunglasses, wig, and mustache, trying to seem inconspicuous as we silently downed our food.

After we escaped the Mexican restaurant without incident, the bells on the door jingling behind us, we pulled off our blond wig and fake mustache and realized that we—a couple of privileged white kids who had broken no laws, hurt nobody, had no drugs on us, didn't even have outstanding traffic tickets—had just sat through an entire meal feeling totally paranoid just because there were cops next to us and we were dressed funny. Silly as the incident was, it showed us that the stories we'd been hearing had really shifted our perspective. We—like Gary, Delbert, Randal, and the others—used to think that if you hadn't done anything wrong, they couldn't do anything to you, except maybe under extraordinary circumstances. Over the past few months, we'd found out that wasn't always true.

Sobered, we got back on the road to Clarence's house. He lived on a cul-de-sac in the Houston suburbs, one of those roads full of brand-new, big, beige houses all made from the same mold. We pulled into the driveway in front of his two-car garage, opened our car doors to a blast of overwhelmingly hot, thick air, and hoped Clarence had air-conditioning as we walked up to his door.

The fiftysomething black man who answered the door introduced himself as Reverend Brandley. He stood around six feet tall, strongly built, with dark skin and graying hair; he wore a T-shirt and jeans. He shook our hands firmly and led us through a house that was clearly under construction—half-painted, floors bare—into the living room.

He sat us down on his couch and proceeded to blow our minds completely. We'd read about his case, but we didn't know all the twists and turns until he told us. What happened to Clarence was closer to legalized lynching than any of the other cases we'd encountered, even in Mississippi, even in Florida. And it didn't happen in some distant, unenlightened past—it all went down in the eighties.

In August of 1980, Clarence began, he was working as a janitor at the public high school in Conroe, Texas. He'd grown up in Conroe, a tiny town with a long and violent history of segregation and racial hostility; a Klan stronghold for many years. Clarence's great-grandfather had died as a result of racist violence; white mobs were not uncommon, even into the seventies. Clarence had left for a while—he did a tour of duty in Korea during the Vietnam War—but had returned to Conroe to be with his family. He was a hard worker, holding down several different jobs; once he started as a custodian at the high school, he was quickly promoted to supervisor. He was the only black janitor at the school; the four others were white.

That August, Clarence told us, school was out for the summer, but the gymnasium was still being used for athletic activities. On August 23, there was a volleyball game, and Clarence and the other janitors were there to neaten up after the kids, restock the bathrooms, that kind of thing. As they were cleaning up after the game, Clarence and another custodian made a grotesque discovery—a white, sixteen-year-old girl's raped and murdered body, stowed in a loft above the gym. Word got out almost immediately, and parents panicked: school was supposed to start up again the next week. Authorities publicly promised the community that they would have a suspect in custody before the school year began, and they started talking to the janitors who'd been at the school that day.

Clarence, trusting that his innocence would protect him, immediately cooperated with police, giving them hair samples, DNA samples, blood. Then Texas Ranger Wesley Styles brought Clarence in for interrogation, along with Henry Peace, the other janitor who had discovered the body with Clarence. According to Peace's later testimony, in that interview Ranger Styles said to the two of them, "One of you two is going to have to hang for this," and then he turned to Clarence and told him, "Since you're the nigger, you're elected."

Clarence passed a polygraph test the next afternoon, and his blood type was not consistent with blood found on the victim's blouse. (The blood on the shirt was type A; Clarence is type O.) Nevertheless, Styles continued to pursue Clarence. The authorities, Clarence told us, didn't obtain hair or blood samples from the other janitors for testing. The white janitors all provided alibis for each other and incriminated Clarence. Five days after the crime—after an unbelievably quick investigation—Clarence was brought before an all-white grand jury, which indicted him for the rape and murder of Cheryl Ferguson.

Four months later, in December of 1980, Clarence was brought to trial, again before an all-white jury. The prosecution claimed that Clarence raped Ms. Ferguson, then strangled her with his belt. No physical evidence implicated Clarence—in fact, the blood evidence seemed to rule him out. Further, sperm found inside the victim's body had apparently been destroyed before it could be tested. The only evidence against Clarence was the testimony of the white janitors. One juror was not convinced of Clarence's guilt; he held out, triggering a mistrial. In the following weeks, that juror was bombarded with hateful mail and repeated anonymous threatening phone calls, including one in which the caller referred to him as a "nigger lover" and said, "We're going to get you."

In February 1981, Clarence was tried again, by another all-white jury. This time, one of the janitors who had previously testified against Clarence wasn't called as a witness by the prosecution. Later, Clarence told us, it came out that this was because that janitor was no longer willing to go along with the prosecution's version of the story. At that point, nobody but the prosecution knew that, but the janitor obviously felt strongly—he refused to repeat his testimony, despite having apparently been threatened with a perjury charge. The other custodians continued to back each other up, though, and Clarence was convicted and sentenced to death.

Nearly a year later, Clarence's new attorneys discovered that some important evidence had been "lost" by the prosecution—including a Caucasian pubic hair and other hairs found on the victim, and photos of Clarence taken on the day of the crime that proved he hadn't been wearing the belt that was supposedly "the murder weapon." Of the original 309 trial exhibits, 166 had mysteriously vanished. Clarence's attorneys appealed repeatedly, citing the apparent destruction of evidence. But the court refused to accept their arguments, and Clarence continued to languish in prison.

By this time, Clarence had been on death row nearly five years. A movement was growing on the outside; supporters were raising money for Clarence's legal defense, and the case was in the news. A local woman named Brenda, Clarence told us, apparently saw a TV broadcast about Clarence's case—and came forward to authorities to say that an ex-boyfriend of hers, James Robinson, a former janitor, had told her he'd been involved in a crime that sounded eerily like this one. Initially, authorities moved to suppress her statements, calling them unreliable. So Brenda sought out Clarence's attorneys and told them.

By now, based on what they had uncovered in the past few years, Clarence's attorneys also suspected a second man—one of the other janitors, a guy named Gary Acreman. At Clarence's next hearing, Acreman's father-in-law testified that Acreman had told him where the victim's clothes were stashed—two days before they were discovered. Then John Sessum got up to testify; Sessum was the janitor who had testified at Clarence's first trial and not the second. This time, he testified that he had seen Acreman and Robinson follow the victim up a staircase just before hearing her scream; that Acreman had told him not to tell anyone; but that he had told someone—Texas Ranger Styles—who, Sessum said, had then threatened to arrest him if he didn't keep his story consistent with those of the other janitors. Clarence was granted a new trial.

At this point, Jim McCloskey and Centurion Ministries came on board. Centurion Ministries is an independent investigative firm dedicated to reinvestigating cases where there is substantial evidence of wrongful conviction. It's a nonprofit organization with an extraordinary reputation that survives solely on private donations; its dedicated, small staff has worked tirelessly to free dozens of innocent men and women. They were a godsend for Clarence; Jim McCloskey began discovering more and more evidence implicating Gary Acreman and pointing to Clarence's innocence. But as Jim was investigating, Clarence was given an execution date. Clarence came within six days of execution, he told us, before a judge granted a last-minute stay.

If it weren't for that stay, an innocent man would likely have been executed. At Clarence's next trial, an enormous amount of evidence finally emerged implicating Acreman and Robinson—and suggesting that Texas Ranger Styles may have skewed the investigation against Clarence from the start. Gary Acreman admitted on the stand that James Robinson had been at the high school that morning. Evidence came out proving that the blood on the victim's shirt matched both Acreman's and Robinson's. More evidence surfaced that Acreman had been seen leaving the scene just after the murder, that he was seen following the victim just before her screams were heard, and that he'd told various people afterward that he knew who "the real murderer" was. And Texas Ranger Styles admitted that Clarence had been his only suspect from the start—even *before* he started investigating the case.

After nine years on death row, Clarence was finally freed.

Not long after his release, Clarence was ordained a minister and started preaching at a nearby church. He also got married and began to rebuild his life. But heartbreak seemed to shadow Clarence: not too long before we met him, he told us, his wife had committed suicide. And now the state was after him for unpaid child support—for his two grown children. The state had, apparently, begun to garnish Clarence's wages to the tune of nearly $26,000—for child support he had been unable to pay because the state had wrongfully convicted him and locked him up. It seemed to us that the state's revenues were the ones that should have been garnished.

Sitting in Clarence's living room, we were enraged. In the last several weeks, we'd heard about prosecutorial misconduct; we'd heard about dishonest cops; we'd heard about investigations tainted by racism. But we had never heard of a case in which all these factors occurred so blatantly—and went uncorrected for so long. It took nine years for all the evidence clearing Clarence to finally come out in court—much of which evidence police and prosecutors had possessed, and seemingly suppressed, from the start. Most death row inmates in Texas are executed after a much shorter period than that. If Clarence hadn't had extraordinary appellate attorneys, world-class investigators, and massive support on the outside, and if one judge hadn't decided to grant him a last-minute stay, he'd be dead right now. All because a bunch of white guys decided to "elect" the "nigger."

The state of Texas never apologized to Clarence. We tried to express how sorry we were for what was done to him, but our attempts seemed ridiculously thin, impossibly flimsy next to the immense concrete weight the state—and the culture of racism—had imposed on Clarence's life. We shook his hand, thanked him for his time, and went back out into the oven-hot air to make our way to Dallas.

We were scheduled to meet with our second Texan in the late afternoon; we had a couple hours' drive ahead of us. We negotiated the tangled tan asphalt freeways, silent as we made our way to Plano, Texas, a mostly affluent, conservative white suburb of Dallas. We drove around for quite some time looking for the address the lawyer had given us; we got lost among the endless strip malls of Plano. Finally we found the address, a small concrete building attached to the local U-Haul center. Kerry worked as a dispatcher for U-Haul, making five bucks an hour; he deserved a lot more, but after twenty-two years on death row he was lucky to find work at all. Most people won't hire exonerated folks no matter how innocent they are; we were sure that in this small Texas suburb it wasn't any different. Perhaps to try to make up for the low-end wage, the company provided a modest apartment for him and his then-eight-months-pregnant wife, Sandra. An attractive white couple in their midforties, you'd never know by looking at them that anything set them apart from the rest of Plano's conservative, sheltered suburban population. But when Kerry sat us down on his living-room couch and started talking, a very different picture emerged.

Kerry was nineteen when he was arrested for the brutal rape and gruesome murder of a twenty-one-year-old acquaintance, Linda Edwards. Prosecutors ignored that Edwards had been having a violently intense affair with her married, older boss; she had recently publicly broken it off, costing him his job and marriage. Instead, prosecutors illegally advanced theories that Kerry was a "homosexual maniacal killer"; despite a lack of any solid physical evidence, Kerry was sentenced to death. Kerry spent twenty-two brutal years in prison, raped, tortured, and carved with invectives before DNA evidence matching Edwards's boss exonerated Kerry.

After all the stories we'd heard during the last several weeks, we thought we'd encountered all possible responses to the experience of wrongful conviction. We'd met so many different kinds of people: black, white, religious, atheists, radical, conservative, pissed off, forgiving; we thought we'd seen everything. But Kerry was different. We could immediately sense the impact of having entered death row barely out of high school—and then living there for twenty-two years (the national record). We'd met others who'd been convicted young—like David—but they'd gotten out after a couple years. We'd met folks who'd been in for long, long stretches—like

Clarence, like Randal—but they were fully formed adults when they went in. Kerry's entire life had been shaped by the system. It seemed to us that he'd emerged from prison a nineteen-year-old trapped in the body of a forty-two-year-old man. His hair was turning silver, but he had the eagerness, curiosity, and energy of a teenager. He'd only been out a year, he told us; he was still rediscovering the whole world. He leaned forward when he talked, animated, excited, with the intensity and instant intimacy of a kid at summer camp. Other people we'd met had been reserved, protective, taken a while to warm up; a half hour into the interview, Kerry treated us like his oldest, closest friends.

Kerry's wife, Sandra, had been a believer in the death penalty when they met, she told us; she was a scientist, pragmatic and conservative. But, she told us, a colleague who worked for Amnesty International convinced Sandra to help Kerry integrate into society after his release. She said yes—and fell in love with Kerry. Now her worldview had changed, the two of them were married, and she was eight months pregnant with a little boy they were planning to name Justice. She sat next to Kerry on the couch, touching him constantly, watching his eyes, taking care of him. She clearly provided a grounding, protective steadiness for Kerry, necessary for someone who'd been deprived of contact with the outside world for twenty-two years and was spending every second taking in as much new experience as he possibly could. Kerry's vulnerability was as palpable as his wide-eyed energy; we could sense how deeply the extraordinary brutality he'd endured in prison had scarred him. But he had someone by his side; Sandra told us how she'd wake up with him in the pitch-black, help him through his nightmares. We were deeply touched by their relationship.

Kerry spent more than five hours detailing the twists and turns of his case—all the cases we'd encountered were complex, but his more than any other: it spanned twenty-two years and four trials. He also talked to us at great length and with great candor about the emotional hell he'd endured in prison—more openly than anyone else we'd met. He was surprisingly candid about his rape, and about his years spent talking openly about the subject on shows like *Dateline* and *Today*. It was an intensely moving experience for us to sit and listen to him. We came away with a much more concrete awareness of how profound the effects of wrongful conviction are, how the experience can shape an entire life. By the time we parted ways with Kerry and Sandra, at nearly 1 a.m., we had acquired an insight into the emotional impact of wrongful conviction that was deeper, more human, than any understanding we'd gained from our nearly thirty other interviews.

We had an early-morning flight out of Houston the next day; we had to be at the airport by five. We left Plano and drove through the night, sleepy but energized. We'd been reading about the Texas death penalty all summer; our heads were full of statistics. But now our hearts were full, too, with an understanding of the lives behind those numbers. In just one day in Texas, we had heard two stories of misconduct, dishonesty, manipulation, and brutality more egregious than just about anything we'd heard anywhere else. These cases followed the same patterns as the ones we'd encountered in other parts of America; all the same factors were involved: interrogation without attorneys, prosecutorial misconduct, coerced witnesses, poor initial representation, media firestorms. But here, those factors were taken to extraordinary extremes.

We knew from the research we'd done that, in Texas, the sheer volume of lives involved was equally extreme. We'd already read that in just three years, under the governorship of G. W. Bush, Texas had executed more people than any other state in America had executed in the last *two decades combined*; that since 1976, Texas had executed over 250 people; and that more than half of these executions occurred during Bush's single term as governor. We'd also found out that in many of these cases, there were significant doubts as to the defendant's actual guilt: the state of Texas doesn't have a public defender's office, so many of the executed had no attorneys working hard to bring potentially exculpatory evidence out in court. And we'd read newspaper article after newspaper article describing how, during his tenure, Governor Bush was repeatedly approached—not only by citizens' groups and international human rights organizations, but also by multiple European governments—to grant stays and/or instruct the courts to reconsider evidence in many of these cases. In almost every instance, he flatly refused.

All that research had instilled in us some pretty strong opinions about the upcoming presidential election. But once we got to Texas and started meeting the people involved, it became less about our personal political beliefs and more about basic compassion—Governor Bush's record on the death penalty had been almost unfathomably extreme, and after just a day down here, we had a real sense of the human costs of such recklessness. Bush repeatedly resisted legislative attempts to ensure decent representation for people accused of capital crimes. His advisers were reported to have given cursory, fifteen-minute glances to numerous requests for clemency from condemned prisoners. Foreign nationals were executed in Texas on Bush's watch (a practice illegal under international law); so were teenagers under eighteen at the time of their crime and grown men so severely mentally retarded they believed in Santa Claus. Kerry Max Cook's requests for clemency were submitted more than once during Bush's term as governor; each time, Bush rejected them. In only one instance did Bush grant a stay of execution: In 2000, when Bush was in the throes of his presidential campaign and the scrutiny regarding his administration of the death penalty in Texas was at its peak, Bush granted a stay to a convicted child killer to allow time for DNA testing—even though most associated with the case acknowledged that the DNA tests were expected to reaffirm his guilt. When the results came back, that's exactly what they did—and in the meantime, Bush had scheduled execution dates for several other inmates with much more convincing claims of innocence.

We'd spent several months shouting at the newspaper or the television when we heard facts like these, ranting and raving, politically and ideologically infuriated. But now, after hearing the people we'd just met, seeing the scars etched so deeply in them, feeling how these injustices could rip a human life apart, we were a little quieter. Shooting our mouths off at the newspaper seemed ridiculous, impotent, in the face of the cavernous depths of the problem. It would take something more nuanced, less ideological, to help people really understand. We understood, this time in a deeper way, why we had set out to do what we were doing. We'd had a life-changing experience, but now we had to relate that experience to others. We had to tell the stories.

Chapter Twelve

When we walked back into our apartment, we glanced around at the piles and piles of transcripts, the mess on our desk, the now-broken answering machine, the Post-it notes tacked all over the living room, and spent a minute taking stock before we dove back in again. In the last two months, we had completed our travels around the country, met nearly twenty extraordinary human beings, had our assumptions challenged and our minds blown, gathered more than enough material to make *several* plays, and, oh, yeah, gotten engaged.

Now the real work began.

We had to somehow translate the experiences we'd had in the exonerated people's living rooms into *theater.* We'd realized when we came back from the Midwest that it would be difficult to convert real people's everyday speech into dramatic language, but we'd repressed our worries about it as we got back on the road. Now we had to address those concerns. And it was tougher, now that we'd met so many more people: we wanted to include *everything* we'd heard over the last two months. We wanted our audiences to go through the entire spectrum of emotions that we had. It seemed impossible to identify which parts of the interviews could be cut; as we waded through those pages and pages of transcripts, we became paralyzed. So we did what we'd done all the times we'd gotten stuck before—we called our friends.

Actors tend to have a lot of immensely talented, out-of-work friends. And most prefer sitting around a theater to sitting around anywhere else; as long as we're rehearsing, we're okay. Allan, supporting our quest to meet his deadline, allowed us to use his theater's nooks and crannies on weekend mornings and weekday afternoons, so we gathered all the actor friends we could find and started reading through the transcripts. First we brought the transcripts in raw—*ums* and everything. As our friends read them out loud, we took a big Magic Marker and crossed out the boring parts, the awkward parts, the parts that didn't translate. Our interviews were beginning—just beginning—to look a little bit like stories.

After workshopping the transcripts all day long, we'd go home and type out new versions, incorporating our edits from that day's work. The next morning, we'd get up at six and spend an hour at our neighborhood Xerox place making copies of the new edits for our actors, and talking to the Indian guy who owned the place. "How is your play *The Freedom?*" he asked us once. We laughed and corrected him, saying, "It's going okay, thanks—but it's called *The Exonerated*, and it's not really about freedom; it's more about miscarriages of justice." "No"—he was emphatic—"it's about freedom. I read it last night. And that is what it's about." We were speechless.

After we finished at the copy shop we'd show up at the theater, pass the new edits out, and go through the same process. We'd go home, enter the next round of cuts, and bring them in the following day. Home, cut, wake up, copy, theater, home, cut, wake up, copy, theater. We sat on the floor, papers spread out in front of us, marking up the pages furiously as the actors spoke. Usually, without talking about it or consulting each other, we'd make the same notes, scribble out the same phrases. We could both *hear* what needed to go and what should stay, which sentences were fat waiting to be trimmed and which ones held the marrow of the stories. We'd elbow each other out of the way to scribble on the pages in a kind of caffeine-inspired little creative dance. We were finishing each other's sentences with our pens.

After a few rounds of this, we started to notice connections in the material we hadn't seen before. A paragraph from the beginning of an interview would link up with something from the very end, connecting thematically, forming an arc. Pieces of text that looked surprisingly like monologues began to emerge.

Another interesting thing happened: the actors started to "channel" the real people whose words they were reading. We purposely didn't play audio of the interviews or screen the videotapes for our workshop actors; we wanted to see and hear interpretations that came straight from the words and the stories, not from actors' attempts to imitate the real people. We gave the actors very little direction, beyond a couple basic "clues." We were shocked to find that, even without any outside input, the actors spoke and looked and moved almost exactly like the exonerated folks whose words they were reading. Different actors read the roles each day, the actors themselves as diverse in looks and mannerisms as you could imagine. But as soon as they picked up the pages and started reading, they all talked and moved just like Kerry or Robert or Brad. The first couple days, we ascribed this phenomenon to chance. But as we saw it happen over and over, without any special effort on the part of the actors, we realized it was coming from the words. As we watched the actors organically and unintentionally adopt whole personas just from reading someone's sentences, we began to understand just how much our psychology is contained in our speech. The rhythms, the words we choose, the order we put them in, the places we pause, stammer, change the subject—they reveal everything about us. We saw that as we cut and pasted the transcripts, ripped them apart to make a new structure, it was imperative that we preserve all the inconsistencies and details, patterns and regionalisms, of each person's speech.

Our actor friends were incredibly helpful, telling us when something rang true and when it didn't, when they could access the text easily and when it took mental gymnastics to follow the logic. Gradually, we broke up the mass of transcript material into about a hundred speeches and scenes.

In the workshops, the text started condensing itself organically. We began to notice that some of the stories were doubling each other. During the interviews, we'd noticed similarities in many of the cases; we'd talked about those parallels at great length while we were on the road. The overlap between the cases was fascinating to hear about and examine in the real world—but as we listened to the actors tell the stories, we realized that onstage it was redundant.

Eventually, ten cases stood out as stories that were unique, compelling, and could be communicated to an audience: Neil, Delbert, Gary, Randal, Robert, David, Brad, Freddie, Wilbert, and Kerry. In the workshops, we started working with the stories of just those men (sometimes accompanied by their spouses), boiling the stories down as much as we could, refining the content while preserving the speakers' individual voices.

* * *

One thing was sorely missing, though—the story of a woman who'd gone to death row and lived to tell about it. We knew from our research that prison, and especially death row, are a whole different experience for women. Women's prisons operate differently from men's; the press deals with female suspects in an unique way; maintaining family connections and reintegrating afterward are distinct struggles for women who survive death row. We knew that to really explore the whole tapestry of innocence on America's death rows, it wouldn't be enough to include stories of men from different backgrounds, races, decades, regions. We had to have at least one woman's story, too.

Two women in America had been exonerated from death row: Sabrina Butler and Sonia "Sunny" Jacobs. We'd spoken to Sabrina by phone as we'd made our initial inquiries, and with the chattering voices of her children in the background, she'd tearfully told Jessica that she just couldn't take any more attention. She hadn't been able to move away from the small, segregated Mississippi town in which she'd been convicted, and the stigma followed her too closely. Every time she got publicity, she said, things just got bad again. It was heart-wrenching. We told Sabrina we understood and didn't bother her again.

Then we tried to find Sonia, but she was *really* tough to track down. Her answering machine always picked up on the first ring, and we couldn't locate anyone who knew another number for her. We left several messages, but never heard back. We called from the road, and between our trips; every few days we'd try her number again. We asked everyone we talked to if they knew her. We sent her letters, but they went unanswered. We were beginning to resign ourselves to not being able to include the voice of an exonerated woman.

* * *

In the meantime, we continued our attempts to bring more and more people on board. We'd raised enough money to get through our travels, but we still had another three months of workshops in front of us, lots of expenses in office supplies and long-distance bills, and ninety-hour workweeks—no time for survival jobs to pay the bills. And then there were the readings themselves. We had to find actors, for one thing. And Allan had promised us the theater for free, but a lot of other expenses were associated with putting on the performances. We'd either have to raise more money or find a *lot* of people who were willing to volunteer—or both. Either way, we had to convince a whole bunch of people to believe in us. As actors, we were used to being hired guns, being told what to do and say, someone else running the show. Neither of us had ever done anything remotely like this project before—we had zero track record.

So we kept reaching out, talking to everyone we knew, looking for experienced folks who would lend their more respected names to back us up. We assembled an advisory board, made up of folks who held top positions at Amnesty International and the ACLU, well-known defense attorneys, and respected playwrights and directors like Arthur Kopit, Moisés Kaufman, and Joe Mantello. Mike Farrell, the actor and dedicated humanitarian activist, added his name early on. We kept working on assembling a strong list of supporters, hoping that people who would otherwise look at us and see two scrappy, untried, inexperienced punks would take our project seriously after seeing the advisory board's names on our flimsy Microsoft Publisher–generated "stationery."

In keeping with this, Jessica's father had set up a meeting for us with his colleague Robert Edgar, former Pennsylvania congressman and current General Secretary of the National Council of Churches. Mr. Edgar would be sympathetic to our project, Dr. Blank said; maybe he would lend his name; at the very least, he'd help spread the word.

We went to meet with Mr. Edgar at his office uptown; he sat down with us in his building's cafeteria and listened intently. He was extremely supportive and agreed to add his name to our list. After lunch, he invited us upstairs to see his office. When we walked in the door, we saw a flyer tacked to the wall, advertising a forum on the death penalty that was being held that weekend at Riverside Church, just a few blocks away.

Sunny Jacobs was a featured speaker.

Even after so many instances of synchronicity, this one still surprised us. We'd been busting our butts to get in touch with Sunny for three months, trying to track her down each way we could think of, and failing every time. We'd almost given up—and then an opportunity to meet her just fell into our laps! That Sunday, we cleared our schedule and went uptown. We brought our little handheld cassette recorder to the church and pressed RECORD when Sunny got up and started speaking.

Good thing, too, because the story she told in the fifteen minutes she was up there was jaw-dropping. Sunny, a white woman originally from New York, was a twenty-seven-year-old hippie mom in 1976, when she followed her common-law husband, Jesse Tafero, to Florida. They soon ran out of money, though, and decided to travel north again. They got a ride partway with an acquaintance of Jesse's named Walter Rhodes. Rhodes was a career criminal, and Sunny didn't like him being around the kids. But he was the only person they knew in Florida, and he was willing to drive them a couple counties north. A little while after they set off, it got dark, and they stopped at a rest area to sleep.

Early in the morning, Sunny said, two policemen came along to do a routine check on the rest area. They looked in the car where Rhodes, Jesse, Sunny, and the two kids were sleeping—and saw a gun on the floor between Rhodes's feet. They ordered Rhodes and Jesse out of the car and asked for their IDs. They called in the ID information, and the police radio came back with the information that Rhodes was on parole; possession of a gun is a parole violation.

One of the policemen drew his gun and said, according to Sunny, "The next one to move is dead." And then the shots began. Sunny, in the car, terrified, shielding her children, didn't know who'd been hit. When it finally got quiet, she looked up and saw that the two policemen were dead. According to Sunny, Rhodes pointed his gun at her and Jesse and told them to get into the police car: he kidnapped the family and took them on a wild ride, stopping only long enough to carjack an elderly man and force Sunny and her family out of the police car and into the second vehicle. They sped along the highway—and then Sunny started to hear helicopters and honking horns. She knew there must be a roadblock ahead, she said; she breathed relief: they were about to be saved. But Rhodes veered to avoid the roadblock, and policemen opened fire on the car. Rhodes was shot in the leg; Sunny and her family were uninjured. But the cops dragged everyone out—and brought them all in as suspects.

Sunny was terrified, but she believed from the start that the police would figure out she hadn't done anything and let her and Jesse go. The police performed a paraffin test on her hands as well as on Jesse's and on Rhodes's and determined incontrovertibly that Rhodes was the only one of the three who had fired a gun that day.

But Rhodes had been in prison, Sunny said; he knew the system. He immediately started arranging for a plea bargain—one in which he would receive three life sentences and immunity from the death penalty, in exchange for serving as the star witness against Sunny and Jesse.

Sunny and Jesse were convicted in separate trials, and both were sentenced to death. At the time of Sunny's conviction, she said, she was the only woman in America who had a sentence of death; there was literally no death row for women. So prison authorities cleared out an entire wing of the women's prison and put Sunny there alone. Completely isolated, Sunny stayed sane by practicing yoga, meditating, and continuing her relationship with Jesse through letters. Sunny and Jesse wrote to each other almost daily for fourteen years. They kept each other alive.

In the meantime, Rhodes was writing letters, too—several letters, to judges and prosecutors, in which he disavowed his previous testimony against Sunny and Jesse and took sole responsibility for the crime. But Rhodes was too skittish to get up on the stand and reverse his statements under oath, and Sunny and Jesse both remained on death row. Rhodes recanted his recantations several times—he'd reach out, then back off again, over and over.

Meanwhile, a childhood friend of Sunny's named Micki Dickoff heard about Sunny's plight. The more she learned about the case, the more she became convinced of Sunny's and Jesse's innocence. She got in touch with Sunny and began bravely, tirelessly advocating for her, bringing new defense lawyers on board, and ultimately going so far as to make a TV movie about the case to raise public awareness.

In 1990, despite Micki's efforts, Jesse Tafero was executed in the worst-botched execution in twentieth-century America. The electric chair malfunctioned, and the executioner had to pull the switch three times, sending three jolts of electricity through Jesse's body that lasted a minute each. The execution took more than a quarter of an hour, and before it was over, Jesse's head burst into flames.

Two years later, Sunny was freed in large part on the theory that Walter Rhodes was the lone shooter.

One would expect someone who'd been through that experience to be bitter or beaten down. Not Sunny. She was the perkiest, most joyful person we had ever met—and it was clearly a *real* joy, not one that's based on comfort or privilege or ease. Sunny had been to some of the darkest places human beings can go: not only had she been wrongly imprisoned for nearly seventeen years under threat of electrocution, she also lost her parents to a plane crash while she was in prison, was torn away from her two children for the entire span of their childhoods, and lived through the brutal execution of the man she loved. But Sunny didn't live in the darkness, she said, and she wouldn't let anybody lock her up. Sunny told the crowds at the church that Sunday that right in the midst of prison, she had found real freedom: "If you sit there, rubbing two sticks together and crying on your sticks, they're never gonna make a spark. But, you know, if you stop feeling sorry for yourself, just because you're determined not to believe in hopelessness, then a spark happens, and then you keep fanning that little spark until you got a flame. And I realized that it was like a big trick! I wasn't just a little lump of flesh that they could lock inside a cage." Sitting up on that panel at Riverside Church, Sunny insisted that building a meaningful life and helping other people do the same were the best revenge she could take for what happened to her. "I was in there seventeen years; I'm not gonna give them one more minute of my life."

Sunny, a tiny yoga teacher in granny glasses, was not exactly an intimidating figure. But we were so unbelievably inspired by the story she'd just told, so blown away by her strength, that we were a little nervous in approaching her. We waited for the crowd that had formed around Sunny to clear (crowds often form around Sunny when she tells her story) and explained what we were doing there. "Oh, yeah!" she said. "I heard about you guys! You were trying to reach me or something!" Um, only for about three months. It turned out she had been visiting her boyfriend, Peter, himself an exonerated death row inmate from Ireland, and hadn't gotten our messages till that week. She gave us permission to use what she'd said in her talk, and we scheduled a more complete interview with her. It was worth the wait.

Chapter Thirteen

Election season was fast approaching, and we needed to start thinking about how these three readings were actually going to come together. We had a theater already; our advisory board was at least keeping people from laughing in our faces; we'd established a routine with our workshops, working on the text of the play several hours a day. The next thing we needed was a director. Erik had worked with veteran actor/director/producer Bob Balaban the previous year—in fact, Bob had directed Erik in the Arthur Kopit play that had been the site of our first date. Erik dug up Bob's number, called him, and asked if he'd be willing to direct the evenings. Bob, as always overworked and overcommitted, said he'd be willing to take a look at what we had.

At that point, "what we had" was about 150 pages' worth of monologue- and scene-like fragments, in no particular order, which in no way resembled a play. But Bob must've seen something in it, because he said he'd direct the readings and asked us if we'd mind if he showed it to a couple of friends. We said go ahead, thanked him for his support, and went back to our workshops.

In the workshops, we were starting to get more specific with the text. It was still a sprawling mess, but less so than it had been when we'd started. At first, we thought condensing and shaping the transcripts would be simple—hard work, but simple. Making this play was like carving a statue out of a big hunk of marble, and thus far we'd been taking out big chunks. We'd seen eye to eye on almost every change we'd made; we could both hear what needed to stay and what needed to go, and we'd nod our heads in assent as we watched each other make cuts on the paper.

Now, as the changes got more detail-oriented, we started to disagree—and fight. As writers, we worked from opposite ends of the spectrum: Jessica looked for the most condensed, vivid moments, the little specificities that illuminated the characters, one sentence or phrase that opened up a whole world. Erik had his eye on the larger narrative arc, focused on keeping the stories moving along at a fast clip, hooking the audience in. In hindsight, we can see how our differing points of view complemented each other, how crucial each perspective was—actually, it seems pretty obvious. But back then, at times we each thought the other was making a total mess of things. Erik thought Jessica was being precious, hanging on to moments that didn't serve the play just because she found them beautiful. Jessica thought Erik was too ruthless with the text, stripping away the very things that illuminated the hearts of the stories, throwing out the baby with the bathwater. We got in some rip-roaring arguments, complete with tears and yelling. The actors would back off the stage, go outside to smoke or chat, and come back inside after the storm had passed.

At stake was something that had become deeply important to us both, and we both fought hard for it. It was scary at first: we'd done everything together, we felt so deeply reliant on each other, and now, all of a sudden, there were times when each of us perceived our closest collaborator as a threat to the thing we held so dear.

The first time we had one of those fights, it kept us up till 3 a.m. We'd disagreed about something in the workshop that day, and we carried the argument home with us, clinging tenaciously to our positions, raising our voices, upsetting the dog. The hours ticked by as we butted heads, each attacking the other's creative modus operandi, until finally we wore each other out and fell asleep. The next morning, we had to wake up, make our photocopies, and head back into the workshop with our actors. Not an hour in, we heard the answer to the question we'd been fighting over—as one actor read the text, he spontaneously cut three sentences Erik had insisted we get rid of but hung on to the one phrase Jessica had been fighting to keep, inserting it into a later paragraph. It was perfect. We scribbled down identical notes about it at the same moment, then looked at each other sheepishly.

That experience taught us two things that we would spend the next year and a half learning how to put into practice. The first was that we had to trust that the text itself would always settle all our arguments—whatever change or cut we were fighting about, we would eventually hear the solution in the words themselves. The second—and more important—thing was that no matter how hard we fought, how fiercely each of us believed that he or she was right, we would still always have to get up the next morning and set our differences aside in order to get back to work. Those arguments could have bogged us down forever. We might've gotten really personal, freaked-out that we didn't see eye to eye, dragged out our power struggles endlessly. But we couldn't anymore. We had a purpose and a deadline, and in the end we always had to sublimate our personal, petty complaints, our little stings and bruises, to the greater good of the play.

Only a few years later did we realize that in those months, we worked out a lot of power struggles that might otherwise have plagued us as a couple for our entire lives. Collaborating so intensely brought all those struggles to the surface—and having a larger purpose forced us to work them out quickly, find ways of solving problems together, and move on, because there was always more to do, and it was always more important than our little arguments.

Our actors helped a lot, too. We created the initial draft of the play in the most luxurious creative circumstances any playwright could imagine: with actors there at every step to help us hear the words. We worked with a pool of about thirty; each Monday, we'd figure out which characters we were working with that week, and we'd call around to our actor pool, finding out who was available. Some would come in once; others would come in a couple times a week; and some were with us almost every day. David Brown Jr., Schantelle Cason, Gretchen Krich, Bruce Kronenberg, Curtis McClarin, April Thompson, Ben Wilson—these folks formed the core of our workshop process, and their input was invaluable. Their insights and impulses were right on target: they'd illuminate things in the characters that we'd missed; point out double meanings, patches of subtext; pull us back on track when we got carried away. They knew we didn't have any money, that no full production was planned, that there wasn't even a script. They voluntarily showed up almost every day out of sheer creative drive, just to be part of making something. In return, we did our best to create a work environment that matched what we as actors had always held as an ideal. We tried to create a process for our actors like the one we always hoped our directors and collaborators would create for us. We kept the focus on them: we provided guidance when they needed it; tried to give them clear direction that was less about producing a particular result and more about exploring the life of the characters and the piece; kept things on track. And other than that, we let the actors lead. When they wanted to talk about a section, we would talk about it; when they wanted to improvise around an idea, we would improvise. What organically emerged in those workshops was one of the most pure, creative, collaborative working environments that either one of us had experienced.

Given the content of the material, the openness of the atmosphere, and the racial diversity of the characters, we also wound up having quite a few conversations about politics and race with our workshop actors. American theater is one of the more segregated art forms; nontraditional casting has done quite a bit to remedy this, but still, most American plays are either white, black, or other, and there's not a lot of crossover. Working with both black and white actors in a play whose content was largely—but not exclusively—about race provided a tremendous space for dialogue; and not the canned, strained, overcompensating-guilty-white-people kind, but the real kind. We learned a lot in those workshops, on a lot of different levels.

Several weeks into the workshops, we were on our way home from the theater when our pager buzzed. Calling our voice mail, we found a message from Bob Balaban, asking us to please give him a call. We did, and he delivered the news that he'd gone ahead and shown the materials to some friends, like he'd said he was going to—and that "Susan and Tim" had agreed to do the first reading of the play.

"Susan and Tim" being Susan Sarandon and Tim Robbins.

That was one of the moments that are burned on our brain—like the feeling of making the first phone call to an exonerated person, or hearing actors read the interview transcripts aloud for the first time. We both still remember standing on the corner of lower Fifth Avenue, getting that piece of news on our shared cell phone. Everything just opened up.

Susan and Tim represented a kind of career/relationship blueprint for us: a couple who created incredible work, both together and apart, and who'd managed to meld deeply held political convictions with their art. There aren't a lot of actors like the two of them—brainy, thoughtful, radical, courageous; artistic equals with a real partnership, a powerful force both individually and together. We'd both looked up to them for a long time. We were untried writers, still a little naive about what we were tapping into. It was sort of unfathomable to us that they were going to do *our* play.

Needless to say, we jumped around the sidewalk when we got the news. Then we tried to calm down; people were looking at us weird. Then we jumped around some more, unable to keep from acting like huge dorks. We thanked Bob profusely and headed home to figure out what the hell we were going to do next.

We should've been nervous that actors of Tim's and Susan's stature were going to perform these words, but we didn't have time. We had too much work to do—all of a sudden, these upcoming readings felt very, very real. We had two amazing actors on board; now we needed to assemble a whole cast for each evening. We didn't know where to start.

We continued with the tried-and-true strategy of calling our friends for help and rang up Eve Battaglia, a casting director we knew and loved from our rounds as actors in the city. Eve is one of the smartest and most creative casting directors we know, not to mention a really good person with loads of integrity. She was the perfect person to call. We explained our project to her, and she agreed to cast the three readings for free.

Eve read the material we had and understood the essences of the characters perfectly, right off the bat. Eve's suggestions of potential actors were right on target; she started putting together three separate casts for each of the evenings. By early October, Steve Buscemi, Vincent D'Onofrio, Charles Dutton, William Fichtner, Cherry Jones, David Morse, Harold Perrineau, Martha Plimpton, and J. K. Simmons had committed to the readings; Eve was getting more and more to come on board each week; and Bob was talking to more actor friends of his. Things were gearing up.

In the meantime, we had to finish a version of the play that would be worthy of its actors. And a *lot* of other things needed to be done: we had to find someone to stage-manage the readings, figure out some sort of poster, advertise the evenings, alert the press, schedule rehearsals, cobble together some kind of light and sound plot, deal with many famous actors' schedules, and all the other thousands of things that go into making a performance happen. As we got closer to the readings, Allan was an angel: he let us use the infrastructure of his theater—the box office, the phones, the ancient copy machine—and he also introduced us to a lot of friends of his who were willing to help. The theater's artistic director, Darrell Larson, gave us advice on our evolving script. Allan recruited Richard Hsu, an immensely talented and experienced designer, to create a poster and program for the readings. And Allan and Darrell connected us with their theater's light and sound people.

And we kept calling our friends. Arthur Lewis, a veteran stage manager who's run everything from the *Vagina Monologues* to *Cosby* to the millennium festivities in Washington, D.C., agreed to stage-manage the show, which was a real coup—Arthur is more capable and organized than all the other people we know combined. And through Colin Greer, we were able to hook up with Riptide Communications, a progressive publicity firm that specializes in the intersection of the arts and political issues. The folks we'd brought on board started talking to each other; a team began to coalesce.

Only thing was, we were running out of money again. By this time we were in such a constant rush of adrenaline that we had no room to panic; we just kept going, running on sheer momentum and trusting that everything would work out *somehow*. We sent out a mailing to all of Jessica's parents' friends; almost every single one of them responded with some form of support. Some even sent a couple hundred dollars, which went a *long* way. In the meantime, we also came across a journalist named Curtis Ellis, who introduced us to a documentarian friend of his, Eames. Curtis thought Eames might be interested in documenting the making of the play, and maybe that might help bring in some much needed funds. We met with Eames—a big, effusive, bikerish kind of character in sunglasses who bought us whiskey at a bar in Chelsea and asked us about what we'd been up to the past few months. We told him; he said he might be interested in helping out.

By this time, it was becoming clear we were in over our heads professionally. We hadn't thought about any of the business aspects of what we were doing; we had our hands full driving all over the country, having our lives changed by the exonerated folks, trying to make art out of what we'd learned, and dealing with the mechanics of making three major readings happen in a three-hundred-seat-theater. Outside of getting solid release forms from the subjects of the play, we hadn't thought about contracts or options—and even if we had had time, we wouldn't have had the foggiest idea where to start. All we'd done was act. We had little clue how the business side of the theater worked, and all of a sudden we were mounting readings of a play we hadn't even finished writing in a major off-Broadway theater, featuring movie stars. When Eames started talking to us about wanting to option rights from us, we played it cool—but really, we couldn't even follow half the vocabulary he was using.

Erik had been keeping his acting manager, Cathy, up-to-date on the project, and around this time she realized we were in over our heads. As a favor, she set up a meeting for us with an old friend of hers, Kara, a literary agent; Kara said she'd like to bring her colleague John. Two days later we poured ourselves into a conference room at the Gersh Agency, all adrenaline and caffeine and sleep-deprivation, and started talking over each other, interrupting and overlapping as we told the story of the insane six months we'd been having. Erik may have ripped open a Mars bar and eaten it during our meeting. We were kind of a wreck by that point, too exhausted to be very businesslike—we must have made a crazy first impression—a couple of Ritalin kids popping out of their seats with excitement about what had transpired over the last few weeks, jabbering a mile a minute. But before the meeting was over, John and Kara said they'd like to take our project on.

We know it's really boring the way actors and writers and directors are forever thanking their agents; it always seems like too much business and not enough humanity. But Kara and John related to us in a human way from the start. It didn't seem to bother them one bit that we were untried, untested, with no real writing credits to our name, not even a finished script. They saw two people with one idea, and they took a chance. Whether or not they actually believed in us from that first meeting, they sure acted like it. It was yet another instance of synchronicity: if we hadn't found good agents at that point, we might've made some dumb moves that could've cost the play its future. Kara and John kept us from doing that—and they did a lot more, too. We couldn't have taken things much further without their help.

Kara and John were the final piece in the puzzle: in a month and a half's time—with no plan, no strategy, no overview, no MO beyond doing the next thing we had to do to get through the next few hours, over and over again—we'd assembled a team of people, all working together to pull this thing off. We had a director, a publicist, designers, a theater, a stage manager, a casting director, agents, and almost a full cast (and let's not forget our tireless interns, still very much on board)—all working selflessly on the project for no reason other than that they believed in what it was about. For two actors who were used to just playing a part, being pieces in other people's puzzles, it was pretty incredible to see something big begin to come together from this perspective. And it had all happened, seemingly, by accident, synchronicity, and goodwill.

Chapter Fourteen

The final couple weeks leading up to the first reading were a blur. Our sixteen-hour-a-day routine had expanded to eighteen hours a day. The phone would wake us up at seven in the morning, and we wouldn't even hang up till six at night: we'd just click the call waiting to pick up call after call after call. We were still working on the text (which was finally beginning to resemble a play): as soon as the phone quit ringing at six, we'd hustle over to the theater to run workshops till nine; then we'd come home and type our edits into the computer till 1 a.m. Then we'd make our to-do list for the next day and crash. The phone would ring the next morning at seven; we'd groan, roll out of bed, and do it all again. One morning we got a phone call at 8 a.m.; that call was interrupted by call waiting, and for eight hours all we did was pass the phone back and forth and hit the flash button as calls piled on top of calls. The only thing that brought the cordless marathon to a halt was the battery running all the way down. We were practically possessed. No, we were definitely possessed. All practicality flew out the window. We had to remind each other to eat.

When we were on the road, we'd gotten the idea to invite the exonerated folks whose stories were in the play to the readings. Now that the readings were less than two weeks away, of course, we had no idea how to make that happen in the real world: we were late on the rent again; we didn't exactly have the cash to pay for multiple plane fares and hotel rooms. But they needed to be there; we knew it was important. As usual, we pressed forward and figured it would fall into place.

Eames the documentarian was still hanging around; he was interested enough to start collecting some footage. He interviewed us on camera, sent a crew to our tiny apartment to film us pretending to work (footage of us *really* working would've come out looking like the cartoon trails that linger behind Roadrunner when he whizzes past Wile E. Coyote), and tracked us through the week leading up to the first reading. The artifice of it got under our skin a little—having cameras follow you around is weird—but we grinned and bore it: the week before, Eames had also agreed to fly some of the exonerated folks to the first reading.

Ideally, we would've brought all the exonerated folks whose stories were in that version of the play. But we couldn't get the money together to fly eleven people and their spouses in; we had to choose.

Since Eames was footing the airfare bill, we let him decide which actors he wanted to film meeting their real-life counterparts; so, ultimately, we wound up making arrangements to bring Delbert, Sunny, Randal, Robert, Kerry, and Brad. Allan and the theater sprung for the hotel accommodations. Most of the exonerated folks had never been to New York, so we recruited volunteers to show them around, help them navigate the city, check into their hotels, negotiate the subway. We called friends of ours whom we knew from all over—spoken-word poets, filmmakers, organizers—to partner up with the exonerated folks for the few days they'd be in the city. We chose the hosts carefully, according to how we thought their personalities would mesh with the exonerated folks they'd be showing around. Our friend Chris Ajemian, a theater director and *highly* organized person—Erik compares him to George Stephanopoulos in the Clinton White House, except more organized, if you can believe it—served as the coordinator for the exonerated people and their hosts; he sent itineraries to the volunteers, briefed them on the exonerated people's backgrounds, kept a phone list. Two days before the first reading, we had a tech run with our workshop actors. The exonerated folks were due in the city the following afternoon. The reading was the night after that. Tickets were already sold-out. It was all becoming real.

The afternoon before the first reading, the exonerated people started trickling in; Brad arrived first and spent an hour or so hanging out in the theater's upstairs office, gregarious and clearly glad to be in the city, chatting with the staff. Robert and Georgia had caught a cab to their hotel, where they had promptly been informed by the staff at the front desk that there was no reservation in their name on the books. Having never been anywhere like New York before, the two of them were obviously a little rattled by the prospect of showing up in the big city, weighted down with suitcases, with no place to sleep. Luckily, their host found Robert and a near-sobbing Georgia in the hotel lobby not long afterward and called us; we had a firm talk with the folks at the front desk. It turned out they'd misspelled the last name in the reservation. We made sure they knew to treat Robert and Georgia *very* well for the rest of their stay.

Then we got a panicked call from Connie on her cell phone. She'd volunteered to show Delbert around while he was in New York (we thought the two of them would be a perfect fit) and had gone out to the airport to pick him up; she'd waited by his gate, and he'd never come out. She'd been down to the baggage claim; he wasn't there. She'd had him paged; he hadn't responded. Had he not made it onto his flight? We panicked, too. There was no way to reach Delbert—he didn't have a phone back home in Chicago, and he didn't have a cell phone either. We weren't even sure he knew how to reach *us*. Connie didn't know what Delbert looked like beyond the description we'd given her; even if they did cross paths, there was no guarantee they'd recognize each other. Connie said she'd hang around the airport some more and look for him; it was all anyone could do. We asked her to stay in close touch, she promised she would, and we ran back downstairs to the theater to keep working out the kinks in the light cues.

In the meantime, Randal and Brenda arrived safely and made it to their hotel; so did Kerry and Sandra, who brought their newborn son, Kerry Justice, and a couple friends from Texas. Sunny was coming the next day; she had friends to stay with in New York who would serve as her hosts. We spent the rest of the afternoon running around like Chihuahuas on speed and worrying about Delbert. We met with the publicists and our sound designer, Alan Rowand, who'd volunteered his engineering talents and equipment. We finished up with the light cues and spent five bucks we didn't have on a ten-block cab ride home. We weren't lazy—we just couldn't spare the fifteen minutes the walk would have taken. We had to get home, run up the five flights to our apartment, get changed, and make it back to the theater to meet all the exonerated folks and Allan for dinner at six thirty.

We whizzed around the apartment at warp speed, getting dressed for dinner and fielding phone calls. Zooey thought we were playing with her and scampered along, trying to jump on us. By the time she could find her stuffed duck under the couch and present it to us for a game of tug, we were slipping out the door.

We ran the ten blocks back to the theater; Jessica tripped on her girl shoes while Erik, his legs six inches longer, kept turning around and telling her to hurry up. We piled into the theater, breathless, and took the elevator upstairs to find Allan. When we spilled out, whom should we find sauntering through the hallway, toothpick in his mouth, mellow as all get-out, but one Mr. Delbert Tibbs. "Hey, man," he said, nodding his head like an old blues guy and extending his hands to us. We fell all over ourselves asking him what had happened at the airport, trying to make sure everything was okay, terrified that we'd somehow inadvertently stood him up. Turns out his flight had gotten in early; he'd headed outside for a smoke. He was standing by the taxi stand, watching the world go by, while Connie was running around looking for him inside. Eventually, Delbert stubbed out the cigarette and strolled back in. He wandered around for a while, till he thought he heard his name come faintly over the loudspeaker (for the fifth time). He made it into the city just fine.

Soon, all the exonerated folks and their hosts were gathered in the lobby; Allan, looking dapper with a silk scarf draped around his neck, greeted everyone warmly; and we headed to the restaurant where he'd made a reservation, a cozy bohemian SoHo hole-in-the-wall that served hearty and sophisticated Turkish-French fusion cuisine. The host shepherded us in, and we all sat down around a big round table surrounded by exposed brick, weathered wood, and lots of flowers. Allan made a beautiful toast; we beamed. We were proud

Allan had set up the dinner at such a nice place, sure that the exonerated folks would be glad to be fed gourmet food in a chichi SoHo joint. Then they opened up their menus.

Delbert, the big-city guy, scanned his comfortably, looking pleased with the range of choices before him. But everyone else was trying *really hard* to be polite. They tried valiantly to hide it, but we could tell: they thought the food was weird. They were all from the South; they would've loved some ribs, probably, or a good steak. The menu was full of things like tagines and goat cheese and quinoa. Oops. We went through the menu, translating, trying to identify the dishes that most closely approximated things they'd actually enjoy. They were good sports, and when the unfamiliar food arrived, they dug in. But after a couple bottles of wine and two hours of rollicking conversation, we noticed that significant piles of food were left on most people's plates, albeit creatively and artfully rearranged.

Everyone was happy, though; many of the exonerated folks had met briefly at that famous Northwestern University conference a few years back, so they had a starting point with each other. And they all seemed to be getting along really well with their hosts—especially Delbert, who spent most of dinner ensconced in an impassioned conversation with Connie about art and revolution. It was a joy to watch Allan start to get to know all these people he had heard so much about—he was so openhearted with them, and we could see the reality of what he was involved with start to sink in for him. For a couple hours, we got to sit back and watch all these men and women we knew from different areas begin to mesh together. We didn't have to orchestrate anything; the music started happening on its own. For a couple hours, anyway; then we'd go back home and the phone would start ringing again.

* * *

We set the alarm for eight the next morning, although it wasn't really necessary; neither one of us could sleep. Caffeine had become an organic component of our blood by then, not to mention the adrenaline and nervousness that were creeping in. Before the alarm could go off in the morning, the phone rang; it was Jessica's family, calling to say good morning. They'd arrived in the city the night before and were staying at a nearby B and B. They told us to let them know if there was anything they could do to help; otherwise, they'd see us later on that evening at the theater. We were all set.

Then Jessica took a pair of scissors and headed toward the bathroom.

Erik was too busy making coffee to notice; the next thing he heard was loud swearing from the bathroom, and then—was that crying? He rushed in and surveyed the scene: the sink looked like an unswept barbershop floor, Jessica held the scissors in her hand, and her hair, which had previously been in a shaggy, shortish, complexly layered haircut, was now sticking out from her head in horribly uneven chunks. Tears were streaming down her face. Erik looked at her, astonished. "I didn't have time to get a haircut," Jessica stammered.

Erik took Jessica by the arm and said, "Come on. Get dressed."

"Where are we going?" Jessica demanded.

"I'm taking you to my barber," replied Erik.

Jessica threw a fit. They didn't have time! It was a Monday; the salon would be closed! There were all kinds of TV people coming to the show that night! She wasn't letting some hairdresser she didn't know cut her hair! No no no no no! Erik took Jessica by the shoulders and made her look in the mirror at what she had done to her head. "You need someone to fix this," Erik said. Jessica couldn't really argue with that.

We headed down the street to Erik's hairdresser, Leslie, who turned out to know a whole lot more about hair than Erik did. He sat

Jessica right down, and within minutes he and Jessica were off in their own world. Leslie fixed everything; it only took half an hour. And Erik had something to make fun of Jessica about for the next three years.

That disaster averted, we headed over to the theater. When we got there, we were greeted by a strange lack of chaos. The designers were calling out cues; the exonerated folks were out with their hosts; the box office staff was going over the guest list we'd given them; Allan was on the phone with the caterers. We'd been tweaking the script up to the last minute, and while we knew we hadn't written the final, definitive draft, we had something decent enough to put onstage. The scripts were bound, labeled, and stacked. The actors wouldn't show up for rehearsal till three; it was only eleven. There wasn't anything for us to do. We hadn't had that feeling in over six months. It was weird. We sort of stood around, waiting to see if anything was about to explode. It wasn't. Finally we decided we might as well go get something to eat.

Later that afternoon, we came back to the theater to meet Bob Balaban and the actors. Bob was outside on the sidewalk, hunched over, an enormous yellow, plastic Sports Walkman–looking cell phone clasped to his ear: a sight with which we would come to be quite familiar over the next couple years. Eventually, Bob followed us inside, and we took our seats several rows back as the actors trickled in for rehearsal: a couple of our workshop actors, then David Morse, then Tim and Susan. Then one of the actors called to say his train would be late (he was coming from several hours away). Another called to say his kid had the flu and the babysitter had flaked; he couldn't be there till the evening. Erik swallowed hard, climbed up onstage, took a seat, and filled in. He sat under the hot lights, sweating, watching the backs of Tim's and Susan's heads. Erik doesn't remember much of those two hours; he was too busy being terrified that the script was awful. The presence of our workshop actors at least provided an anchor; when it got too scary listening to the words roll around in the big stars' mouths, Erik would just focus on the familiar voices coming through.

Bob gave the actors a few clues; he had them stop and start a little, skip ahead sometimes; a few sections he went cue-to-cue. Mostly he wanted to familiarize them with the text: with eleven exonerated people's stories in play, plus several girlfriends and wives, many of the actors were playing two parts each; the stories were interwoven, so the structure was complicated. Jessica, perched at the back of the theater, got frustrated listening to the stops and starts; she was outside the action enough to be excited rather than terrified, and she wanted the actors to just keep going. Mostly, though, that rehearsal was a blur for both of us: we'd heard that version of the script so many times by then that it was starting to sound nonsensical, like when you stare at a word so long it loses its meaning.

After a couple hours, Bob sent the actors off for dinner; we stayed at the theater, wrung our hands, and watched the press begin to trickle in. Some of the press people knew that exonerated folks would be there that night, but we swore them to secrecy till after the show: the actors and ticket holders had no idea that the subjects of the play were coming. Sunny had gotten into town that afternoon, and now all the exonerated were off with their hosts; they'd be shuttled into the theater right before the lights went down.

By the time the actors got back, the lobby was full of TV crews, and Susan, Tim, and David Morse stood under the lights and talked eloquently about wrongful conviction while we looked on, still wondering whether we'd really pulled this off.

Then the audience started showing up.

We had to hold the doors open till nearly eight twenty, the crowd was so big. It was chaos. The house was more than full; we had to squeeze in folding chairs to accommodate everyone. The TV cameras were still in the lobby; Eames's documentary crew was tracking us as well as several actors and audience members, navigating the crowds. We raced around, greeting the seemingly hundreds of people we knew and recognized: Larry Marshall had flown in from Chicago; Barry Scheck, the well-known attorney, author, and cofounder of the Innocence Project, was there; seemingly everyone who'd helped us get this far was packed into the teeming lobby. Adrenaline was coming out our ears. A couple minutes before the doors closed, we grabbed our tickets and raced into the theater.

Our seats had an obstructed view.

Now, really, in the grand scheme of things, this was not a big deal. But in that moment, it sure felt like one to Jessica. We didn't know if the play would go anywhere after these readings; all our work had so far been directed toward this night. This was it. After all the buildup, Jessica found the notion that she wouldn't actually be able to *see* the performance heartbreaking. The stress and the nervousness and the speed of things got the better of her, and she threw a little temper tantrum. Not a big one; it probably wouldn't have been audible or visible to anyone more than a foot or two away. Except that when we turned around, there were Eames's cameras—pointed straight at us. Impulsively—and ridiculously—we both held our hands up in front of the cameras as if we were fending off paparazzi. Eames graciously pointed his camera in the other direction—but our absurd stressed-out behavior had already been captured on film for all eternity.

Just before the lights went down, we wound up giving up our obstructed-view seats and sitting on the floor of the aisle up by the sound booth. We took a deep breath as the lights dimmed and the music started.

For one hundred minutes, the actors channeled the stories of eleven exonerated people while the audience watched. It was brand-new for us: as actors, we'd both always been on the other side of things. When you're onstage, you can feel the audience, but you don't think about them; you just focus on what you're doing, the actions you're carrying out, your interactions with the other characters. But this was different. Sitting in the back of the theater, we could see the audience take in the play—it felt as if we were watching them watch *us*. For Jessica, it was invigorating. She was fascinated to see the audience respond en masse to moments we'd gone over and over in our heads and on paper. They laughed at the things we thought were funny; sometimes they gasped; sometimes they reacted in ways we would never have predicted. For Erik, it was terrifying. He sat there sweating, scanning the audience for sleeping theatergoers, watching like a hawk to see if anyone was shifting in his or her seat. Erik was petrified that the audience would hate what we'd written, completely unable to tell if it was any good or not, how people were actually responding. For the entire performance, he dug his nails into his palms, waiting to see if the audience would boo or cheer.

When the last words were spoken and the lights came up, Erik's fears were finally assuaged: the audience applauded wholeheartedly, and many stood. They clapped for a long time. Then Allan took the stage, quieting the audience. He introduced Larry Marshall, who stood up, announcing that he had some special guests to present. One by one, Larry brought up the six exonerated people who were with us: Sunny, Randal, Kerry, Brad, Robert, and Delbert.

The audience jumped to their feet and roared. The actors—totally shocked to find out that their alter egos were in the audience—started weeping. The exonerated folks joined the actors onstage; the audience went on applauding at top volume for what seemed like five minutes.

Neither of us expected how that moment would feel. We knew it would be powerful, but we had no idea how intense it would be to see everything come together like that: art and life, the play we'd put together and the real people it was based on. We clenched each other's hands as chills ripped through us. We both had goose bumps; tears streamed down our faces. It was the highest moment of either of our lives.

Compounding the intensity was our knowledge that some of the exonerated folks onstage were shunned by their communities, unable to shake the stigma that clung to them like shadows. Not here, though. Tonight, in this theater, they were getting a standing ovation from movie stars. We breathed deeply as we watched these incredibly courageous souls get the respect they so deserved. It wasn't justice—but it was a start.

Afterward, we had a party upstairs in Allan's loft. We had intended to keep it small—just the actors, the exonerated, and people who'd helped the play come into being—so that the exonerated folks and the actors would have a chance to get to know each other a little without being mobbed. We were expecting a quiet little cocktail party; but even though we kept it to the guest list, it got pretty big and loud. We didn't realize just how many people had been part of making this play happen.

The actors and the exonerated people they played talked and talked—and talked. Susan and Sunny went off in a corner for what seemed like hours, deep in conversation with each other, immune to the rest of the room. Tim slung his arm around Randal's shoulder; Randal beamed. Even though J. K. Simmons had a flu-stricken kid at home, he stayed for a while, talking it up with Brad. David Morse stood with Kerry and Sandra, holding little Justice in his arms.

It was incredible to watch the effect meeting the real exonerated had on the actors. David Brown Jr., one of our most dedicated workshop actors, had been playing Robert for the past two months; now, we could see the reality of it hit him on a whole new level. He didn't leave Robert's side the entire night. And the extraordinary Charles Dutton had come in earlier that evening seeming overworked and a little skeptical of the goings-on; we'd had little contact with Charles before the performance, and it seemed like he was reserving judgment on whether we had really done justice to the subject matter. He gave his all as an actor, but we weren't sure how much he liked us or our work. But as soon as Charles saw Delbert stand up in the audience, his eyes lit up. His heart opened wide; Charles talked and joked for hours not only with Delbert, but with all the exonerated. He stayed at the party till literally everyone else had gone home, smiling for cameras, talking to press, and most of all giving the exonerated folks his undivided attention. He was extraordinarily generous.

Everyone was. That party was nothing like your typical Manhattan fancy-pants opening-night cocktail party, full of air-kisses and schmoozing. The interactions that happened in that room were deep and real and human, informed by the weight and joy that had passed between the actors and the exonerated and the audience. These were real people's lives being communicated and touched and transformed: three years later, we would be back at Randal and Brenda's Alabama home and see nearly ten photos from that evening, arranged impeccably in gold and wooden frames, above their bed.

Chapter Fifteen

After that first performance, the rest seemed relatively easy. Two more readings at the theater, on November 6 and 13, both sold out, with casts that included Steve Buscemi, Vincent D'Onofrio, William Fichtner, Cherry Jones, Martha Plimpton, and several other incredible actors. At the start of the reading on the sixth—the day before Election Day—Allan got up to introduce the show. He talked for a few minutes about the suspense in the air that evening, how next week's reading would carry a whole new set of connotations and associations, depending on the outcome of the elections. Even though both presidential candidates were pro–death penalty, Bush's extreme record and position on the issue were in a category all their own.

After the experience of last week's reading, we had a new sense of what a blow it would be to thousands of people if Bush were to become president. A palpable tension infused the audience; whichever way it went, we all knew that tomorrow's decision would powerfully impact the lens through which the play was viewed.

The next week, though, the same tension was still in the air. The 2000 election result was of course unexpected; everyone had assumed that we'd have the answer on Election Day. It was surreal; as the audience filed in for the performance on the thirteenth, it was like being in exactly the same place we'd been a week earlier, except with a different cast onstage. Allan said something to this effect as he introduced the show; his remarks got a big—and heavily loaded—laugh. We were in the midst of unprecedented political events, and over and over again the play reminded us how deeply those events would impact people's lives. When Gary Gauger and his wife, Sue—who'd taken a couple days away from the farm to fly in and see the show—stood up at the end of the second performance, it hit home for the audience, too.

As the electoral chaos unfolded, we were asked to present a fourth reading, at the United Nations. For that performance, in late November 2000, Eve Battaglia and Bob Balaban put together a cast that included Ossie Davis, Arliss Howard, Parker Posey, David Strathairn, and Debra Winger; Gabriel Byrne and Marisa Berenson introduced the play. The reading took place in a U.N. auditorium, complete with sixties architecture and orange and brown carpeting. The marble halls leading into the auditorium looked just like all the pictures we'd seen of the United Nations in magazines and newspapers. Many U.N. staffers attended, in addition to members of the public; it was pretty incredible to us to imagine that this play was being performed for people whose everyday actions could impact events internationally. Sunny came back for this performance, along with her boyfriend, Peter, an exonerated death row inmate from Ireland, just as joyful and strong as Sunny. Peter is the very picture of an Irish fisherman, with a ruddy face, snow-white hair and beard, and a thick brogue. The musician Steve Earle introduced Sunny and Peter at the end of the performance; both spoke, their presence together onstage reinforcing the international scope of the event.

After the U.N. reading, we finally had a chance to step back and look at what had happened over the past several months. Up till now, we had been aware of what we were doing from moment to moment, but everything kept happening so fast that we didn't have much time to think about the big picture. The intensity and speed with which we were working forced us to exist totally in the immediate present and didn't allow us any room to think about past or future. We were constantly being thrown new challenges, and it took our full attention just to meet them one by one. Even at the most expansive point—when the exonerated folks stood up at the end of the first reading and everything came together—the moment was so overwhelming that we couldn't really think about anything beyond what we felt right there, right then.

But now, all those events that we'd been hurtling toward for half a year were over. All the moments had added up; we'd pulled it off. After sleeping for about four days straight, we woke up and surveyed the new life we'd created in the last several months. The last time we'd lived at normal speed, we were a couple of comfortable, mid-level actors, leading familiar, emotionally easy lives, who'd just met and started to sort of like each other. Now we were collaborators about to get married; playwrights as well as actors; stretched so far beyond our comfort zones that those old boundaries had ceased to exist.

Our view of the country we lived in had been deepened, transformed, made immeasurably complex. Our own relationship had been boiled down, accelerated, concentrated, as we'd struggled hard about what was most important to both of us, thrown manners out the window, duked it out. Now we knew each other inside out. We'd covered a lot of territory together in the last several months. We felt entirely changed, with a whole new set of relationships to people we'd never thought we'd know, and a brand-new, almost overwhelming sense of responsibility.

And then there was the future of the play. The readings made it evident that the play needed to continue; that it should have a full production in New York. Although several producers, attracted by the readings, had approached us, it was also clear to us that the 45 Bleecker Theater was the play's home, and that Allan and Bob should be at the helm of any future production. They were there with us when the exonerated stood up and everyone cheered; they understood what was at stake and cared deeply about the real people involved. That understanding and care made it obvious that we couldn't entrust the future of the play to anyone else, no matter what kind of offers were dangled in front of us.

It was also clear that the script wasn't finished. It was strong enough to have made an impact, but we knew it needed surgery. Our audiences had been quite responsive; people had approached us after each reading to say how moved they were by the stories, how spurred to ask new questions, how disturbed and touched and opened up. But over and over, they also asked the same question: *How does this happen?* Audiences understood *what* had happened to the people portrayed in the play, and they understood how the events had made the exonerated *feel*. But people couldn't see *how* this had happened to these people, how the system could go so terribly wrong. They were confused; they wanted to know more about the cases, what had happened at the trials, how justice could be subverted so seriously in a system that prides itself on its fairness. They didn't understand.

We knew this was due, in part, to the way we had structured the script. All the stories we'd heard had impacted us so strongly; we had wanted to include as many of them as we possibly could. Any of them that didn't double each other, that translated powerfully to the stage, we'd incorporated into the script. But now, as we grappled with the question "How does this happen?" we realized that we were trying to tell too many stories. We regretfully concluded that to fully explain what had happened in each case, we had to reduce the number of stories we were presenting. We were so attached to all of them, but there was just no way to fully tell eleven complicated stories, spanning up to twenty-two years each, in a ninety-minute play.

We decided to cut the number of stories in half. We picked the six stories we felt were most representative—not just of demographic qualities like race, gender, and geography, but of other factors, too. We chose some people who had support from their families and communities, and others who'd lost everyone. We chose some who'd spent three or four years in prison, another who spent twenty-two; some folks who'd had brushes with the law, and others who were as squeaky-clean as you could possibly imagine. We chose some people who had been wrongly convicted of killing people they knew well, others who were hauled in for the murders of people they'd never even met, and one who was at the scene and actually witnessed the crime for which she was wrongly convicted. We chose lots of different personalities. We tried to cover as much emotional territory as possible, selecting people who had processed their experiences in wildly varying ways.

We also took pains to use more than one case in which the accused was also a family member of a victim—Gary Gauger was accused of the murder of his parents; Kerry Max Cook's brother had been murdered (in an unrelated case); and Sunny Jacobs's husband was executed, just two years before Sunny was exonerated on the grounds that a third man had likely acted alone. We wanted to make sure the play didn't contribute to the polarization between victims and the accused. We wanted to illustrate that sometimes they're the same.

After much agonizing, we decided to hold on to the stories of Kerry Max Cook, Gary Gauger, Robert Earl Hayes, Sunny Jacobs, David Keaton, and Delbert Tibbs.

Without editing, it's impossible for good writing to exist. It's said that writers have to be willing to kill their children—to cut anything that doesn't serve the text, ruthlessly, no matter how much they love it, no matter how precious it is. Nowhere is that more true than in the case of writers who are trying to fashion a ninety-minute work—about forty-five single-spaced pages—from literally thousands of pages of material. Creating this play was like carving a statue out of a huge mass of rock. Had we not been willing to chip away at it ruthlessly, we would have been left with rough edges, undefined lines, coarse masses of words. We could not, without that kind of decision-making, have created a play with the ability to impact people's emotions, opinions, and lives. As writers, we had to cut those stories. But because this play deals so directly and intimately with the lives of real people, it has never been an ordinary piece of writing. And we didn't realize, when we halved the number of stories, that it would be hurtful to some of the folks whose stories were cut. Had we understood that, we would have handled the situation with kid gloves, called them immediately, broken the news gently. At the time, we looked at the cuts as just part of the writing process. In hindsight it seems obvious that, for some of the exonerated folks, it would be much more than that. Our one major regret—our biggest failing during the making of the play—is that we didn't realize that at the time and thus didn't act accordingly. Though we had promised no one that his or her story would definitely wind up in the play, the people who we'd flown to New York had all felt part of the play's brand-new community; they may have felt betrayed by our cutting their stories. Our only explanation is that we'd never done this before; we didn't know, we didn't predict people's feelings carefully enough, and we made a mistake. We want to extend an apology in print to anyone whose feelings we might have hurt. If it's any consolation, we learned something from our mistake and have tried to evolve from the experience. Please know that we so deeply value all the stories that we heard, and the courage it took to tell them.

After we settled on which stories would remain in the play, we faced the task of presenting those cases in more depth and detail. We knew we had to stick with words that were actually said by real people; anything else would undermine the play's impact—but we wanted to present the cases in ways that were compelling and that didn't come from just a single point of view. So far, the play contained only monologues culled from the interviews we'd done with the exonerated. We knew we needed to expand our sources beyond that. We hit upon the idea of going to the trial transcripts and working with that text to create scenes.

Around the same time, Bob said he'd like to meet with us to talk about where the play was headed. We took the train up to a café on the Upper West Side to sit down with him; over granola and yogurt, Bob leaned in and said, "I think what you guys should do is cut the number of stories and go back into the court transcripts to find more material. From the transcripts, you can construct scenes. That'll theatricalize the play, give it some movement, some energy. If you do that, I'd love to be involved with the future of the play." Clearly, this was the right direction to go.

At first, we thought finding the transcripts would be easy. We started by calling all the lawyers we had relationships with: we called Paul Nugent, Kerry's lawyer; Barbara Heyer, who'd been Robert's attorney; Larry Marshall, who'd represented Gary; and Kent Spriggs, David's lawyer. We didn't know Sunny's attorneys and couldn't find the public defender who'd represented Delbert, so we left those for later. We asked the lawyers we spoke to for any material they might have kept. Most of them had their closing arguments, as well as assorted briefs and motions, and Paul had kept almost everything—over 150,000 pages of material. (He sent us the opening and closing arguments from each of Kerry's three trials; we were still broke and didn't have money to pay what it would have cost to copy and ship the whole thing.) The rest of the lawyers mailed us what they had, and their assistants spent lots of time on the phone with us, explaining how we should go about acquiring the rest of the material.

Court transcripts are supposed to be public records. That's the law, and it's the law for a reason—it keeps everything out in the open, so any citizen can examine the events of a trial, so the people who run the system know they're being watched by the rest of us. Concealment breeds abuse: when the powerful are allowed to conduct their business in secret, they're no longer accountable to the people. That's why one of the hallmarks of a free society is an open court system—and an open court system includes court documents being available to be examined by anyone who cares to do so. In America, we have that kind of open system—according to the law.

But in reality, we found, court documents are *really hard* to get your hands on.

As we made phone call after phone call to track down the transcripts, we discovered that this is yet another area where the way the system works on paper is vastly different from the way it plays out in the real world. We should have been able to call the courthouses where the trials took place, pay a reasonable fee for copying and postage, and receive any documents we requested. Instead, we got responses like "Well, but that case was an acquittal in the second trial, and we don't make a transcript for a not-guilty verdict." Or: "We destroy the records after five years." Or: "If you want that, you're going to have to call the judge, but he's retired and moved to Texas two years ago. No, I don't know his number." We even got a letter from a court reporter who—even though these documents are supposed to be available to anyone who requests them—had gotten wind of what we were doing and sent our check back, claiming that she wanted to keep the records to herself so she could write her own book or movie! When she thought we were law students or paralegals, it was hunky-dory, but bring storytelling and the "entertainment industry" in and people get weird. They start to think that there are fortunes to be had (there usually aren't), and that their fifteen minutes of fame are just around the corner. It even makes them write and sign letters denying access to records—when the denial of that access is against the basic tenets of our supposedly transparent legal system.

But even when people were willing to grant us access, the elusive records were stuffed in the backs of musty warehouses, hidden under piles of cardboard boxes, unmarked. In some counties, the only people who had access to the transcripts were private court-reporting companies, who charged five dollars *per page* for copies (a trial can run up to fifty or seventy-five thousand pages). Every state had a different system from the next; within each state, all the counties operated differently; none of it was computerized, and none of it was cheap. On paper, all the documents we needed were part of the public record. In reality, they were all but inaccessible to the average citizen.

We must've spent a hundred hours on the phone with Broward County, Florida, and McHenry County, Illinois; with circuit court in Texas and district court in Florida. Lucky for us, we had sold one of Erik's guitars and yet more books, scraping together enough cash to cover the long-distance bills; we had time to spend on the phone, we weren't in a big rush, and ultimately we only needed the transcripts to make art with. We could only imagine how difficult it must be for an innocent person, locked up, who needed access to court documents to make the case for her freedom—and who was unable to sit on the phone, to call up twelve retired court reporters, to pay fifty dollars for a records search and another several hundred in photocopy fees.

We pieced together what we could from our initial requests of the attorneys, and we had some small successes ordering things over the phone—a brief here, a motion there. But when we put it all together, we hadn't gotten anywhere close to what we needed. We'd learned through our research that a lot of the records were stored at the county courthouses on microfiche, or in warehouses nearby; we could go through them ourselves for free and make copies of the ones we wanted for relatively cheap.

Time to hit the road again.

Chapter Sixteen

We had structured the initial readings as benefits. And though we hadn't promised anyone any financial reward—and although there was no actual profit to distribute—the exonerated people all got a shiny new check. The rest of the proceeds had gone to pay for lumber, advertising, box office staff, hotels for the exonerated people, and other expenses related directly to the evening. Allan actually lost money on the readings, but he didn't complain once. Bob and the actors had waived their fees as well; so had a lot of volunteer ushers, designers, and envelope lickers.

So our bank account was pretty drained; we needed to conserve what little money we had for transcript fees and records searches.

Also, Erik had gotten a role in a Martin Lawrence comedy (playing, naturally, a bumbling revolutionary who gets wrongly locked up in a dungeon and sentenced to death) and was about to be stuck in Wilmington, North Carolina, for three months without any real freedom to travel. We scrutinized our calendar and our savings account, trying to figure out a way to get to all the counties where the cases had been tried; but financially and time-wise, we just couldn't make it work. We had to prioritize.

Paul Nugent had almost all the material from Kerry's trials, so Texas got knocked off the list first. And we'd had zero luck with Delbert's documents: his defense attorney had died, we'd discovered, and we weren't about to call the prosecutor to ask for help. Also, Delbert had no idea what his case number was, and without a case number it's virtually impossible to track records in a case. His trial had taken place a *long* time ago, and any newspaper articles that would have given us the specific dates or other leads had long since deteriorated. We dug into LexisNexis for some details, but we needed to make certain that all of our material came strictly from the public record. We didn't know how we were going to find Delbert's records, but we knew traveling to look for them would be an expensive wild-goose chase.

Larry Marshall had given us his summary of Gary's case, which contained significant excerpts from his trial, as well as documentation of his interrogation; that was enough to work with, for now. And the folks at the courthouse near Quincy, Florida, had told us that all their records from David's case—which was over twenty years old by then—had been destroyed. That left Sunny and Robert—both of whose cases had been tried in Broward County. We scraped together enough money for two plane tickets, and three months after the election fiascoes that made south Florida famous, we were headed down to meet the bureaucrats of Broward.

We had four days. Our schedules didn't allow for any more wiggle room, and we couldn't afford to be away from home for longer than that. But we could do it; we'd just spend all day, every day, becoming really good friends with the microfiche.

We crashed with an old friend of Jessica's, Bekah, and her husband, Ken, both Unitarian ministers. They lived in a big high-rise in a forest of angular, glinting-glass high-rises, right next to the beach, in Hollywood—about a half hour's drive from the Broward County clerk's office. We flew to Fort Lauderdale, rented a car, and drove into the weird world of south Florida, with its condos and construction and retirement communities, its swimming pools right beside the ocean, every inch of land developed all the way up to the white sand and palm trees. It was February; it was eighty-five degrees. In our grungy East Village clothes, we were almost as out of place there as we had been in Alabama. Bekah and Ken didn't think so, though; they greeted us warmly, broke out the air mattress in the living room, and cooked us white-bean soup. We did our best to fall asleep early; we had to be at the clerk's office the next day at 8 a.m. sharp.

The alarm woke us up at six. We hadn't been up that early for months, and we grumped at each other all the way to the IHOP, where the coffee helped us gradually become nice again. We got lost on the way to the clerk's office, but finally we found it, on the fringes of downtown, in a neighborhood that was all sleek office buildings and Starbucks on one side, trash-strewn, weedy train tracks on the other. The clerk's office was right in between, a tiny, squat sixties brick building surrounded by asphalt.

Inside, a tiny counter was separated into two sections: one for criminal trial records, the other for birth, death, and wedding certificates. The records-request form we filled out had space for criminal-record queries on one side, and marriage-certificate requests on the other. It was weird, the way Broward was weird. The office had rust-colored carpeting; the walls were painted a sort of khaki; the microfiche machines were ancient and brown. It looked like a school library from 1974. The staff stared as we walked in; we found the friendliest face, gave her the case numbers, and told her that we needed to go through the entire case file for each one. We didn't explain why. The staff assumed we were law students; we said nothing to contradict their assumptions.

They hauled out the microfiche files on each case, showed us how to thread them through the machine, scroll through the pages, and which button to press to get a page to print out. It cost a dollar a page; we were supposed to keep track of the number of printouts we made, check that number against an oft-broken counter on the side of the machine, and write a check when we were done.

The case files were *huge*. They contained portions of the trial transcripts, as well as all the motions—at least fifty or sixty for each case—and every piece of written material that had been entered into evidence, including depositions, letters, and partial transcripts of police interrogations. We sat ourselves down in the seventies orange plastic chairs and started in on Robert's case file.

After we slogged through twenty or so motions, struggling to decipher the legal language, we got to the depositions and the transcripts of police interviews. During an investigation, the police interview all potential witnesses in a case; they then turn over the results of the investigation to the prosecution. Then the prosecution takes depositions from many of the same people. Later, the prosecution is required to turn over this evidence to the defense, which can then take its own depositions from the witnesses it chooses. In Robert's case, the prosecution and police talked to quite a few workers at the racetrack where the crime had occurred—there must've been over fifty interviews and depositions from those workers, each one running around twenty-five pages. The clerk's office closed at four, and it took us until then to get through that first group.

Reading them, it started to become clear to us how Robert had been convicted at his first trial. Those interviews were full of gossip and hearsay; most of the track workers were eager to help the police and racked their brains to come up with anything they could think of about Robert that seemed the least bit suspicious. Several of the workers were clearly swept up in the drama and excitement of the investigation, painting with broad strokes, offering highly embellished opinions, making theatrical, melodramatic statements. The racetrack was clearly a gossip-fueled environment, and all kinds of rumors and opinions floated around. Many of the white workers said they'd "heard" things about Robert. Fistfights were common at the tracks; Robert had a temper, which fueled endless speculation. People brought up questionable or violent incidents that happened at other racetracks Robert had worked at, offering these as a rationale for suspecting him of murder—while completely neglecting to acknowledge that a huge number of workers follow races from track to track, and any of those people could have been the thread that connected those incidents. Some of the workers even strayed off the topic of Robert and gossiped about each other in their interviews. It wasn't immediately obvious, reading the transcripts, which subjects were white and which were black; but the way that investigators questioned the workers offered some clues, as did the position that each worker held. Some people tried to broach the subject of racism at the track in their interviews, but were passively rebuffed. Here it was again, this ugly side of America rearing up and staring at us. At the tracks, whites tended to work as vet assistants, bartenders, security guards; while blacks generally worked as stable hands, grooms, and janitors. The police, it seemed, conducted a less formal kind of questioning with the whites while seeming to doubt, contradict, or pass over statements made by African-Americans that didn't match up with their theories.

Put together, we could see how those depositions—and a case built on their more inflammatory contents—could trigger suspicion in a jury. We even got sucked into some of the rumors ourselves—until we went back and reread the depositions, this time critically, and noticed that virtually none of them contained actual facts directly related to the case. It was opinion, conjecture, and guesswork; not evidence.

At four, the staff came in and started putting the chairs up, switching off lights. We got the message. We gathered up our copies and staggered out, our eyes burning, our muscles stiff, and our brains overfull. We both felt toxic and scared—reading Robert's case file, we'd been immersed in the events of the investigation, and it was dark stuff. We could see how the violence and rumormongering of the racetrack culture had contributed to Robert's arrest and, we surmised, his conviction as well. As our eyes had flicked across the microfiche screens, we'd temporarily gotten absorbed in that culture, and now the rawness of it combined with the burnout from eight hours in front of the machines and no food made us feel creepy and irritable. Emerging from the records room was a very different feeling from coming out of an interview: darker; more abstract, less human.

We slept heavily that night. In the morning, we dragged ourselves back to the clerk's office and planted ourselves in front of Robert's case file again. The documents were organized chronologically; as we plowed ahead, we began to notice what information came out in the police investigation, what emerged at the first trial, and what came to light during the second trial. For example, early on we found a deposition from the forensic hair expert who had investigated the crime scene, saying that he had been instructed by his superiors to search the scene only for "Negro hairs" and to ignore all others—including, apparently, the fistful of Caucasian hair that the victim was found clutching. We read that deposition the first day; but as we continued reading, it looked to us as if that information wasn't made fully clear to jurors until Robert's second trial in 1997. And we were able to follow the way Robert's attorney, Barbara, had tracked down Scott, the racetrack worker who, by the time of Robert's second trial, had been convicted of an eerily similar rape-murder in Ohio. Then we backtracked to the initial interview that police had conducted with Scott—and realized that said interview had not yielded any real information as to his whereabouts the night of the murder. The questions were not as probing as they should have been. Scott's answers seemed short, abrupt, not overly helpful—as distinguished from those of the dozens of other witnesses whom police had questioned. A chill ran up our spines.

Reading the case file, we traced the paths of evidence to identify when prosecutors knew things and when the defense found them out; to track a piece of information from the time it was first discovered to when it finally came out in trial, years later. On the page, we watched Barbara work for years to finally be allowed to present certain pieces of information to a jury. We realized how clogged the arteries of the system are, how information that should be flowing freely instead gets blocked, stopped, gummed up.

In the early afternoon, the clerk lugged in several more cardboard boxes containing additional case material; apparently only part of Robert's case file had been put on microfiche, and she'd turned the rest up in a warehouse. We pulled our bloodshot eyeballs away from the machines long enough to count the cardboard boxes: there were five. We were only halfway through the microfiche. We had just two more days here, and we hadn't even started on Sunny's case file yet.

We decided to divide our forces; Erik continued to go through Robert's case, copying the most pertinent documents, while Jessica started in on Sunny's.

Erik didn't get far, though: right away, Jessica started gasping every few minutes, telling Erik he *had* to come look at what she'd just found. Sunny's case file was incredibly dramatic. Sunny had been at the scene of the crime, and after the murder Walter Rhodes (who later, in a letter, confessed to being the sole killer) had taken Sunny, her husband, Jesse, and the kids at gunpoint on a wild ride, which ended only when he crashed into a police roadblock. Everyone was hauled to the station and questioned immediately, including Sunny's nine-year-old son; portions of those initial interrogations were preserved in the case file, and they were transcribed word for word, pause for pause. These were incredibly loaded; emotion seeped off the pages. Hearing Sunny tell us her story had been intense enough, even twenty-three years after the fact. But reading a word-for-word record of what had actually happened—what the cops said as they leaned on Sunny; how she broke down and begged them not to take her kids away; how, terrified, Sunny at first tried to claim that Rhodes and Jesse were strangers who'd picked her up hitchhiking—was overwhelming. The interrogation of her son was even more disturbing. Why had these men questioned a nine-year-old? It was not at all clear from this transcript that this child had a lawyer present. Were the police pursuing convictions based on evidence, or would they stoop to coercing a child to make the evidence match a predetermined conclusion? It was hard to tell.

The case file also included the text of Sunny's death sentence, in which the judge said, "You are hereby sentenced to die by lethal injection. You will have twenty-five hundred volts of electricity run through your body until you are dead." Sunny had talked with us about how stunned she had felt when her sentence was handed down;

but reading the sentence ourselves, seeing the actual words, dated and signed, we got an eerie glimpse of how shattering it actually was.

And then we got to the letters from Rhodes. The dates on the first few weren't too long after Sunny's conviction, but they kept coming: there were lots of them, spanning years and years. Over and over, Rhodes—who had pled guilty to a reduced charge and received three life sentences in exchange for immunity from the death penalty—sent letters through official channels, detailing how he had been the only one responsible for the murder. He changed the particulars of his story several times, and he would always retreat at the last minute, refusing to testify on the stand; but there it was in the file: repeated confessions from Rhodes, trying to make peace with his "creator," absolving Sunny and Jesse of guilt. It took seventeen years before those confessions could come to light sufficiently for Sunny to be freed—and by then it was too late for Jesse. He was executed two years before Sunny was released.

Neither of us had ever experienced anything that even approximated the feeling of going through those case files. The interviews had been intense, but each one still took the familiar form of a conversation. The stories we heard changed our lives, but the process itself—of listening to someone tell a story—wasn't unfamiliar. Reading these case files was.

When the exonerated people told us their stories, the events were filtered through their consciousness, organized by history. Now, reading the transcripts, with the intermediary of a storyteller removed, we were somehow getting even closer to the actual events. We were examining the detritus of incidents that had caused immeasurable upheaval in so many people's lives. We felt like archaeologists. The order of the documents followed the order of the real events, tracing their outlines; reading them, we were plunged headfirst into the worlds of the investigations and trials. It was all there, all so immediate: Rhodes's real letters confessing to the crime. Sunny's real words as she was being interrogated. Robert's letters to the judge from prison, asserting his innocence. The exact sentences the judges uttered condemning Sunny and Robert—and the words the jury foremen uttered years later, reversing the convictions and setting them free. Those words carried so much weight, so much history. They were like fingerprints, marks that the events themselves had left behind. Their *realness* was overwhelming. Reading the transcripts was almost like being there in the courtroom, the interrogation rooms, the places where all those letters had been written and received. We'd never had this kind of window in.

The emotional effect it had on us was exhausting—and we knew it was just a vague shadow of what it must've been like to actually be part of the events. We spent the rest of our time in Broward dazed, not talking much, just trying to get all the way through the files, taking in more and more. It got hard to process after a while, but we knew that once the emotional overload wore off, we could utilize this material to bring a whole new dimension to the play. In the initial version, we had wanted to share with our audience the experience we'd had as we conducted the initial interviews: the feeling of sitting down with someone and hearing them tell a story that opens your heart, upends your assumptions, breaks open your view of the world. We still wanted our audience to have that experience; the text we'd culled from the interviews would remain primary, first-person storytelling the heart and spine of the play. But now we had an additional experience to bring to our audiences: this feeling of being *in the room*, the immediacy and weight that lived in words taken from the actual events. The words carried a trace of the power of the events themselves, gave us a vicarious, visceral understanding of what had happened in each of these cases. Reading them was haunting; seeing them performed, we hoped, would be even more so.

Chapter Seventeen

We returned from Florida with several hundred pages of material. The overload gradually wore off, and as we read and reread the material we'd gotten, we started to think about which parts of it might translate well to the stage. Not long after we got back, Erik had to leave for North Carolina; Jessica held down the fort at home, acting in New York and continuing to gather transcript material for the remaining four cases.

Almost nowhere are transcripts and case files stored in computers, so what we got was all hard copy, and Jessica—with the help of our newest intern, Zoe Tanenbaum, a spunky, smart Harvard student—began the long task of retyping it. Our plan was to workshop the court transcripts in much the same way as we had workshopped the interview text: working with actors to refine and condense the material. We'd edited the interview text into monologues; now we would edit the court transcripts into scenes: between defense and prosecution, accused and interrogator, judge and jury. But before we could begin to workshop it, we had to gather it all—in the end, we would amass more than 250,000 pages of material—and enter a lot of it into our computer.

We also had some other things to do before we could begin the next round of workshops: our wedding was in three months. We were too broke to visit each other more than twice before then, so we spent lots of time on the phone, seamlessly switching topics of conversation between the feasibility of doing a records search in Plano, Texas, and the prudence of having an all-vegetarian menu at a wedding that would include grandparents. Erik's father, on hearing of the meat-free nuptials, threatened to bring prepackaged beef and demand that the chef cook it just for him. The idea of Steve Jensen slipping a steak into our veggie wedding lit the fuse for faraway-fight number one. So Erik gesticulated from his chair atop a fake moat in North Carolina while Jessica, with her mom on the other line, tried to decide if the Robert's Supreme Court order overturning his conviction was more gripping than Sunny's. It was bizarre, to say the least.

Jessica was occasionally ticked off that Erik wasn't around to keep lists of florists and guests, but again, actors don't get to argue with their shooting schedules—and even if Erik had been home, Jessica would've probably just bossed him around and then done it all the way she wanted to anyway. Erik dutifully did his best to follow wedding orders from a thousand miles away, Jessica faxed him copies of new transcript material as it came in, he edited it in the hotel bar at night, and in this way our life in the three months leading up to our wedding became a strange mishmash of capital murder cases and floral arrangements, and we almost didn't have time to be nervous. Almost.

The three months Erik was filming sped by, and we all worked our butts off on the wedding, and pretty soon we were on Block Island, a little island off the coast of Rhode Island, getting married in a meadow on a ninety-degree June day surrounded by a circle of seventy of our closest friends and family members. That, to this day, is the only moment we've experienced that tops the moment at the end of the first reading, when the audience rose up for the exonerated folks. Bekah—Jessica's old friend whom we'd stayed with in Florida—conducted the ceremony, which the two of us wrote together. One of our better collaborations. We'd hardly had a chance to breathe in the last year, let alone step back and take stock, but in the middle of the circle of our family on that June day, the whirlwind slowed enough that the air around us was still. Everyone stayed on the island for the whole weekend; we remember every second.

After the wedding, we took a five-week honeymoon. The only thing Erik had in common at this point with George W. Bush was that Erik had never traveled abroad—despite his protestations that he'd "been to Canada," which Jessica insisted didn't count—and Jessica wanted to take him to some of the places in Europe where she'd backpacked around. But she also wanted to go somewhere new, and Erik wanted to go somewhere non-Western. So we came up with an itinerary that covered all the bases: we flew into Amsterdam and headed south by train, stopping in Paris and Madrid, then took the boat from Spain to Morocco. We traveled in Morocco on the cheap for almost three weeks, spending our days in the labyrinthine medinas and our nights under the huge desert sky, smoking apple-flavored tobacco with Moroccan families in Fez, getting as far off the tourist map as we could and immersing ourselves in a culture that stretched our imaginations and understandings further than they'd ever been stretched.

One afternoon, in a corridor four or five twists and turns off Fez's main drag, we were pulled into an amazing secret world when a man who'd stopped us to paint traditional wedding henna on Jessica's hands invited us to stay with his family for dinner. Honored by his generosity, we spent the afternoon playing with his kids, trading jokes in French, and eating couscous. After a while, he asked us what we did for a living; we were actors, we told him, but right now we were writing a play, too. We didn't have the French to fully explain the subject matter, so we just said the play was about "justice." His ears pricked up: Was this Allah's justice, or man's justice? he asked. Man's, we replied. Ah, he said. God's justice was like an arrow: it went straight to the heart and always achieved its objective. Man's justice, he said, was none of those things. It was misguided and jealous and often caused more problems than it solved. If we remembered the difference and strove for God's justice, he said, our lives would be blessed. He then went on to tell radical-feminist us that he hoped we would return the following year, that Jessica would be pregnant, and that the child would be a boy. We tried, in French, to explain that our work was our child, at least for now. We got intensely quizzical stares from everyone at the table. "That's up to God, too?" said Erik. "*Oui, exactement*," our Moroccan friend replied.

Afterward, we made our way back up to Amsterdam, stopping in the French Pyrenees on the way. We actually had to *leave the country* to stop working on the play long enough to have a honeymoon. We're glad we did. We came back with our minds and hearts expanded by a whole new set of adventures, wondering how they would seep into our work when we returned.

In early August, we arrived back in New York, slept off the jet lag, and started making preparations to go back into workshops. We spent a month or so organizing our transcript materials, compiling an updated list of workshop actors, refining the monologues, and identifying what materials we still lacked. By now, we'd tracked down transcripts for all the exonerated folks—except Delbert. Not only was his defense attorney dead, but none of our other leads had panned out. We'd been trying to get Delbert's material for six months now, and realistically, we were realizing it wasn't going to happen. We'd turned up one lead: a ninth-degree black-belt conspiracy theorist who'd been compiling material on Delbert's prosecutor for years. This guy supposedly had a garage filled with all sorts of papers, pictures, transcripts, and the like. But every time we called him, he'd sound off for several minutes and wind up referring to his perpetually under-construction website. He was obviously extremely dedicated and intelligent, but he was also a little territorial about his materials. Finally, after a last-ditch effort to bribe him for access to his files, we gave up. We admired his crusade, but our Batman-and-Robin style did not suit his go-it-alone Superman kung fu.

We were really stressed-out about it; the total lack of coherent case material on Delbert seemed to ruin the vision we had constructed for the final version of the play. But as we wrestled with what to do about that, we realized that maybe there was another way to handle things. Maybe Delbert's story could come entirely out of his mouth, and we didn't need to dramatize scenes from his courtroom battle. That courtroom stuff wasn't really the most important aspect of his story, anyway: Delbert was a philosopher and a poet, with so much insight into the roots and effects of wrongful conviction, a highly articulated political and spiritual metaview. Already, we knew his mode of storytelling differed from that of the others. Maybe we could solve the problem of not having Delbert's transcripts by making him a sort of narrator, with a similar dramatic purpose to that of the

Stage Manager in *Our Town.* We had to be careful about setting him up as the Wise Old Black Man, a dumb, racist stereotype that still manages to wiggle its way into hundreds of Hollywood movies; but we felt pretty positive that if we stuck to the truth of Delbert as a human being, we could sidestep that ugly trap. Erik's old obsession with Greek drama had finally found a point of entry into our play. Delbert would be our chorus.

The chorus is an ancient dramatic element, a bridge between the story and the audience that elucidates and clarifies elements of the action onstage that might otherwise be confusing. Here, we could play with that function and give it a twist. Usually, the chorus exists in a separate reality from the other characters, entirely outside the action. Here, the character of Delbert could straddle both worlds. He'd had the same basic experience as the other characters, but also articulated it in a different, more macrocosmic way. As we went back through the monologues we'd edited from our interviews with Delbert, we noticed things he said that applied directly to each of the other stories, that connected with moments in the other five cases and filled in the gaps. We realized it was a blessing that we hadn't been able to find Delbert's case material. It had led us to the structure of the play.

Now that we had a clearer game plan for the script, we could see that some things were missing—we didn't have an account from Gary, for example, of how he'd spent his time in prison; we didn't have a clear picture from Sunny of how she got out. We started another round of interviews, this time by telephone, asking targeted questions, honing in on the gaps in the information we had.

One Tuesday in early September, Erik had set up a phone interview with Gary. Gary was smack in the middle of harvest season, so they'd agreed to talk first thing in the morning, before Gary headed out to his fields. Around eight thirty, Erik was fiddling with the tape recorder, making sure it was hooked up correctly before he called Gary at nine. Jessica was putting on coffee, goofing around the living room with the dog, distracting Erik. Then the phone rang, and Erik pressed RECORD, figuring he'd test his wiring, make sure the tape recorder was taping calls correctly. On the other end was his mom, calling from Minnesota, audibly upset. "Turn on your TV," she said. "A plane just hit the World Trade Center."

The next weeks were complete upheaval for us, as they were for all New Yorkers. We were lucky: we didn't lose anyone, nor did anyone close to us. One of the early and constant supporters of our play lost her sister on one of the planes, but that was as close as we got. We were still circles away from the center of the tragedy. Compared to other acquaintances we had who'd lost family, friends, partners, jobs, the physical substance of our lives remained relatively intact. But it sure didn't feel like it.

We live downtown, about a mile and a half from the buildings, and for a while our neighborhood was closed off to anyone who didn't live there: we had to show ID to military men in full camo, with enormous guns strapped to their chests, to get back into our neighborhood anytime we left. The streets around us were closed to traffic; the city went silent, eerie, and tragically beautiful. The air smelled like burning plastic and poison. In the parks near our building, people kept vigil, every inch of the asphalt around them layered with wax from candles that were always burning; twenty-four hours a day, people were in the park talking to strangers, drumming, chalking the statues, painting murals on newsprint stapled to the "keep off the grass" fences, right next to all the missing-persons flyers. It was a spontaneous outpouring of human expression and connection; in any other moment, one might call it art. In that moment, though, that word, with all its connotations of craft and purpose and audience, seemed hollow. What was happening was more real, immediate, direct; people did it because they needed to, desperately; because there was nothing else to do.

In the face of that immediacy, the overwhelming realness of what had happened in our city, our little project seemed pretty tiny. We had the same crisis of meaning as every New York artist we knew: all our ideas and understandings about why we did what we did seemed flattened, empty, abstracted. Privileged. They'd emerged from a context that seemed to no longer exist, from a world where the stakes were lower, where thousands of people didn't just die out of nowhere, where we had the luxury of trusting that we'd have time, years and years, to make things, to open other people's minds and our own. That world felt over. Now, the only things that made sense were immediate and basic: staying alive and loving each other. Anything more complex than that—theater, writing, art—seemed hollow.

That crisis of meaning was further complicated by the fact that the art we were making was explicitly political. The stories were the heart of it, sure—not any kind of ideology or preaching—but the impetus to tell those stories came out of wanting to correct an imbalanced system, to awaken people's compassion and help them see the human consequences of injustice, to trigger questions, and in so doing, to inspire change. Going into this project, we possessed pretty developed political worldviews; those worldviews informed and guided our work, even as they were transformed by the experiences we had. But now, everything was thrown into question. The most basic, spiritual underpinnings of our political views—our beliefs in humanitarianism, egalitarianism, the essential value of all beings—those things were challenged, but remained unchanged at their core. But everything we thought we knew about how to manifest those beliefs in the world was totally up in the air. Again, it seemed like we'd formed our belief systems in a different, sheltered world, in a context that no longer existed, and we had no idea which parts of them applied anymore. The events of September 11 didn't really change what we thought about any of the stories or ideas in the play, per se; but the play had been built on a solid foundation of ideas and understandings that now seemed to have disintegrated. We didn't trust any of our beliefs anymore, because we didn't know or trust the new world we'd been thrust into. We didn't know what to do.

We spent a few weeks just surviving, absorbing, trying to help; we couldn't sleep at night, and it took us a week just to turn off CNN. Sometimes we clung to each other tight, and other times we turned on each other in ways we didn't even understand, terrified and confused. After a while, we started forcing ourselves to leave the house again, to get out and go on, even if it felt bizarre. One of the first "normal" events we attended, a few weeks after September 11, was a panel discussion at Lincoln Center called "Making Movies that Matter." HBO had gathered a fascinating group of filmmakers and intellectuals to discuss the idea of politically and socially conscious film. The group included Oliver Stone; Christopher Hitchens, the contrarian English intellectual; Christine Vachon, the independent producer who made *Boys Don't Cry* and *I Shot Andy Warhol*, among others; bell hooks, the radical political theorist who's written for twenty years about gender, race, class, and media; and Raoul Peck, the Haitian/French filmmaker who made the film *Lumumba*, about the assassinated revolutionary leader and former president of Congo. The event had been planned months before the events of September 11; it had then been postponed, but now it would go on. An audience of hundreds settled into the theater, and the moderator began by asking each of the panelists how they felt September 11 had impacted their views on artmaking and the world. Each of the panelists' comments began along the lines of what we and all the other artists we knew had been saying and feeling over the past month: it was an end of one context and a beginning of another, it made everything immediate in a profoundly disconcerting way, it triggered a radical reorganization of ideas and beliefs, et cetera. Until they came around to Raoul Peck, who'd grown up in Haiti. "You know, everyone is saying how September eleventh changed everything, changed the world," he said. "For me, and for all the other people who grew up in the countries where these things happen all the time, it didn't change the world. It just brought the rest of the world to America."

In hindsight, it seems sort of ridiculous that we didn't think of this before. Of course the events of September 11 wouldn't be brand-new to the rest of the world. Seventy percent (at least!) of the planet is mired in violence much of the time. Our experience of a life free from extreme political violence is quite unusual; to most of the rest of the world, violence or the threat of it is a part of daily existence. Something clicked for us when we heard Raoul Peck articulate that. The rest of the world doesn't stop everything because of violence and war. Living under the threat of violence is profoundly different from living at peace, of course, but people who live under violence in the rest of the world don't stop creating, believing in things, having worldviews, struggling to make things better.

Experiencing the violence of September 11 affected us profoundly. It deepened some of our beliefs and shifted others. It made us powerfully aware of what was important to us and what was not. It confused us, it clarified us, and it changed us. But it didn't have to make us *stop*.

Chapter Eighteen

We knew we wanted to go forward, but as we began to revisit the play, it became increasingly unclear whether we would be able to. As we began to get back to work, we were often distracted by the enormous task of recovering from and responding to the events of September 11. Erik, still anguished from the destruction and havoc that had been wreaked by the actions of just a few individuals, was facing new and unexpected struggles having to do with his own feelings about the death penalty. Still convinced that it is never anybody's place to decide when another human being should die—and understanding that any execution of terrorists could create martyrs and likely *increase* the level of violence—he nevertheless wrestled with unfamiliar desires for retribution, safety, and "closure"—even revenge—gaining a new understanding of how some victims' families feel when violence strikes close to home.

Sometimes it was hard to focus on the play when we were so busy with the more pressing and immediate tasks of mourning our city's losses, joining with the rest of the country in examining how we would fit into this seemingly new world we were living in, fighting not to give in to fear, and struggling to maintain our optimism and faith in what we could do as individuals, as partners, and as citizens of New York, of the United States, and—most importantly—of the world.

Just as we began to recover from the memory of watching bloodied people walk past our neighborhood deli on the morning of the eleventh, we began to see white guys walk into that same deli and treat the Pakistanis who worked there with suspicion and hatred. Middle Eastern cabbies were forced to plaster their cabs with American-flag stickers to keep from being violently harassed. The mosque down the street from our house received bomb threats. As we saw these ignorant and destructive reactions to September 11 unfold, we became increasingly aware of how important it was that our desire for justice not be confused with a will toward vengeance. And we realized that—however small it was—our little play had something to say about that.

We spent hours with Allan hashing out our thoughts about the play's future—and all the new obstacles to mounting a full production. We had been talking about opening in the early spring, but now that was clearly impossible. To open the play in the spring, Allan would have to put a budget together now, and the chances of that happening were slim to none. And we didn't know how soon—if ever—things would change. New York had been thrown into chaos; in our little corner of it, previously successful plays were closing left and right; and the scared-silent political climate didn't leave much room for criticism of the system. Which meant investors weren't exactly clamoring to put their money into a play that critiqued the status quo.

The fear of dissent in the months after September 11 was both frightening and paralyzing to us. Frightening, because without dissent and debate, freedom suffocates and withers—and we'd learned firsthand how a lack of freedom impacts real people's lives. Paralyzing, because as New Yorkers we understood people's deep desire to rally around our leaders at that moment. That desire didn't come from weakness; it came from fear. We'd been attacked, and we wanted our leaders to protect us. In that moment, to feel safe, a lot of people needed to believe that our *entire* system was infallible. Nobody was in any mood to look at its flaws. It took the two of us just a few weeks to realize that many of our leaders weren't living up to the hopes we had for them, and to reaffirm our belief in the importance of critiquing the powers that be. But other New Yorkers—and other Americans—weren't necessarily on the same page at that point. And we understood and empathized with the reasons for that enough that it was tough for us to argue.

We believed in our play, but we weren't sure we could get anyone else to. We weren't so sure the play would have a future. Allan, after a pause for reflection and mourning, didn't stop thinking about the play, though—or believing in it. And one day, he came to us with a realization he'd had: "You know," he said, "we've been talking so much about being afraid we won't be able to bring together the resources to mount a play that's critical of the system. But this play isn't just about critiquing the system. That's part of it, sure, but I really think this play is about survival, and about hope. I think people need to see this play even more now than they did before."

The more we talked about it, the more the truth of Allan's statement sank in. The people in our play had *survived*. Each of them, individually, had been to places as dark as those visited by New York—and the whole country—that September. And not only had each of the exonerated folks survived, but many of them had come out the other side stronger. We felt that no matter what the public might think of the play politically, and however the majority's politics might differ from ours, the exonerated people had something to teach all of us about facing darkness—even death—and coming out the other side. For the exonerated, the source of that darkness was a justice system gone horribly wrong; for New Yorkers, the source might be the loss of a family member, the crumbling of a building. Whatever the (very real) differences between their stories and what we were all going through, the exonerated people had something to teach us about survival, endurance, and hope. *That* was the heart of the play.

Now, we had an organizing function—Delbert as Greek chorus—and more important, we had a new understanding of what the play was about that both included and transcended what we'd known before. And we had Allan and Bob still firmly behind us. It was time to get back to work.

Probably, we could have gone right back into workshops at that point, but we wanted to wait a little longer just to make sure our actors were as ready to get back to work as we were. So we spent another month in our apartment, finishing up our supplementary interviews with the exonerated—and revisiting, refining, and organizing the court transcript material. In the end, we'd been through thousands and thousands of pages' worth—and at least half of them were sitting in our apartment, stretching the limits of our creaky file cabinet. On the page, *all* of it was fascinating. Every prickly exchange between defense and prosecution, every tolerant or imperious judge, every weird moment in depositions taken from strange and slippery characters. The transcripts went off in so many different directions, traced so many hundreds of tangents—and all of them were gripping. We had no idea how we would narrow it down.

After we'd organized and cataloged our material for the umpteenth time, we decided it was ridiculous to wait any longer. If any of our actors were too traumatized to get back to work, they would tell us. So we called them. And it turned out that most of them were hungry—after so much time spent alone in their apartments, getting to know the cable news anchors—to start creating again. Especially with other people.

All our actors had gone through the same process we had—questioning, overhauling, and reassembling their political beliefs and ideas—even some who wouldn't have considered themselves "political" people before. So we slammed ourselves into rehearsal again. Sometimes we didn't bother to crack open the play at all. Sometimes we'd sit there silently, sometimes we'd talk about the current political situation, breathe sighs of relief as friends who'd been out of touch resurfaced.

The discussions we had with our actors as we workshopped the new material covered a lot of territory, and in a newly *lived* way. Life and death were deeply felt things those days, and we saw it in those few workshops. In the meantime, we listened to the words, edited like crazy, and whittled the court transcripts into scenes. Gradually, we began to find connections between the new courtroom scenes and the monologues we'd already created. We matched them up, and a real structure started to emerge.

* * *

One afternoon in February, as we were finishing up our first draft of the final version of the play, our phone rang. We tiptoed over the pages of scenes and monologues, spread out on the floor around us, pressed the speaker button, and said hello; there was a delay on the other end, and then a voice said, "Hey, this is Tim Robbins. Listen, uh, what's going on with *The Exonerated*?"

It turned out Tim was interested in mounting the play at his theater in Los Angeles, the Actors' Gang. Tim and a bunch of his punk-rock theater buddies from UCLA had started the Actors' Gang in the early eighties, and it's been thriving ever since. Now Tim is the artistic director, and the tightly knit company produces and creates a steady stream of new work.

Bob was still riding the wave of *Gosford Park* (which he'd produced and acted in) and wasn't available to direct; he suggested to Tim that we step in and direct the show instead. Allan was amenable to the idea: by that time, the political climate of silence and fear had chilled out a little, the theater world was up and running again, and things were starting to gear up for a fall New York production at Allan's theater. He thought a production in L.A. would give the play some momentum. And we were thrilled: directing together would be yet another big adventure, the opportunity to work with such a legendary and respected company was a great one, and we could use the rehearsal process to work out any kinks and finalize the script.

We had a meeting over at Tim's office, where we all discussed our collective visions of how we wanted things to go, took in the ideas that Tim and Bob threw onto the table, and went home to start figuring out what we needed in terms of sets, props, sound, budget, etc.

Arrangements were made, and soon we found ourselves in sunny, weird, palm-treed L.A., casting the play from the pool of Actors' Gang company members. The Gang even provided us an assistant (!)

for the auditions, and we watched for the first time as a bunch of actors we'd never met came in to show us their work on our script. We continued to enact our philosophy of providing the kind of acting environment we always hoped directors would provide for us, and we spent a *long* time working with each actor who came in. We ran over, but it didn't matter: at the end of two days, we had been granted a wonderfully talented cast and crew.

They were all much cooler and less hyperactive than us, especially a scarily *present* guy named P. Adam Walsh, who seemed to be able to procure chairs, reel-to-reel tape recorders, rehearsal tables, and extra lights out of thin air, before we even realized we needed them. Then there was the theater's managing director, Greg, tightly organized with an entirely inappropriate sense of humor, who'd punctuate really awful jokes with the ring of a bell on his desk; and Leah, a gorgeous, tough, profoundly talented actor, who for this production signed on (at her peril) to be our stage manager—or marriage counselor, take your pick. They were all totally committed, brilliant, and hardworking, and we felt incredibly supported as we embarked on the rehearsal process.

We were still nervous for the first day of rehearsals, though. Erik has an almost religious belief that one's opening sentences set the tone for the entire conversation, and neither of us knew where to start. We'd both lived with the play for so long; we knew it inside and out, but we also knew our actors needed to discover and own it for themselves. We knew, at least skeletally, how we wanted to bring the play to life; but how could we lead our actors there without imposing our ideas about it on them?

The night before our first rehearsal, Erik called up Dave Elliott, an old, close director friend of his—who was also by now a producer of the play's New York production. Dave listened calmly to Erik's anxious questions and finally replied, "You guys just need to tell the truth, man. And always say yes to everyone's first suggestion—" Then he interrupted himself with a flurry of swear words; apparently the monsters in his video game were about to kill him. Erik managed to get a few words out thanking Dave for the sage advice before Dave hung up to continue battling dragons.

We took Dave's advice, and the first rehearsal went smoothly. In the play's new structure, six actors played the exonerated folks, while six other "swing" actors took on numerous roles as attorneys, spouses, police, judges, witnesses, and the like. Many of the actors were longtime company members; others were brand-new to the Gang. The cast quickly coalesced, forming a tight bond. And they indulged us as we worked out a new collaborative vocabulary: early on, we found that directing together was different from writing together.

We warned the actors at the first read-through not to be alarmed if the two of us sometimes argued in front of them about the best way to approach a problem; they could trust that we shared the same vision for the play, and through the back and forth we would always wind up on the same page. Later, the actor who played Delbert, Richard Lawson, would tell us that he wrestled over whether to take the job: Delbert was a great role, and he loved the play—but working with two directors, who were *also* the playwrights, who were *also* married, sounded to him like an absolute nightmare. He was right—on paper it sounded like a potentially disastrous situation, and we were nervous about it, too. But our experience this far gave us faith (if not confidence) that we could figure it out.

As we'd written together, we'd discovered that Erik naturally keeps his eye on the big picture, always returning to whether a piece of text serves the larger story, keeping the pace galloping along; while Jessica pays more attention to condensing and distilling the essential moments, finding the connections between scenes, the cores of the characters. In our writing, as soon as we got over thinking we were supposed to work the same way, we found that our styles complemented and augmented each other.

When we started to direct together, we found something similar. Erik thinks fast on his feet as a director, overflowing with ideas for staging, lighting, exercises for the actors. His imagination goes on overdrive. And he's got his eye trained on the big picture as a director, too, seeing all the corners of the stage at once, making sure everything's balanced, that all the spaces are either filled or left empty for a reason. He's always looking to hunt down the larger resonance of things, the links between a character's individual actions and the overall meaning of the play.

Jessica, on the other hand, loves forming specific connections with all the actors, learning their individual styles. Each actor needs a different kind of communication from a director to find his or her way to the character; actors don't always *know* what that kind of communication is; and sometimes what they really need is the opposite of what they think they need. Part of a director's job is to figure out how best to engage with each person to pull out his or her strongest, deepest work. And it's also a director's job to maintain a relationship in which the actors consistently feel supported, safe enough to take risks—but not so safe they get complacent. Jessica naturally gravitated toward these interpersonal aspects of directing. Once again, we found that if we allowed ourselves to be complementary—instead of being afraid of our differences or nervous about our respective strengths and weaknesses—our whole became much greater than the sum of its parts. It was also an opportunity for us to learn these skills from each other.

(Another thing keeping us humble, honest, and gloriously off our guard was that Kelly, the guy Jessica had been on a date with two years previously when she first met Erik, had been cast in the play. He had mounds of dirt on both of us and threatened to pull it out whenever we misbehaved.)

The rehearsal period whizzed by, and soon we found ourselves in tech rehearsals. Tim was in and out, as was Bob; both of them had witnessed disastrous rehearsals where the play had run three hours when it was supposed to run ninety minutes. We were floating on adrenaline and fear. Because we were rehearsing things in pieces, nothing really seemed to hold together.

We'd purposely kept the aesthetic sparse: the set consisted only of two tables and twelve chairs that were arranged variously by the actors to create sketches of courtrooms, prison cells, living rooms. There were no blackouts: the actors made quick entrances and exits, the scenes dovetailing as the stories interlocked. We wanted to highlight the power of the exonerated people's stories, and we knew keeping the aesthetic spare, simple, and actor-oriented was the way to do that. But the lack of sets, combined with the multiple settings and stories, also meant we were quite reliant on sound and lights to help create and define environments. A couple weeks before the first previews, as we started to build the cues, we found that we had inadvertently created a *very* technically elaborate production, with over a hundred sound and light cues. Tech rehearsals are always an all-day, all-evening proposition, but ours went way past that, stretching late into the night. Sometimes, because of the hours, we crossed the line of reasonable, polite behavior and became demanding. Our actors and designers seemed to laugh this off, but we are certain that they left rehearsal and went home to burn us in effigy, throwing darts and spanking the two-headed effigy with a wooden spoon.

After the first tech rehearsal ran over significantly, we came home to an even-more-hyper-than-normal Zooey—she'd been alone for almost thirteen hours. That'd be tough for any dog, and Zooey is famously sensitive and high-maintenance. She wouldn't let us get to sleep for hours; after that, we decided to bring her along to the few remaining tech rehearsals. She stayed in the greenroom while we worked with the actors and designers and became quite popular with the cast. Sometimes after we finished working out a technical problem, we'd notice that the stage was strangely devoid of actors; after a while we figured out we'd find a gaggle of them clustered in the greenroom, spoiling Zooey rotten.

Once, during a *very* late night running cues with Leah, long after the actors had gone home, Zooey came trotting up to the lighting booth, wagging her tail. She'd escaped the greenroom without us noticing. She pranced right up to Erik, looking particularly proud, and dropped at his feet a small blue cube she'd apparently found. Erik didn't know what this gift was and wanted to know what the dog had had in her mouth. Clearly not having the best instincts when it came to mysterious blue cubes, he picked it up and took a bite. Then he cringed. It was rat poison.

A round of frantic 2 a.m. calls to both the human and animal poison-control centers ensued. After an hour or two, neither Zooey nor Erik had started convulsing or frothing at the mouth, which the poison-control centers told us meant they were going to be fine. Of course, in the meantime, we'd spent a half hour making the poor dog throw up. If we had any dignity left in the eyes of our production team, that night eradicated it completely. Once everyone was done slapping Erik on the back, each individually confided in him that he needed to stay married to Jessica or he would probably die in some horrible incident, like stepping on a lawn rake or feeding his head into a blender.

The humor and goodwill flowed like watery molasses. But, in all honesty, we were a little stuck again artistically. The staging worked. The actors were honest and their performances were solid. But the whole thing was missing a spark. We'd taken the play as far as we knew how to—but it wasn't quite there. In the last days of rehearsal, Tim came in, watched us work, and gave us notes. His input kicked everything up a notch. He noticed that the current characterizations in the play spanned the gamut, covering a huge amount of emotional territory—except anger. The justified—and necessary—anger that many of the exonerated folks had about what had happened to them wasn't reading. Part of the picture wasn't being painted. This didn't apply uniformly to all the characters—part of what's astonishing and surprising about Sunny, for example, is that she's moved through most of her anger, and anger really doesn't read as part of her personality—but with the actors' input, we identified the moments and characters for which the note made sense. Almost immediately the play became much more gripping, conflict-ridden, *alive*—and the repercussions of what had been done to the exonerated people were so much clearer.

After that, we were ready to open. The first previews took place in April, and both Sunny and Delbert came out to see the play early on. We kept their presence a secret from the actors, just as we had at those first readings in New York, and again the looks on the cast's faces as the real exonerated were introduced were priceless. Richard, the actor who played Delbert, is enormously charismatic; wherever he goes, he's always the coolest guy in the room. But it was clear he'd met his match in Delbert. The two of them stayed up late into the night, talking over drinks, outcooling each other. Sunny and Adele Robbins, the woman who played her, had actually met before; Adele and her husband, Brian (who played Gary in the Actors' Gang production), have been involved in the anti-death-penalty movement for quite some time, and Adele and Sunny had encountered each other several years before. But now, they were meeting on new ground, with a new level of connection.

Small-theater people (including us) are known for banding together and busting their collective butts to make plays happen. They're also known for large amounts of interpersonal theatrics. This production was different. *Everyone* approached the process with an enormous amount of respect and reverence. The character of the actors, designers, and crew had something to do with that, of course—but we could tell that it also had a lot to do with the material. That the play dealt with real people's lives infused rehearsals and created an enormously strong sense of collective purpose among the cast. They wanted to do justice to the stories. We recognized that desire, because we had been feeling it ourselves for two years. We hadn't *tried* to instill it in our actors at the Gang—they came to it themselves, through their own relationship to the material. It was the first time we got a glimpse of the life this play would take on as it passed from our hands to others', as it went out into the world.

Chapter Nineteen

The Actors' Gang production ran into the summer, and we stayed on till June, rehearsing understudies, tweaking the actors' performances, and generally being around. The cast had developed into a tight-knit ensemble; we felt like part of that, and we hated to leave. But we had to: casting for the New York production was about to begin.

We drove home, all the way from L.A. to New York. It was the first time we'd been on the road since our interview trips two years before; it was interesting to note how the country inside the coasts had and hadn't changed since then. There were a lot more American flags; a lot more bumper-sticker references to war, including a truck with "Terrorist Hunting Permit" on the rear window; we also saw "I

Visited Ground Zero" T-shirts in places like Utah, Indiana, West Virginia, and Missouri. The commodification weirded us out: that was our city they were wearing T-shirts about, and the last time we'd been in these parts of the country, they weren't exactly welcoming to New Yorkers. But, we found, that had changed, too.

This time, as before, in the more rural areas people could tell we weren't locals. Now, though, instead of just staring, they often asked us where we were from—and when we said "New York City," their eyes invariably went wide, and the questions started pouring out. "Were you there on September eleventh?" was always the first one. Then: "What was it like?" and "What part of the city do you live in?" and "Has everything changed there?" and inevitably "Did you lose anyone?"

Two years before, we'd been looked at as vaguely threatening aliens because of the city we came from; now, people seemed to identify with us. Or needed to. All of a sudden, just being from New York made us some sort of moral authority in people's eyes. It made us sad, in a way: it seemed to take some sense of false unity against a dangerous Other to make people overcome their mistrust of the big city and open up to us.

But as the conversations went on, it became clear that they didn't identify with *us*, really, but more with some sort of 9/11 narrative of which we, to them, were the embodiment. The differences between what 9/11 meant to us and what it meant to the people who inhabited the conservative, mostly rural areas we visited were often profound. And the ideological and cultural differences between us were still just as stark as they had been two years ago. But now they knew a little bit of our story—and wanted to know more—and that created a little piece of common ground. Telling that story didn't erase the differences between us, and it only sometimes bridged them. But it created a space in which a conversation could happen, where there wouldn't have been one before. In a certain way, it reminded us of what had happened the last time we'd traveled across the country—except this time, the roles were reversed.

After two weeks of driving, we arrived home, eased back into our New York life, and started showing up at the theater almost every day. The play was scheduled to begin previews in October, and preparations were well under way. While we were in L.A., Allan had been assembling a producing team; by now there were five producers, almost none of whom we'd ever even met. It was pretty amazing to us to realize that people whom we'd never even talked to were now putting thousands of dollars into producing this play we'd written. It was getting bigger than us, fast.

Over that summer, things came together, and Bob started rehearsals in September with a cast that included Tony-winning stage actor Charles Brown, Jill Clayburgh, Richard Dreyfuss, and Sara Gilbert—as well as several of the actors who had workshopped the play with us from the very beginning. It was great watching acting giants like Jill and Richard work, but it was almost more gratifying to see actors who had been with us since the play was just a pile of interviews finally inhabit their roles onstage.

We came to almost every rehearsal. Playwrights are always at rehearsals for their play's first New York production, working with the director to make final improvements on the text. It's a collaborative process, and Bob was great with us, letting us sit in on entire rehearsals, checking in with us on breaks, talking with us every couple of days about his vision for the play. But we were still terrified. Thus far, we'd had artistic control over most of the play's incarnations—first, during the nearly two years we spent writing it, and then later at the Actors' Gang, where everything onstage was a manifestation of what we saw in our heads. Sure, along the way we'd gotten notes from Bob, and later from Tim, but mostly, we were in charge. Now we weren't anymore.

Even though we knew from our experience as actors that the director is the only person who *ever* gets to talk with the actors about their performances in progress, it was really tough for us to keep our mouths shut in rehearsal. Especially since many of the actors would ask us questions about the exonerated people's case histories, their backgrounds, their personalities. We were allowed to answer those questions, but we had thought so much about the exonerated people—what they'd been through and who they were—that it was hard for us to stop talking once we started. We'd spent the last two years figuring out how to translate these real people to the stage, learning to help actors find their ways of talking and moving, inventing shorthand that would give the actors access to the exonerated people's personalities. But now that wasn't our job anymore; it was Bob's. Our job was to give the actors facts about the real people's lives, share our research with them, and tweak the script; anything else had to go through Bob. We had to bite our tongues a *lot* to keep from crossing the line between information and direction.

It was also really scary for us not to know how the play would look in the end. Bob's staging of the play was very different from the way we'd staged it in L.A. At the Actors' Gang, the aesthetic was sparse, but the actors moved around, changed environments, made entrances and exits; only one exonerated person was onstage at any given time. We knew from early on that Bob's staging would be less elaborate, but only in rehearsals did we see just how stripped-down his production would be. The actors sat in chairs: eight actors who played the six exonerated people and their wives sat in a row, with one male "swing" actor seated on a raised platform on either side of the row of exonerated. All the actors remained seated onstage throughout the entire play; Bob told us that they'd be isolated by lights as they told their individual stories. Initially, Bob said, he had thought of having the actors stand during certain more dramatic, active scenes, but as rehearsals went on, he became more and more convinced that simpler was better. He wanted to stage the play like an old "story theater" piece, more like a radio drama than anything else. "The power's in the stories," he said, and he wanted to highlight that as much as he possibly could.

We agreed with him in principle—and we thought the story-theater idea was great—but we couldn't see it in our heads. Our fear had nothing to do with Bob's direction, the actors' work, or anything we saw in the rehearsal room. All that stuff was going wonderfully. It was simply that we didn't *know* how the play would turn out: it was out of our hands, and that scared the hell out of us. It was our baby, and now someone else was bringing it into the world.

Playwrights are famously nervous during the first rehearsals of their plays. It's a scary thing to turn your work over to a director, to trust someone else to take what you've imagined and bring it into being for the world. We were even worse than normal, though. First of all, we'd never done this before. We'd always been actors, not writers; when you're acting, your work is just your work, and nobody else interprets it for you (except critics, but that's a whole different story). Second, we'd just directed a production of the play, so we had a lot of ideas and thoughts about how certain moments worked onstage. And third, our entire process had been unusual: we didn't write this play alone in our apartment in front of a computer. It—and the real people whose stories it contained—had overtaken, defined, and transformed our lives over the last two and a half years. It felt like the play was our whole life. We were so scared about what the public's response would be when it opened in New York. Audiences had seen it before, but the stakes were always lower for us: at the first readings, we knew the play was a work in progress; we'd only been working on it for six months. In L.A., we knew that even if something went wrong, another production was coming up—and putting up the play in L.A. felt less risky, since it wasn't our home. But now a full production of the play in New York was about to open; this is what we'd been working toward for two and a half years. And New York audiences can be brutal. In New York, "been there done that" is what people eat for breakfast. You better be damn sure you have something new to say in front of an audience that's seen fifteen plays in the last three months, many of them written by people we don't even deserve to be in the same room with: Pinter, Albee, Beckett, Shepard. This was it.

Bob was very patient; he never got annoyed when we'd talk a little too long in rehearsal, present him with pages of notes we'd taken, ask incessant questions. He knew how close we'd been to the play from the beginning, and he'd met the real people involved, so he understood how high the stakes felt to us. After a couple weeks of rehearsal, he gently suggested we take a few days off, come back at the end of the week when some of the light cues would be added in. Later we realized that we were making everyone nervous. They needed us out of there as much as we needed to be out of there. We followed Bob's gently worded advice and spent the rest of the week in our apartment biting our nails.

We could have left our fingernails alone: by the time we came back, the production had taken several rapid steps forward. It looked beautiful. Bob and the lighting designer had worked out light cues that shone down on the exonerated characters as they told their stories, isolating each of them completely. As each of them spoke, he or she would seem utterly alone; then the lights would come up slightly at the end of each monologue, and you'd see the rest of the exonerated there, too, a reminder of how many people share this story. The actors' performances were deepening. And now there was music, too: Jason Pendergraft, an actor/musician friend of ours who'd been helping out with the play since the first workshops, and David Robbins, the sound designer and composer for both the L.A. and N.Y.C. productions, had collaborated on beautiful, bluesy incidental guitar music that framed some of the more poignant moments. Bob had added layer upon layer to his stark, minimalist framework, creating a rich texture while preserving the simplicity of the storytelling. We were finally able to see what Bob had been envisioning since the beginning of rehearsals.

That night, we went home; we had a few free hours and some long-neglected chores to take care of, including cleaning out our filing cabinet, which was overflowing with two and a half years' worth of research. As we were going through our files, we came across the notes we'd made at that conference at Columbia nearly three years before, when we'd gotten the idea for the play. On the back of a flyer, we'd sketched out our first thoughts. In the middle of the page we'd drawn a single chair, with a single light shining down on it. Next to that, we'd drawn a shadowed row of ten identical chairs, each with an identical, solitary light above it. We'd forgotten about those scribblings, but somehow the idea had preserved itself. Bob's staging was identical to our very first brainstorms. We stopped worrying.

A week later, it was time for the first previews. We watched each one from the back row, pens poised to scribble notes. We didn't have many, though. The play felt pretty complete. We were still nervous: not only did we know critics were in the audience that week, we also knew who they were, which papers they wrote for, and what nights they'd be there. It's one thing to face critics as an actor: what they say makes a difference, sure, but the critic's job is really to critique the play itself, and as an actor you're not responsible for the whole thing, only your small part of it. This was different, though, and brand-new for us. We'd never been *authors* before. If they hated the play, it was on our shoulders. And we really didn't know what they would say. We knew that we had put everything we had into this play: money, time, our whole relationship. We'd been over the text with a fine-tooth comb, reshaping and honing it again and again, tightening it where it dragged, shuffling scenes until the connections between them were clear and the flow of the play was uninhibited. But we were so close to it that we had no idea what would happen when other people picked it apart.

Ultimately, though, we knew it didn't matter: we could already see that the play was doing its work—in a way that had nothing to do with critics or reviews. Allan and the producers had flown the exonerated folks in for the whole week of previews; all of them were able to come except Gary (who was harvesting his crops) and Sunny (who was in Europe). After every performance, Allan introduced the exonerated people; always, that moment was as powerful as it had been at the first reading two years before. Each time, we were able to see the intersection between art and real people's lives; and each time, we could see the audience see it, too. Thanks to the hard work of an entire community of people, our audiences in New York were having the same experience with the play that we'd had in that workshop at Columbia University. The human stories—so different from a newspaper article, a list of statistics—were coming through. Often, audience members stayed long after the show, talking to the exonerated people, even asking for autographs. Sometimes they'd come up to us, too, and want to talk, telling us how they had been pro–death penalty when they walked into the theater but now they weren't so sure, rethinking their ideas out loud. Strangers asked us lots and lots of questions, and they told us stories of their own. A conversation had begun.

By the time opening night rolled around, six days later, we were exhausted. We'd spent every night that week at the theater, and every day with the exonerated folks. Watching the show repeatedly was tough on some of them—cathartic and healing, but *very* emotional—and navigating the city was sometimes overwhelming, especially to the few who'd never spent any length of time in big cities. We hadn't thought it was necessary to fix them up with full-time hosts this time, since things had gone so smoothly when they'd visited two years ago. But back then, they were only in the city for a couple days; now, they were here a whole week. It was a different group of people from the one we'd brought here two years before—some of the people in this group had never been to New York. And, we guessed, the experience of watching the show was more intense this time: each of their stories was told much more fully, and the play had been boiled down, its emotional impact concentrated. We wound up spending most of the preview week with the exonerated folks: we'd written this play for them, and it was so important to us that their experience here be good. We knew that for some of them it was complicated: healing, cathartic, beautiful, but also raw and overwhelming. We spent that week providing as much support as we could. We were bone-tired, but grateful for the opportunity. It was a beautiful reminder for us: whatever impact these stories were having on audiences, however exhilarating the process of making of art from life and putting it out into the world, the *most* important thing about these stories was the real people behind them.

Opening night was a whirlwind. It was sold-out, and both the show and the party afterward went off without a hitch. The theater seemed about to burst at the seams, spilling people out into the street. To survey the packed lobby and see that just about everyone there had helped bring this play into being was pretty incredible. We—with Allan and Bob's crucial support—had spearheaded the effort; our hands and minds and phone lines had served as a clearinghouse; we'd gathered, sculpted, and honed the text. But none of it could have happened without everyone who was in that room. Western culture has sustained the myth of the solitary artist—the idea that real art is sparked by individual imaginations, made by individual pairs of hands. And maybe that myth holds true, occasionally, for painters, for novelists. But not in the theater—and not here. We were here, in this room, tonight, because of the faith and work and risk-taking of an entire community of people, all of whom had come together not because it was their job, not because they had to, not for profit or recognition or payback. They'd put their creativity and support into this project because they believed in the idea, because they thought the stories were important. We hadn't done this alone.

The next morning, Jessica's parents roused us from a dead sleep by reading aloud from the play's *New York Times* review. We breathed a sigh of relief heard round the world (or at least round the East Village)—the review was a good one. This meant the play would have a real life, that it would run for at least a few months, that theatergoers who weren't already in line with us politically would come and see the play. But that wasn't what really got us. As Jessica's dad read on, we grabbed hands, tears welling up in our eyes: most of the review was devoted to communicating the deep impact and profound implications—both human and societal—of the exonerated people's stories. Ben Brantley, the toughest critic at the *Times*, was articulating precisely the insights and experiences we had hoped to communicate to our audiences. And as the other reviews came out that morning, the same thing continued. The reviews—all good except for one in a conservative local paper that didn't like our "liberal" politics—were less about *us* than they were about the heart and message of the stories. Praise is nice, and good reviews make a practical, material difference in the life of a play. But what was really important to us was that people (even critics!) were having some of the same emotional and intellectual experiences in watching the play as we had had in the exonerated people's living rooms. The power of these people and their stories translated—we hadn't gotten in the way. We'd done our job.

Chapter Twenty

Over the next couple of months, the play caught on fast. Ever since the winter of 1999–2000—when Governor Ryan declared a moratorium on executions in Illinois and a landmark study came out of Columbia University detailing the extraordinary risk and reality of executing the innocent—a national dialogue about innocence and the death penalty had been fomenting. We got the idea for the play at the beginning of that conversation; one reason we worked so frantically at first was that everyone expected the issue to die down after six months or so. But it didn't. Instead, it was all over the country.

By the time the play opened in New York in October 2002, more and more Americans were grappling seriously with the fact that over one hundred people had been released from death row, their convictions overturned. And those one hundred were the lucky ones—the ones with pro bono lawyers, free defense investigators, teams of college students on their side. With each new release, it became increasingly apparent to the mainstream American public that innocent people were being jailed and sometimes condemned to die. And that opened up a space for dialogue where previously there had been only polarized argument.

For many years, the national debate around the death penalty had been framed in black-and-white terms. On one side, the pro-death-penalty camp argued that if someone intentionally took another person's life, they deserved to die. On the other side, the anti-death-penalty camp argued that it was wrong for the state to take a human being's life, no matter what the circumstances. The disagreement was so morally basic that the two sides might have remained locked in opposition forever. But now, as Americans were watching more and more innocent people walk off death row—some having come within hours of execution—it shifted the conversation from an abstract ethical debate to a concrete conversation about the ways in which the system fails innocent people. With many of those exonerations backed up by unarguable DNA evidence, and still more based on overwhelming mountains of physical evidence and witness testimony, even the most ardent death-penalty supporters were being forced to acknowledge the serious flaws in America's capital punishment system. And it was becoming increasingly clear that—because human error and bias are unavoidable, we could probably never be assured that no innocent person would ever be sent to death row.

Most lawmakers hadn't caught on yet, but the American people were starting to reevaluate their thoughts about the death penalty. And our play was becoming a part of that process, in its own small way. The first few months of the New York run were almost entirely sold-out. We were shocked—and heartened—to see how eager people were to grapple with the issue. The great thing about being a playwright, we found, is that nobody recognizes you in the audience: sometimes we'd hang out in the lobby after the show, eavesdropping on conversation after heated conversation as the audience filed out of the theater. At the bar across the street, the discussions would continue late into the night.

Sometimes we'd get caught up in them ourselves. A month or so after the play opened, Gary had finished his harvest; he was finally freed up to come see the play in New York. We accompanied him to the theater and sat a few seats down from him to watch the show. As the lights dimmed, a loud rustling began: the woman sitting behind Jessica—a white woman in her fifties, sitting with a twentysomething woman who was clearly her daughter—was rifling through her purse. Bob's production of the play is incredibly intimate; its intensity is quiet, and the three-hundred-seat theater is close quarters. The audience—and the actors—heard the rustling, which continued intermittently through the entire first half of the show. Jessica turned around and glared a couple times, to no avail. Soon after, the rustling was drowned out by loud whispering. The younger woman leaned in repeatedly to her mom, making disgusted noises, muttering, "This is bullshit," as a scene between Robert and his trial judge unfolded, saying, "Fuck that," as the actor playing Gary performed a monologue detailing how police had intimidated and threatened him just hours after he'd found his parents' bodies. Most everyone in the theater could hear her comments—including Gary. She seemed immune to other audience members' dirty looks or shushing: she continued muttering through the entire performance.

At the end of the play, the audience stood to applaud, and Gary made his way toward the stage; Erik headed up with him to lead a talkback with the audience. Jessica waved off Erik's invitation to join them up onstage and turned around to face the younger woman who'd been commenting during the show. Without identifying herself as one of the playwrights, she said, "You know, whatever you might think of the play politically, these *are* real people's lives up there. No matter what your opinions are about the issue, the people themselves deserve a little respect."

Jessica had been fuming throughout the performance, but her tone with the woman was controlled, even gentle. The woman's response, however, was nothing of the sort. She turned on Jessica, eyes blazing. "How *dare* you," she snapped. "How dare you tell me what my response should be! If I'm angry, I'm angry. I think it's bullshit. I don't give a shit what you have to say. It's none of your fucking business."

Jessica was stunned. She tried to stay calm. "I'm not trying to tell you what response to have," she said. "You can think whatever you want. I'm just trying to point out that those are real people's stories up there, and one of the real people was sitting right in front of you, and it's disrespectful to talk that way in the middle of a play, no matter what you think of it. There's a talkback about to happen right now. That's a much better time to voice your—"

"Don't tell me about disrespectful," the woman spat. "You don't know me." And then she continued in the same vein, her voice rising louder and louder. People were starting to stare.

Finally, Jessica saw that the conversation wasn't going anywhere. "Look," she said. "I'm not trying to take away your right to feel however you feel. I was just trying to remind you that those are real people's lives up there, not just some writer's ideas, and to take that into account when you criticize them." Rattled, Jessica walked off.

A few minutes later, Jessica was standing down by the stage, her pulse gradually slowing, as the audience filtered out of the theater. The young woman approached Jessica again, her mother at her side.

The young woman's body was still visibly tense, her eyes flinty. "I'm sorry," she said to Jessica, an edge in her voice. "I didn't mean to snap at you. But it really pissed me off, the way these people were portrayed as some kind of victims, like they're just innocent."

"Well, actually," Jessica pointed out, "these people's convictions were all overturned by the courts because the system made mistakes, and some of them were freed on the grounds that someone else committed the crime. Didn't you hear that part?"

Then the mother stepped forward confrontationally, interjecting, "I used to work in the system. All the guilty people always say they're innocent. Innocent doesn't mean anything. I know something about the system."

"Well, I do, too," Jessica said. "I cowrote the play."

Pause.

The mom backed off; the daughter slowed for a moment, but lost none of her edge. "I'm a *victim*," the daughter said. "I was *raped*. And I'm sorry, but I'm not going to feel sorry for these people like they're some kind of victims, too."

Jessica stood there in silence for a moment, absorbing what she'd just been told. It made total sense, knowing that this woman had been a victim of violent crime. Her (*entirely* justified) anger at what had been done to her explained her refusal to quiet down during the performance; it accounted for the intensity of her response when Jessica asked her to remember the real people behind the stories onstage. Jessica chose her words carefully.

"That's the whole point, though," Jessica finally said. "These people aren't at fault here. The system made a mistake in each of these cases. And in all the cases but one, the *real* guilty person is still out there walking around, free. The prosecutors won't go after the real perpetrators because they don't want to admit that they made a mistake. And that doesn't help any of the victims in those cases." The woman looked at Jessica warily, weighing her words. "I am so sorry for what happened to you," Jessica continued. "You didn't deserve it. And you're right—I *don't* know you. I don't know your story, or what you've survived. But the people up there are victims—and survivors—too. And not just of the system. Gary, the guy who was sitting in front of you, lost both his parents to violent crime. Kerry talks in the play about being a rape victim, too—*and* about his brother being murdered while he was in prison. They're not so different from you."

The woman, still guarded but listening now, took in Jessica's words. "Yeah, I guess I can see that," she finally said. "But look, I came here tonight. I didn't just write it off. I wanted to hear the other side."

"I appreciate that," Jessica said. "I totally give you credit for that. And you have the right to whatever response you have; if you totally disagree with the politics of the play, that's fine. All I was saying is remember that the people in it have their own stories, too." The woman nodded, and Jessica nodded—making an uneasy, but real, truce—and then they parted ways.

That interaction was the first direct contact either of us had had with someone who had come to her pro-death-penalty position through an experience as a victim of violent crime. We'd spent some time with Murder Victims' Families for Reconciliation—an organization of victims' family members who are opposed to the death penalty—and as Jessica had said, several of the people portrayed in our play had been crime victims themselves. But those people all ultimately arrived at the same conclusions that we had; for example, Gary publicly asked for his parents' real killers to be spared from the death penalty. We'd never had the opportunity to hash it out with anyone from the pro-death-penalty victims' lobby.

We knew that lobby was formidable and resolute, with some of the most determined activists, often fierce in their insistence on the strongest possible punishments for violent criminals. In talking with the young woman in the theater, Jessica understood something about why that was the case. What had been done to that woman was heinous, violent, and hurtful. That was unarguable. And the rage she so clearly felt was entirely justified. But that rage was such a powerful force that it became diffuse: it was no longer directed only at the person who had hurt her, but also at many others who *hadn't* hurt her—who, in fact, hadn't hurt anyone—just by virtue of the fact that they were part of the same category as her attacker: the category of "defendant."

This woman had obviously wanted someone to pay for the crime committed against her. We empathized with her, but the deep need she had to find someone to punish seemed to inform her perception of *everyone*. It turned every suspect into a criminal without the benefit of trial or counsel. It came from a deep emotional place—a place that can be quite dangerous when it comes into too close contact with the law.

One of the things we'd learned over the last three years is that it's incredibly important that the law and its implementation *not* be informed by emotion. Ethics, yes; compassion, sure—but not emotion. Violent crime, by its very nature, triggers intense emotions in all of us. But it is imperative that we not replicate those emotions within the legal system; that we let reason, analysis, and a dispassionate search for the truth lead the way. Whenever emotion runs the show, whether it's in the form of a desire for vengeance, a deeply felt need for a quick resolution or "closure," a real fear of further violence, or a prosecutor's personal desire to get ahead at all costs, it inevitably obscures the truth and leads to wrong decisions—often with tragic consequences. In this new world where real wars have their own sweeping and crescendoing sound tracks, and real-time cable-news "journalists" deliver hotheaded commentary on jury trials, it is more important than ever that we strive to remove our emotions from our legal system. We'd spent the last three years witnessing what happens when communities forget to do that.

Seeing this other side of the story in person, we also understood something new about how the system pits victims against defendants, often without a truly critical eye to whether those defendants are actually guilty. Many victims and victims' families—with good reason—want so much to have an object for their anger that often they accept whomever the police and prosecutors present as the guilty party. But sometimes those police and prosecutors are wrong. And when they are, their refusal to admit it does a deep disservice not only to the accused, but to the victims, too.

Our political education hadn't ended when we finished with our research: the first months of the play's New York run were full of lessons like the one we got from that young woman. We spent a lot of time down at the theater, engaging with strangers of all kinds of viewpoints and backgrounds. Sometimes our audiences reinforced our beliefs; other times they challenged them. The play's new public life opened up a thousand conversations.

The play wasn't the only thing that had gone public—as the authors, we had a new public life of our own, too. All of a sudden, people from newspapers were calling us up; we were going live on the radio, doing interviews with magazines. We quickly learned that talking to the press is a whole different animal from regular human interaction. Every word is recorded, each phrase can be disseminated to thousands of people—either in or out of context. Once the words leave your mouth, you have no control over how they're used. Both of us tend to be pretty loose in conversation—we think out loud, circle around new ideas till we land on them, shoot from the hip, try on thoughts that we're not even sure we agree with. It only took an exhausted, overworked Erik shooting his mouth off spontaneously at one after-show talkback—getting impatient and saying a particular pro-death-penalty argument was "bullshit"—for us to realize that communicating in the public sphere is different from communicating in everyday life. We were talking to strangers, who would quote us on every word. We had to make sure that everything we said—and every way we said it—reflected exactly what we meant. (Erik whispers, *Even if what we were responding to was bullshit.*)

Sometimes being in the public eye was scary. It's one thing to make work in your own living room with your friends as collaborators, or to work in a small theater with a tight ensemble that grows close during the collaboration. It's also one thing to be recognized occasionally for a part you played in someone else's movie or TV show. It's another thing entirely to have thousands of strangers experiencing, interacting with, and critiquing work that you *wrote*. Don't get us wrong—it's incredibly gratifying to reach so many people, and having the ability to do that was more than we could have hoped for. But, especially when it's happening for the first time, it's also sometimes surreal. Not long after the play opened, we were walking Zooey in our neighborhood, off in our own little world, when a woman strode up to us: "Hey! I know you—you guys wrote *The Exonerated*! Good work!" We chatted for a little while about the play; when she walked off, we both felt strangely naked. Our own little world wasn't just ours anymore.

Those first months were so overwhelming and absorbing that we decided we needed to escape for a little while, just to take a breather.

This play had been our life for two and a half years now. We'd worked twelve-hour days, six days a week, unpaid, in our one-bedroom apartment for those two and a half years, and we needed a break. We'd expected that when the play finally opened in New York, we could take a step back, watch it unfold, enjoy the fruits of our labor from a bit of a distance. The opposite turned out to be true. It was so easy to walk the few blocks from our house to the theater, and people were working on the play there practically around the clock. Three of the ten roles in the play were rotating; Bob was constantly rehearsing new actors, and we always wound up coming to the rehearsals. It was pretty tough not to when the likes of Gabriel Byrne, Mia Farrow, and Aidan Quinn were showing up to read through our play. Sometimes new actors would ring us up to ask questions about the exonerated folks they were playing. Sometimes we got called to fill in for actors who couldn't make it to a rehearsal here, a performance there. And we were perpetually doing press. The play was still very much our life, and it showed no signs of stopping. We couldn't even begin to absorb what had happened in our lives in the last two and a half years, let alone imagine beginning other projects. We needed some breathing room. Jessica had some acting opportunities in L.A., and we made a plan to spend a couple months there, beginning in January.

In the meantime, though, something very important was happening in Illinois.

Back in January of 2000, when he declared a moratorium on executions in Illinois, Governor George Ryan also appointed a blue-ribbon, bipartisan commission to look into what was causing so many innocent people to be sent to his state's death row. After two years, the commission came back with their findings: by a narrow margin, they voted that Illinois's death penalty was fatally flawed and should be abolished. Further, they were unanimous in their identification of serious defects in the system, all of which had the potential to cause the executions of innocent people. The commission recommended eighty-five reforms in the state's capital punishment system, including improved training for defense lawyers, guaranteed access to DNA testing, limits on the prosecution's use of confidential informants in capital cases, mandatory videotaping of murder suspects' entire interrogations, and the establishment of a statewide commission to review any case in which a prosecutor sought a death sentence. Despite widespread support—including from several police and prosecutors' organizations—by that winter the legislature had enacted *none* of these proposed reforms, due at least in part to what author, attorney, and commission member Scott Turow calls "the chronic timidity of officials when it comes time to take positions that can later be labeled as 'soft on crime.' "

Granted, enacting these reforms would likely have cost tens of millions of dollars and entirely revamped the state's bureaucracy. (This is one reason several members of the commission suggested that a better way to avoid executing the innocent might be to simply abolish the state's death penalty.) But whatever the reason for the legislature's failure to act, that failure left Governor Ryan in a difficult situation. Because of the commission's work, Ryan was acutely aware of the serious flaws in the system; he knew that many people on Illinois's death row were possibly innocent, and that the specificities of their cases had not adequately been addressed. The system remained in exactly the same sorry condition that had impelled Ryan to declare the moratorium in the first place—but now, he understood so much more about the horrifying extent of its flaws and inconsistencies.

And both candidates to replace Ryan as governor had discussed lifting the state's moratorium on executions if elected. But none of the reforms that might reduce the chance of innocent people being executed had been enacted. Like a factory that had been shut down because of rusty, broken gears, but was now sending its workers back to the assembly line without having repaired its faulty parts, the state's capital punishment machinery was possibly about to roar back into operation—but it hadn't been fixed.

Ryan seemed painfully aware of what this meant: that innocent people would likely be executed after he left office. What he had hoped, when he declared the moratorium and appointed his commission, was to prevent this through legislative channels, but now it was too late for that. And regardless, drafting and passing laws weren't within the scope of his powers as governor.

One thing was within his powers as governor, though: clemency.

In fall of 2002, after both candidates to replace him had declared that they might lift the moratorium if elected, Governor Ryan began to publicly consider granting blanket clemency to all 171 people on Illinois's death row. He wouldn't let the prisoners out; he would simply commute their sentences to life in prison, so they could live long enough for the courts to examine and rule on the flaws in their cases. If any of them were actually innocent, the courts would have time to discover this and act accordingly. If they were guilty, they would remain locked up. There was some precedent for Ryan's proposal: Ohio governor Richard Celeste had commuted eight inmates' death sentences just days before he left office in 1991; and New Mexico governor Tony Anaya commuted the death sentences of all five men on death row on his way out of office in November 1986. And governors—as well as presidents—are known to exercise their clemency powers in select cases just before retiring from public life. But no governor had ever proposed exercising his or her clemency powers on such a scale. The scope of Governor Ryan's proposal—and the number of lives it would affect—were entirely unprecedented. His announcement met with an enormous public uproar.

Police federations, prosecutors' organizations, and many families of victims came out in force against Ryan's proposal. Some of them argued that everyone on Illinois's death row had correctly been prosecuted, that those who had been released had gotten out on "technicalities," and that there was no reason whatsoever to revisit the convictions. But most opponents of Ryan's proposition had a more compelling argument. They argued that to grant a blanket commutation would be to ignore the very real differences between the cases and would be to treat the actually guilty the same as the potentially innocent. They claimed that by taking the same action in all of the cases without examining their individual details, Ryan would in effect be undoing the work of those attorneys, police officers, and judges who had *not* acted wrongly and, further, would do a disservice to the family members of victims whose murderers had *correctly* been convicted.

They had a point.

Ryan responded to these concerns by agreeing to hold individual clemency hearings in 142 cases. He would hear the details of each crime, each trial, each conviction, and would look at each case on its own merits. In this way, he hoped to be able to separate out those inmates with convincing claims of innocence from the worst of the worst: those who admitted to their crimes, who bragged about the murders they'd committed.

In October 2002—just after the play opened in New York—the clemency hearings began in Illinois, with the fourteen-member Prisoner Review Board split into four panels, all working simultaneously. The Prisoner Review Board is a bipartisan group, made up of former law-enforcement professionals, prison officials, and former state lawmakers. It is, as one official was quoted as saying in the

Chicago Tribune, "not a panel of bleeding hearts." The board had just a couple of months to hear an enormous number of cases, and they worked around the clock, with Governor Ryan sitting in on the hearings.

When the hearings finally drew to a close in December 2002, Ryan found that his position had hardly improved. He had hoped that the clemency hearings would help him sift through the cases, identify the most egregious miscarriages of justice, distinguish the actually guilty from the actually innocent. But if anything, the hearings made things *more* confusing. Many cases that had looked cut-and-dried before were now much more difficult to define—on both sides. Some cases in which the defendant had appeared unmistakably innocent now inhabited a decidedly gray area. And other inmates who had at first appeared to have no convincing claim to innocence were introducing evidence that raised serious questions. It would take months or years to sift through and analyze all the new evidence in even a few of the cases—let alone hundreds. The more the commission learned about each case, the more elusive any kind of certainty became. Instead of clarifying the facts, the hearings just raised more questions.

Ryan was in a bind. He took seriously the victims' families pleas that he not treat the correctly convicted identically to the wrongly convicted. But the more that came out about each case, the harder it became to tell the difference between the two. The system was so tangled that untying the knots of each case was becoming a nearly impossible task. By all accounts, Ryan really didn't know what to do.

So mostly, he listened. He spent hours on end with the victims' families; used nearly every free second to read and reread case summaries, court opinions, the recommendations of the board. He went over and over the findings of the blue-ribbon commission. He spoke to retired judges and to lawyers' associations. He talked to prosecutors, and he talked to defense attorneys. And he talked to the Center on Wrongful Convictions.

The controversy gripped the state of Illinois. Nearly every day, the papers ran impassioned editorials advocating for both sides of the argument. At Northwestern University, just outside Chicago, the folks at the Center on Wrongful Convictions were trying to figure out how best to participate in the conversation. Finally they settled on a plan: in just weeks, they would pull together a second conference of death row survivors, like the one they'd held in 1998 but even bigger. They would hold a relay called Dead Men Walking: the exonerated would walk thirty-seven miles from death row at Statesville to the governor's office, carrying a letter imploring him to commute all the sentences. And after the relay, the exonerated people—and the governor—would attend a performance of *The Exonerated*.

Larry Marshall called us up in late November to ask us if we'd be amenable to the play being performed in this context. We were a lot more than amenable. We were blown away, honored, and totally humbled. Governor Ryan was in the midst of making a decision that would affect the lives of hundreds of people. He had opened up a dialogue with thousands of experts from both sides. And now *we* were going to get to be a part of that conversation? We thought back to that conference at Columbia nearly three years before, and the notes we'd typed back and forth on Jessica's laptop. We'd been grappling with the question of how to bring an understanding of the human experience of wrongful conviction to people who weren't already opposed to the death penalty, who were engaged in a struggle with the issue. We'd been looking for a way to raise questions not just on a political level, but on a *human* level. We'd also been trying to figure out how to start a conversation with those who had more decision-making power than ourselves, who were perhaps more conservative, who controlled the system in more direct, immediate ways. We could imagine no more perfect venue for the play, no situation in which it would fulfill its purpose more directly, than this. We told Larry we'd be delighted and put him in touch with Allan and Bob to work out the details.

Allan, Bob, and Larry worked hard to find a Chicago theater that would be available on such short notice; they also worked hard to figure out what actors would perform the play. Bob was in New York; there wasn't really any conceivable way to cast and rehearse a whole new group of actors in Chicago, and our New York cast was busy performing the show off-Broadway. They did have Mondays off, though. The producers couldn't require the actors to perform on Mondays, nor could they even request that they do so. But the cast and crew of the play are a tight community, and when the actors found out about the event that was about to happen in Chicago, most of them jumped at the chance to participate. They couldn't imagine *not* performing for the governor. Eventually, a cast came together that included some of our New York actors, as well as Richard Dreyfuss, Mike Farrell, and Danny Glover. Bob, with the Center on Wrongful Convictions' help, found a Chicago theater that was willing to host the play for a single night. The performance was scheduled for Monday, December 16, less than a month before the last day Governor Ryan could announce his decision—whatever that decision might be.

By the time mid-December rolled around, Erik had been cast in another movie. It was a great part for him—his first romantic lead in a long time—and we were both excited. Unfortunately, though, the film's shooting schedule required Erik to stay in town until Christmas Eve. He wasn't going to be able to attend the performance in

Chicago. He was incredibly disappointed, but Jessica promised to take lots of pictures and call every hour with full reports. We canceled Erik's ticket just a few days before Jessica got on the plane to Chicago.

In the few days before the Chicago performance, buzz was mounting. We'd been notified that a full press conference had been scheduled, and that several local channels were going live on the governor immediately after the show. That meant something big was in the works—news channels don't go live when nothing's going to happen. There were murmurings that Governor Ryan was going to stand up onstage after the performance and announce that he'd arrived at a decision to commute all of Illinois's death sentences. The event was shaping up to be far more exciting than we'd even imagined.

Jessica arrived in blustery Chicago a few hours before that afternoon's rehearsal. The exonerated men had finished their Dead Men Walking relay just hours earlier, Mike Farrell was going over his lines on the second floor of the theater, and the New York actors were adjusting to the new space. Jess met Danny Glover when he arrived, making herself available to answer any questions he might have about the script (Danny was the only actor there that day who hadn't had any previous contact with the play). Everyone did newspaper interviews in the lobby; adrenaline was running high when the news came that Governor Ryan, who'd been in intensive meetings with some victims' families, had apparently just made a public statement. He was still undecided about what he was going to do, he told the cameras, but whatever it was, he seemed fairly sure that it wouldn't be a blanket commutation. The news came as a blow; people had been growing more and more excited at the possibility that Ryan might announce a blanket commutation after the show that night. That was obviously no longer in the cards.

There wasn't much time to be deflated, though; CNN was setting up in the greenroom. Even without the governor making a big announcement after the show, the event was still big news. Jessica did her first press junket, going from station to station with the actors, practicing her sound bites. We're not sure what (if anything) made it on air, but talking to the national news, with their enormous cameras and blinding lights, was pretty heady stuff. The chance to reach that many people was exhilarating; at the same time, the reporters didn't interview anyone for more than a few minutes, and there was little chance to get into any substantive discussion. We knew intellectually that cable news generally deals out information in small doses, edited MTV-style, but it was a new thing to experience that from the inside: to be asked a complex question, barely scratch the surface of the answer, and then be shuttled along to the next set of cameras. It was illuminating—and a little frustrating—to realize that reaching millions of people on television news usually means forfeiting the ability to say more than a few sentences; that almost always it's a choice between communicating with smaller numbers of people in greater depth, or reaching millions with a sound bite. CNN was exciting and all, but Jessica was looking forward to the audience of just a few hundred who would come see the whole play—and then talk for hours afterward.

However, she was also more than a little intimidated by that audience. Governor Ryan would be there, of course, as well as several members of the state legislature and everyone from the Center on Wrongful Convictions—and so would over fifty exonerated death row inmates, many of whom we'd never met. Having politicians and luminaries in the audience was exciting—but having so many exonerated folks there whom we didn't know personally was kind of scary.

In the play, we tell the stories of six individual exonerated people. But we're also telling a bigger story, the story of the phenomenon of wrongful conviction as a whole. The play belongs to the six individuals whose stories it depicts, but metaphorically, it also belongs to all the exonerated, including the ones we've never met. We were terrified that even one of them might think we got it wrong.

As the lights went down, Jessica watched the audience like a hawk, finally understanding some of the anxiety Erik had grappled with early on as he watched our audiences watch the play. Jessica tried to watch Governor Ryan respond to the play, but he was sitting too far away to see much more than his shock of white hair. But the exonerated folks were much closer. She recognized most of them, even the ones we hadn't met, since we'd researched all their cases—and she kept her eyes on them throughout the performance, attempting to discern their reactions. Some of them whispered to each other; others watched, intense and silent; some nodded at stories they clearly recognized; and others "Uh-huh"ed at key moments. The laughs came in different places than usual: the exonerated folks in the audience would chuckle at things that an audience of civilians would never recognize as funny. And one exonerated audience member—a man whose case we knew quite well—walked out in the middle, along with his wife. He'd been sitting right in front of Jessica and didn't seem particularly disturbed before he left (although his wife was clearly distraught). But Jessica spent a long time trying to figure out what might have made him leave, and wondering if it was our fault. We never did find out.

After an hour and a half of suspense, Danny Glover spoke the last words of the play, the lights came up, and the audience applauded. Then Larry Marshall took the stage and introduced Governor Ryan. Ryan tried just to stand politely for a moment, but the audience applauded thunderously and ceaselessly, insisting he come down to the stage. Finally, he did, looking slightly overwhelmed and entirely undecided. He stood, eyes cast down, listening, as Larry read an eloquent and moving statement exhorting him to "err on the side of life." And then he stayed for a long, long time as all the exonerated folks came down to talk with him individually, thanking him for the immense courage he'd exhibited thus far. Coming from the exonerated, the statements were as weighty as they'd ever be: many of them wouldn't have been alive to talk to the governor that night if it hadn't been for actions like his. And you could tell by the look in the governor's eyes that he knew it.

As Jessica called Erik to catch him up on the latest developments, the gathering moved into the next room; and several exonerated folks we'd never met approached Jessica with compliments and appreciation. She deflected all the compliments—the exonerated themselves deserve them so much more than we ever could—but she gratefully accepted the thanks. The exonerated folks who approached Jessica didn't seem to think we got it wrong—in fact, several said how familiar the content was, how much the stories reminded them of their own. It was a huge relief: their opinions were more important to us than any others. This play is their story—we're just the conduits—and not having been to death row and back ourselves, we're always hoping that they feel we've done it justice.

These days, people sometimes ask us what "secrets" we've learned about how to create art that has a political impact without being preachy. We always say the only secret we've learned is that sometimes it helps, instead of ranting on and on about your own personal political beliefs, to simply tell stories that encapsulate and embody those ideas. And sometimes that's easier to do well when the stories aren't your own: your ego never has a chance to get involved, and you're free to focus on what the stories do and mean. The stories in our play were never *ours*. It was our job to get out of the way and let them come through. Our duty was to tell those six stories, of those six cases, as best we could and let the stories themselves do the rest of the work. And so it was pretty incredible to see those stories do that work in Chicago—and to hear other exonerated people say that the play told not only the six stories onstage, but also parts of their own stories, too.

Governor Ryan stayed late into the night, listening to everyone, closing out the party. At the end of the evening, after talking to him, it was no clearer to Jessica what action Ryan was planning to take. It was probably no clearer to the governor himself, either. But we knew we had been part of the conversation, and we knew he'd listened to us and to the voices in our play. That in itself was an enormous honor. We had written the play with the intention of bringing the immediacy and poignancy of the exonerateds' stories to an audience of the undecided. As far as we were concerned, if that evening in Chicago were the only performance the play ever had, it would have been enough.

Chapter Twenty-one

By January, we were on our way to Los Angeles for our little sabbatical. The play was going gangbusters in New York, with new cast members each week, and the producers had also planned a short five-week tour to Boston, Chicago, and Washington, D.C. Janet Reno was expected to attend the Washington production; so were Senator Patrick Leahy and Supreme Court justice David Souter. The Boston and Chicago runs were selling well in advance. We were well on our way toward raising over $400,000 for the people whose stories appear in the play (early on we structured a profit participation system with multiple revenue streams: they receive donations from the audience as well as a share of the profits and of our pay). The play had also already helped raise significant amounts of money for several different organizations. The whole operation was all safely in the hands of Allan, Bob, and the other producers. And by now, the play had overtaken Allan's life as much as it had overtaken ours: the exonerated folks and the larger issue had come to be immensely, deeply important to him, and we knew the play would thrive under his stewardship. People at the theater were even starting to get a little annoyed when we kept checking in constantly on our baby, forever making sure everything was running okay, acting like mother hens. It was time to leave it in their hands for a little while, to let it grow.

So we went on the road again, this time driving down the Pacific coast from Oregon to L.A., Zooey jumping around in the backseat as always. We wound through the redwood forests, everything green and glistening around us, finally breathing after all the chaos of the past three years. Our little life was crammed in cardboard boxes and we clasped hands over the gearshift, watching the mountains roll by for days through the rain-spattered windows.

After several days camping in the woods and driving down the coast, drinking in our newfound quiet, we got hungry for a little of the outside world. In rural northern California, there's not much on the radio besides the Humboldt State University station, which mostly plays a lot of conga drums and didgeridoo. But after several minutes of dial-fiddling, we landed on a staticky AM news station. We sat through several promos for scary-sounding talk-radio shows as we waited for the headlines. Jessica whined about having to listen to commercials, but Erik, desperately needing a news fix, insisted we sit through them for just another minute.

When the ads finally let up, an announcer came on with breaking news: "Today in Illinois," the announcer began, "Governor George Ryan has just announced a historic decision." We veered off the road onto the shoulder, put the car in park, and turned the volume way up.

The announcer continued, "After months of controversy, and just days before he is to leave office, Governor Ryan has announced that he will commute the sentences of all one hundred and sixty-seven of Illinois's death row inmates to life in prison."

We gaped at each other, both our eyes filling with tears. He had done it. As Larry Marshall had urged him, Governor Ryan had "erred on the side of life." A hundred and sixty-seven lives, some quite possibly innocent, had been saved because of the courage of one man and the diligent, unwavering work of hundreds of people. The announcer went on to say that Ryan had also granted six full pardons—four to wrongly convicted inmates who'd been in prison until that very day; one to Anthony Porter, a Chicago man who'd been exonerated and freed from death row several years before through the work of the Center on Wrongful Convictions; and one to Gary Gauger, the Illinois organic farmer whose story appears in the play. The pardons erased the wrongful convictions from those six men's records forever. Gary's record was now completely clear.

As we sat listening to the rest of the report, we thought about those 167 lives, how vast that number was, how much this action meant to so, so many people. Certainly some, if not most, of the people whose sentences had just been commuted were guilty and would remain in prison—but now, perhaps, they'd have a shot at rehabilitation, a chance to turn their lives around. And now the people on Illinois's death row who had strong claims of innocence might have an opportunity to prove them—and, hopefully, to walk free again.

And, we realized, one of those people was Leonard Kidd—the man whose tearful phone call to a classroom at Columbia Law School had started this whole thing. The man whose words had first opened our eyes to the human experience of being on death row and innocent was now, three years later, off death row himself. And the play had been part of the dialogue that had made that happen.

We would never presume to take credit for triggering Governor Ryan's decision. Many, many factors contributed to the choice he made, most of them much more compelling than our little play. Ryan consulted with thousands of experts more knowledgeable than we are; talked to hundreds of people closer to the issue; and most of all, followed his own strong conscience. But—as we have felt over and over through our three years of work on this play—it was an honor to be a part of the conversation.

We are different people now than we were in that Columbia University classroom in the spring of 2000. Of course, in some ways we're not—we're still scruffy and in love and take our dog with us on car trips. We still work out of our living room. We still make art together, squabble over it, and work it out, always finding better things through our disagreement than either of us could stumble across alone. We have the same families and the same old friends. But the few new friends we've made—the exonerated—have changed us forever.

We no longer believe that our system functions in reality the way it does on paper. We no longer believe that the system handles the poor using the same hand with which it handles the wealthy. We no longer take for granted that we are safe just because we're innocent. We've seen that closing our eyes and praying our leaders will keep us safe isn't what creates real safety. We know that *everyone* is human: each of us has the capacity to make mistakes, act carelessly, be selfish—including ourselves, and also including lawyers, judges, politicians, and police. And we also know that every one of us also has the capacity to do the opposite: to ask questions, to listen closely and carefully for the truth, to learn to act out of compassion and wisdom instead of fear. And we've seen just how far one person's conscience can reach—how it's possible to help save lives just by asking questions and acting ethically on those rare answers we find.

We've seen just how much one person can live through; we've seen how love and courage make it possible for any of us to take the ugliest circumstances imaginable and come out the other side with something beautiful. We've also seen that none of us can do that alone. We have a much more profound sense of our responsibility as citizens and human beings—we've seen that freedom isn't something that just happens because our leaders promise it, or because it's supposed to, or even because we want it and believe in it. We have to *work* for it, case by case, person by person, life by life.

Afterword

In that Columbia Law School classroom back in 2000, we thought we'd better get this play up quick, that we had just a little window of time before the American public tired of the issue of wrongful conviction and turned its attention elsewhere. Boy, were we wrong. The number of death row exonerations tracked by the Death Penalty Information Center—89 when we first started out—is up to 123. Three-quarters of Americans now believe an innocent person has been executed in the last five years (*Criminology and Public Policy*, February 2005), and according to an October 2005 Gallup poll, support for the death penalty is down to 64 percent, the lowest since 1978. When the option of life without parole is added to the equation, support for capital punishment drops—to 47 percent, according to a May 2006 Gallup poll: the lowest in twenty years. Even in Texas, the landscape is changing: in 2004, 64 percent of Texans said they supported a moratorium until problems of accuracy and fairness could be solved. In March 2005, the Supreme Court forbade the execution of individuals who were minors at the time of their crimes, citing a "national consensus" against the practice. And in 2004, the number of Americans executed was the lowest since the reinstatement of the death penalty in 1976—a decline that is the result, according to the *Washington Post*, "in part of events such as the exoneration of some death row inmates by DNA evidence."

Against this remarkable backdrop, the life of our little play has continued to expand. During its second year Off-Broadway, a touring company brought the show to seventeen American cities, including Fort Worth; New Orleans; Philadelphia; and Washington, D.C. The play won the Drama Desk, Lucille Lortel, and Outer Critics Circle awards, as well as awards from the National Association of Criminal Defense Lawyers, Death Penalty Focus, Court TV, and Amnesty International. Actors from the New York cast performed excerpts for the Texas Bar Association. *The Exonerated* closed in New York after nearly two years and six hundred performances, and has been taken up by regional theaters across America, finding new life and new interpretations in the hands of directors and actors we've never met. Most important to us, the play has been performed and studied, often as part of a larger curriculum, at universities and high schools throughout the country. It's been translated into French, Spanish, Japanese, and Italian; performed in Mexico City, Kyoto, Edinburgh, Rome, and London; and in 2005, *The Exonerated* was made into a film for Court TV that reached millions of households.

Bob Balaban's deft direction translated the play faithfully from theater to film, and an incredible cast—including Brian Dennehey,

Danny Glover, Delroy Lindo, Aidan Quinn, Susan Sarandon, and original Off-Broadway cast member David Brown Jr.—lent their talents. We were enormously grateful that such artists were making a film from our script, elated at Court TV's unwavering support of the play and its message, and thrilled at the prospect of these stories reaching a greater cross section of Americans. At the same time, the play had been in the public eye for a while, so we thought the film's release would be just another step in the journey, not so different from those that had come before.

We were in for a lesson in the difference between theater and television.

Between 2001 and 2005, *The Exonerated* reached hundreds of thousands of people, roomful by roomful, together, in the dark. After each performance, there were questions, opinions, healthy debates: in San Francisco, we stayed late into the night talking with a high-up official in the police department about his struggles to balance the demands of his job with the very real risks of wrongful accusation. In Texas, staffers from the prosecutor's office spoke up at talkbacks, saying they wished everyone in their workplace could hear these stories. Police, state and federal prosecutors, senators, Supreme Court judges, even a former attorney general came to see the play; many stayed long after to tell us how crucial these stories were, how much they grappled with the problem of wrongful conviction in their work. Not all of them agreed with us one hundred percent, of course, but even in the most vociferous debates people were striving to figure something out *together*, to work toward a common goal of justice, to ask questions and look for solutions as a community, there in the room. And even though some media coverage of the play asked tough questions, they were always just that—questions—and we welcomed them.

The week before the film's first broadcast, the attacks began.

Apparently, when a piece of work is on television, it immediately becomes a hundred times the political target that a play could ever be. We understood the reasoning: the audience for the film was in the millions, while even the most popular play's audience must necessarily be much more limited. Television becomes part of popular culture, part of the zeitgeist, in a way that theater rarely does, at least in America. (In England, it's a slightly different story.) And we knew that there are people out there who thrive on the kind of loud, uninformed discourse we've always so carefully avoided indulging.

But still, we were shocked to discover the ripple effect just a few motivated, well-connected individuals can have in the mass media. The attacks on the film came from less than a handful of people; the overwhelming majority of media coverage was positive and constructive. The American Bar Association even gave the film an award for "helping to foster the public's understanding of the legal system." But a few individuals seemed to want to discredit the play's message: that wrongful conviction is a real and far too frequent phenomenon, with real, human consequences; that sometimes the authorities make mistakes, and that those mistakes concern all of us.

It's hard to argue with the notion that innocent people shouldn't be sent to death row, whether you believe in capital punishment or not. So those who are hell-bent on preserving the death penalty at all costs have only one option when faced with the problem of wrongful conviction: to argue that it doesn't actually exist. That it's a "myth," that all these folks aren't "really" exonerated—despite DNA evidence, witness recantations, and prosecutorial misconduct; despite repeated confessions from the real killers; despite hard physical evidence and study after scientific study proving the system is riddled with mistakes.

Of course, all capital cases are enormously complex and many span decades, and every exoneree originally had a case made against them by prosecutors. If you present facts (or allegations) from those cases out of context—without also presenting the ways in which those "facts" were later refuted—it's not too hard to create a misleading impression. And once you've drawn the public and reporters into a debate about obscure twenty-year-old legal details that have already been repeatedly addressed in court, it's not too hard to steer the dialogue away from the real issue of wrongful conviction.

We spent the week before the film's broadcast on the phone, on the radio, and in TV studios, doing interviews about the newfound "controversy" about the play. We'd spent years researching these cases, reading transcripts and case files, and were able to answer all the "issues" raised by the play's opponents. But we would have much preferred to spend that time debating constructively about how to improve our system.

Five years after we started out, we were still on a sharp learning curve—this time getting a real lesson in the workings of the mass media, and how easy it is for a few savvy individuals with an agenda to create a media firestorm that confuses the issue and stifles real, healthy debate. We feel very strongly that all of us who are concerned with justice—judges, prosecutors, defense attorneys, politicians, activists, ordinary citizens—should be working *together* to solve the problem of wrongful conviction. We found it deeply disheartening that a few prosecutors out there seemed much more concerned with devoting their considerable resources and intelligence to denying that the problem exists.

That same year, we would also get another lesson in just how deep the problem of wrongful conviction goes. Robert Hayes, one of our interviewees, was brought to trial on charges stemming from an unsolved crime, one that took place years before the Florida case portrayed in the play and film. Apparently, Robert's wrongful conviction in the Florida case (before he was exonerated based on DNA and other physical evidence) had caused suspicion to fall on him for this earlier crime, and after seventeen years, he was brought to trial. This time, having been wrongly convicted once before, he panicked and pleaded to a lesser charge after one day in court; he tried immediately afterward to retract his plea, but was denied. According to the New York State Police Forensic Investigation Center, DNA evidence from semen found in the victim's body *does not match* Robert's DNA. That information was never given a chance to come out in court. As of this writing, nobody seems to know whose DNA it is.